# *The*
# *American*
# *Garden*
# *Guidebook*

# *The*

# *American*

# *Garden*

# *Guidebook*

A TRAVELER'S GUIDE TO EXTRAORDINARY BEAUTY
ALONG THE BEATEN PATH

339 Listings

The Finest Botanical Gardens, Parks and Arboreta
Of the 28 States & 4 Provinces
Of the Eastern Half of the United States and Canada

**Everitt L. Miller and Dr. Jay S. Cohen**

*M. Evans and Company, Inc.*
*New York*

Copyright © 1987 by Everitt L. Miller and Jay S. Cohen

All rights reserved. No part of this book may be reproduced or transmitted in any form or by any means without the written permission of the publisher.

M. Evans and Company, Inc.
216 East 49 Street
New York, New York 10017

Design by Lauren Dong

Manufactured in the United States of America

9 8 7 6 5 4 3 2 1

Library of Congress Cataloging-in-Publication Data

Miller, Everitt L.
    The American garden guidebook.

    "339 listings, the finest botanical gardens, parks, and aboreta of the 28 states & 4 provinces of the Eastern half of the United States and Canada.
        1. Gardens—United States—Guide-books.    2. Botanical gardens—United States—Guide-books.    3. Arboretums—United States—Guide-books.    4. Parks—United States—Guide-books.    5. United States—Description and travel—1981-    —Guide-books.    6. Gardens—Canada, Eastern—Guide-books.    7. Botanical gardens—Canada, Eastern—Guide-books.    8. Parks—Canada, Eastern—Guide-books.    9. Canada, Eastern—Description and travel—Guide-books.
I. Cohen, Jay S.    II. Title.
SB466.U6M55    1987        712'.5'0974        87-6857

ISBN 0-87131-499-1

# Table of Contents

## GEORGIA
*Location Map*
*"Don't Miss" Gardens:*
*Excellent Gardens:*

## ILLINOIS
*Location Map*
*"Don't Miss" Gardens:*
*Excellent Gardens:*

# NEW YORK
*Location Map*
*"Don't Miss" Gardens:*

*Excellent Gardens:*

# NORTH CAROLINA
*Location Map*
*Excellent Gardens:*

# OHIO
*Location Map*
*"Don't Miss" Gardens:*

*Excellent Gardens:*

# VIRGINIA
*Location Map*
*"Don't Miss" Gardens:*

*Excellent Gardens:*

# WEST VIRGINIA
*Location Map*
*Excellent Gardens:*

# WISCONSIN
*Location Map*
*"Don't Miss" Gardens:*

*Excellent Gardens:*

GARDEN LISTINGS, PART THREE: SPECIAL GARDENS

# Welcome

North America is blessed with such a wealth of fine gardens that one can only wonder at the many travelers who pass them by unaware. Hence the purpose of this book—to introduce the outstanding gardens of eastern North America in a practical and easy-to-use format.

Although many excellent guides for the garden expert and horticultural enthusiast already exist, this book represents a different approach. *The American Garden Guidebook, Volume I,* is written for the general traveler who may have no interest whatsoever in the Latin names of plants or the characteristics of various species. It is for people who know only that they enjoy the beauty of a breathtaking landscape or the symmetry of a perfect rose.

The bounty that these gardens offer requires no special knowledge or translation—their message is universal. At the same time, there is also something here for the more serious enthusiast, for it follows that the gardens that are the fairest to the eye often possess the finest collections and utilize the best techniques.

Whether you are a general traveler or a garden expert, *The American Garden Guidebook* is your passport to a different kind of travel experience, to a quiet land where beauty is the objective and magnificence the result. Nor is it necessary to travel to the remote reaches of an "unspoiled" wilderness to experience such natural splendor. It exists right here in North America's premier gardens, along the beaten path, beside the busy crossroads. More enchanting than a museum, more holy than a church, these gardens reflect an art form of a different type—alive, dynamic, ever-changing and ever-enchanting—forged from the inspired partnership of man in harmonious concert with nature.

Visit one of these gardens and your definition of beauty will be permanently altered. Here is another reality, an oasis of hushed splendor amid a hectic and noisy world. You will find it not just a pleasant afternoon's outing, but a unique experience and an indelible memory.

EVERITT L. MILLER and JAY S. COHEN

# How to Use This Book

The 339 gardens listed in *The American Garden Guidebook, Volume I,* represent the finest of their kind from among the thousands of gardens, parks, and arboreta of the eastern half of the United States and Canada. Selecting the best from among so many is not an easy process, for there is no simple formula by which all gardens can be measured. They vary in their qualities as much as the people who have conceived and created them. In order that all tastes and interests might be represented, we have attempted to assemble as wide a range as possible. To insure that readers have the opportunity to decide whether a particular garden might appeal to them or their families, each listing is accompanied by a thorough description. Such information includes the following:

---

TYPE OF GARDEN: Botanical garden, conservatory, family attraction, city park, natural swamp, and so forth. (These are described further in the next section, "About Gardens," on pages 21–26.)

GENERAL ATTRIBUTES: Displays (azaleas, roses, other flowers), lovely vistas, natural woodland, Japanese gardens, and so forth.

SPECIAL COLLECTIONS: Orchids, bonsai, rare trees, and so forth.

OTHER ATTRIBUTES: Historic mansions and museums, fountains, educational displays.

LOCATION

ADDRESS

TELEPHONE: Number when available.

HOURS: Times and days open.

FEES: The exact fees are listed for most gardens. *Please note that these are subject to change.*

TOURS: Individual or group tours.

RESTAURANTS: Availability and type.

SHOPS: Availability and type.

WHEELCHAIR ACCESS: Most gardens indicate whether they are accessible by wheelchair. A few will provide wheelchairs upon request.

SPECIAL ACTIVITIES: Flower shows, horticultural exhibits, classes, workshops, concerts, art exhibitions, museum displays, antiques, fountain shows, entertainment, fireworks, and so forth.

---

Beyond this basic information, we have chosen a list of gardens that we call our "Don't Miss" group. These gardens, most of which are famous nationally and internationally, offer displays of such spectacular quality that we feel required to highlight them with extra description and background information. When these "Don't Miss" gardens are at their peak bloom or are offering special floral shows, they are spectacles worth driving several hours to see.

In addition to the garden listings themselves, the book offers four appendixes for your convenience.

Appendix A is "Family Fun," which enumerates ninety-one gardens offering special displays or activities for children. For instance, Florida Cypress Gardens presents world-famous water ski shows, amusement rides, an aviary, and a petting zoo, whereas its namesake to the north (Cypress Gardens, SC) offers an unusual garden tour via swamp boats. Colonial Williamsburg (VA) presents the most authentic colonial American village to be seen anywhere, whereas the Thomas A. Edison Winter Home's garden and museum (FL) has many educational displays regarding Edison's incredible accomplishments, as well as his antique auto collection (which includes gifts from Henry Ford and Harvey Firestone.)

Appendix B is "Free Gardens," which lists one hundred and forty-six gardens that charge no entrance fee all or part of the time.

Appendix C is "Wedding Gardens," which lists eighty-three gardens that offer facilities for weddings, receptions, or wedding portraits. Some of these (Queens Botanical, NY; Bellingrath Gardens and Home, AL) have created special areas with ornate trellises or masses of white flowers specifically for wedding ceremonies. Some gardens possess historical mansions that also can be reserved for such occasions or other social activities or meetings.

Appendix D is "Winter Gardens," which indicates those that have refreshingly green and colorful displays during the usually barren months of winter. As you might expect, most of the outdoor gardens in this group are located in Florida or other southern states, but there are a surprising number of northern conservatories (Chicago's Garfield Park Conservatory and Lincoln Park Conservatory, IL; New York Botanical; and others) that present Thanksgiving, Christmas, and other winter shows. For example, few displays, either indoors or out, match the world-famous Longwood (PA) winter shows for sheer color and elegance.

Following the appendixes is a glossary in which commonly used terms (such as "annual plants," "perennials," "herbaceous," "deciduous," "parterre") are defined.

It has been our goal in creating *The American Garden Guidebook* to produce a book that covers the breadth of eastern North America's public gardens, so that whatever your interest, your age or background, your tastes or those of your family, there are gardens presented herein that will please you, entertain you, and perhaps, inspire you. For beyond their differences in style and design, these superb gardens offer every visitor something special and rare.

# *About Gardens*

Individual gardens, like individual persons, represent different purposes and points of view. For example, some gardens were originally established for scientific investigation; others owe their origins to nothing more than a garden enthusiast with a grand idea or a creatively green thumb. Although the spectrum of garden styles is broad and varied, some general categorization may be helpful in appreciating the origins and styles of those we have included.

## GARDEN ORIGINS

### HORTICULTURAL OR BOTANICAL GARDENS

Horticultural or botanical gardens are devoted to the collection and study of rare and unusual flora. Examples of this type of garden are the New York Botanical Garden, the Norfolk Botanical Garden (VA), and the Fairchild Tropical Garden (FL). Although these gardens are committed to scientific research, many of them also produce dazzling displays for the general visitor. Brooklyn Botanic Garden, for instance, offers an outstanding Japanese garden and bonsai collection, an award-winning rose garden, and the finest stand of flowering cherry trees north of Washington, DC, while at the same time maintaining an internationally recognized educational program for both adults and children.

### ARBORETA

An arboretum is by definition a place where trees and shrubs are collected and studied, but again this label is too restricting. For example, Planting Fields Arboretum (NY) possesses, in addition to an impressive array of trees, a conservatory featuring seasonal displays, a Touch and See Trail for the blind, a schedule of musical programs, plus one of the Northeast's finest collections of azaleas and rhododendrons.

## ESTATES

Many gardens were originally developed as part of an estate or mansion. In some cases, they were specifically designed to complement the manor house or to serve as an outdoor "room." Excellent examples of this type of design can be seen at Nemours (DE), Vizcaya (FL), Old Westbury (NY), Magnolia Plantation and Gardens (SC), and the Biltmore House and Gardens (NC).

## MUSEUMS OR CHURCHES

Some gardens were created to augment a museum or place of worship. Examples of this are the Ringling Museums (FL), the Edison Winter Home Museum and Gardens (FL), and The Cloisters (NY). The Bishop's Garden outside Washington Cathedral (DC) is an example of one of several fine church-related gardens. Some religion-oriented gardens include plants mentioned in the Bible (Temple Beth El, RI) or contain replicas of Jersualem or Palestine (Ave Maria Grotto, AL; Palestinian Gardens, MS).

## TOURIST ATTRACTIONS

Some gardens serve as a vital part of a large tourist attraction, theme park, or resort. Notable examples are Florida Cypress Gardens, and Callaway Gardens, a first-class resort in Georgia.

## COMMERCIAL ENTERPRISES

Several nurseries, hotels, and cemeteries have developed collections or landscaped their grounds with such vast or unusual plantings that they rank among eastern North America's best displays. Mohonk Mountain House (NY), Grand Hotel (MI), and The Greenbrier (WV), for example, all exhibit gardens remarkable in the diversity of their flora. Legg Dahlia Gardens (NY), a commercial nursery, offers three acres of this captivating flower in every color of the rainbow. Mount Auburn (MA) and Spring Grove (OH) represent cemeteries that began with a concern for garden design and attractive displays.

## PLEASURE GARDENS

Many gardens were established for their own sake—to create an island of serene beauty in a busy world. Perhaps the ultimate example of this genre is the incomparable Longwood (PA), but there are many others equally laudable—Bellingrath (AL), Winterthur (DE), Dumbarton Oaks (DC), Brookside (MD), Kingwood (OH), Magnolia (SC), and many more.

Of course, such definitions and categories as those just mentioned are inexact because many gardens manage to fill several roles. Many of the botanical gardens and arboreta have found it necessary to attract the public's interest (and support) by adding colorful displays and seasonal shows, thereby obtaining badly needed funding through gate receipts and memberships, as well as cultivating public support for government subsidies and grants. The Brooklyn Botanic Garden, already mentioned, is an example of this. In fact, all of the botanical gardens and arboreta listed in *The American Garden Guidebook* offer superb visual displays. That is because our selecting them was based solely upon the quality of their public displays, not their scientific reputations.

Just as botanic gardens have evolved into public showcases, many of the more commercial types of gardens carry on noteworthy horticultural and educational activities. For example, Longwood, which ranks among the finest of show gardens, maintains a first-rate educational program for graduate students in horticulture.

## STYLES OR SCHOOLS OF GARDEN ARCHITECTURE

Another way of understanding gardens is from the style in which they are designed. Some gardens can be deemed formal in style, which means that they've taken their design from one of the many traditional schools of garden architecture. An abbreviated list of such schools might include the English, French, and Italian schools, as well as Japanese gardens.

### ENGLISH SCHOOLS

There are many different schools of English gardening, each representing a different era. The *country estate,* with its broad lawns, graceful trees, and wide vistas, became very popular in the late eighteenth and in the nineteenth centuries. Planting Fields Arboretum (NY) and Middleton Place (SC) are good representatives of this genre. An earlier era gave rise to the *cottage garden* of Elizabethan times (the finest examples can be seen at Colonial Williamsburg, VA) and the *traditional herb garden*.

## FRENCH SCHOOLS

If you have visited Versailles, you have seen the most famous of French styles—fountains shooting forth vast quantities of spray, stone and marble statuary at every turn, and the plants themselves trimmed and clipped into elaborate forms. Flowers are widely used in this design, and they are carefully placed and pruned within beds and borders (parterres). Longwood (PA) and Nemours (DE), created by cousins of the famous du Pont family, were conceived according to this school.

## ITALIAN SCHOOLS

Gardens take an altogether different form in traditional Italian design. Historically, because of nutrient-poor soil and the heat and dryness of the climate, flowering plants rarely thrived and were little used. Instead, pools were employed to create a tranquil, cool ambience, and grottoes (cavelike areas) developed to provide shade from the summer sun. Statuary, urns, and fountains were commonly used. Evergreens were also frequently included, usually shaped and planted into designs or avenues. Rows of Italian poplars were commonly employed in this manner. Italian gardens were often designed to be outdoor extensions of the living space of the home; these gardens were oriented to be viewed from a bedroom or parlor. A "secret" garden was often created where the owner could escape the noisy household and catch up on his letters or correspondence. A faithful representative of this style is the opulent Vizcaya (FL).

## JAPANESE GARDENS

A totally different concept from most Western gardens, the Japanese garden is meant as a place for meditation, not sensory stimulation. It is intended to reflect the forest in miniature, at all times of the year. For these reasons, Japanese gardens are primarily evergreen gardens, with only a carefully chosen smattering of seasonal flowers (usually azaleas, rhododendrons, or camellias). Rocks and water play a role as important as the plants themselves, and all are blended to create a mood of tranquillity and contemplation.

# GARDEN FOCAL POINTS OR SPECIALTIES

Many gardens do not fall into a particular school, but they nonetheless have their own focal point or specialty.

## INDOOR DISPLAYS

America possesses many excellent conservatories where collections and seasonal shows are presented year round. The largest and best in the world can be found at Longwood (PA), but Chicago's Garfield Park, Mitchell Park (WI), Whitcomb (MI), New York Botanical, and many others offer outstanding displays. Duke Gardens (NJ) presents eleven individual gardens, each representing a unique culture or era of garden design, a history of civilization, so to speak, through its gardens.

## SPECIAL COLLECTIONS

Many gardens choose to specialize, realizing that a few exquisite collections outweigh a plethora of mediocre ones. For example, many gardens have developed vast collections of orchids or roses. Other plants that are similarly highlighted include azaleas, rhododendrons, camellias, herbs, palms, blossoming trees, and cacti. A variant of this approach is *topiary,* the art of training trees and bushes into the shape of animals or geometric forms. Topiary can be found in several gardens, but only a few, such as the superb Green Animals (RI) and Ladew Gardens (MD), devote themselves exclusively to this pleasingly whimsical art form.

## SPECIAL ENVIRONMENTS

Some gardens exist in a special area or environment, and they devote themselves to presenting their natural flora in an informative and pleasing manner. Corkscrew Swamp Sanctuary (FL) is the Audubon Society's demonstration of the original, natural Florida landscape via a boardwalk built directly into the swamp. Cypress Gardens (SC) is a fine example of a southeastern forest, where moss-covered trees grow out of the water and wild azaleas coat the shore. At this garden, one can tour by boat as well as by foot.

Whatever its origin, style, or focal point, you can be sure that the gardens of *The American Garden Guidebook* represent the best in eastern North America. These are places of rare beauty and unmatched serenity, masterpieces carefully conceived and lovingly cultivated. These are places that offer the public something unique; in return they deserve the public's strong support. They provide a different, refreshing kind of experience for you and your family; an experience not to be missed or forgotten.

*Never lose an opportunity of seeing anything that is beautiful, for beauty is God's handwriting—a wayside sacrament. Welcome it in every fair face, in every fair sky, in every flower, and thank God for it as a cup of blessing.*

EMERSON

# PART ONE

# Garden Listings:
# Eastern
# United States

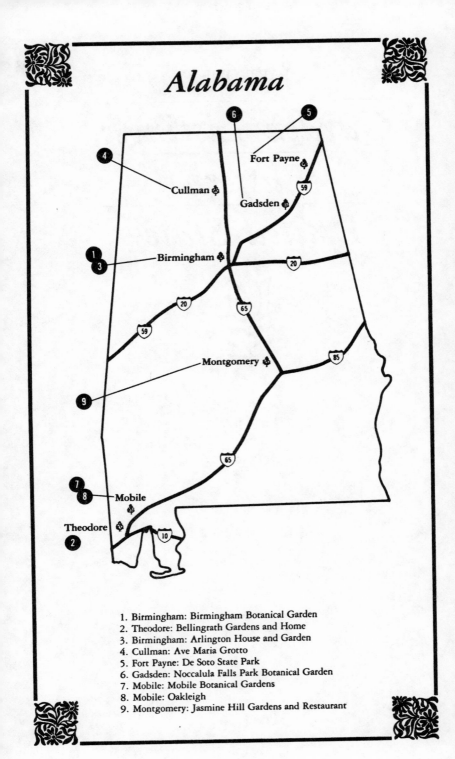

# Alabama

1. Birmingham: Birmingham Botanical Garden
2. Theodore: Bellingrath Gardens and Home
3. Birmingham: Arlington House and Garden
4. Cullman: Ave Maria Grotto
5. Fort Payne: De Soto State Park
6. Gadsden: Noccalula Falls Park Botanical Garden
7. Mobile: Mobile Botanical Gardens
8. Mobile: Oakleigh
9. Montgomery: Jasmine Hill Gardens and Restaurant

# *Alabama*

## "DON'T MISS" GARDENS

### BIRMINGHAM: BIRMINGHAM BOTANICAL GARDEN

*A municipally owned, 67½-acre garden containing several excellent specialized gardens (roses, annuals, daylilies, wildflowers, ferns, iris, and others), a large conservatory, a first-rate indoor collection of camellias, and one of America's finest Japanese gardens.*

Established in 1962, the Birmingham Botanical Garden is operated by the City of Birmingham Park and Recreation Board and supported by donations from individuals, groups, and memberships in the Birmingham Botanical Society. The garden was designed as a pleasure garden, offering interesting and colorful displays throughout the year, and as a resource for the education of the community. Special gardens include the Rose Garden (more than 2,000 plants, 150 varieties), an All-America Selections display garden featuring annuals and vegetables, a lily garden, a wildflower garden created at the site of an old rock quarry, a touch-and-see nature trail with braille labels, a fern glen, an iris garden, a magnolia garden, a crape myrtle collection, and a garden for southern living offering new ideas for home gardeners. Other displays include an intricate floral clock and a naturalized area of fields and forest where over 230 species of birds can be seen. The conservatory offers continually changing holiday floral displays in addition to its permanent exhibits of ferns, bromeliads, orchids, and other tropical plants. Adjacent to the conservatory are propagation houses (open to the public), a desert house, and a camellia house exhibiting 125 varieties of camellias. The widely acclaimed Japanese garden includes a Zen garden, a bonsai display, sculptures, a stone bridge, and waterfalls. This garden was built with donations from both the United States and Japan. The teahouse was a gift of the Japanese government and was featured at the 1965 New York World's Fair. Two large granite lanterns have been presented by Birmingham's sister city, Japan's Hitachi.

LOCATION: In Lane Park and close to the zoo, near the junction of I-280 and U.S. 31, about 2 miles southeast of downtown Birmingham.

ADDRESS: 2612 Lane Park Rd., Birmingham, AL 35223.

TELEPHONE: 205-879-1227.

HOURS: Open daily, sunrise to sunset.

FEE: None.

TOURS: Group tours by prearrangement.

RESTAURANT: Under construction—scheduled to open in late 1987.

SHOPS: Gatehouse Giftshop specializes in garden-oriented items.

WHEELCHAIR ACCESS: Most of garden is accessible.

SPECIAL ACTIVITIES: Full schedule of lectures and classes are held in the Garden Center (near entrance). The center also contains a large horticultural library, plus meeting rooms and an auditorium available to the public. Fiesta plant sale is held the second weekend in April.

---

TIPS: 1. Birmingham Botanical Garden offers fine color year-round, from the camellias in winter to the brilliant foliage of fall. Peak time is spring with its magnolias, iris, wildflowers, azaleas, and rhododendrons. Summer, though quite hot, offers good color via roses, daylilies, and magnificent crape myrtles.
   2. The conservatory presents a succession of shows from autumn to Mother's Day.

---

## THEODORE: BELLINGRATH GARDENS AND HOME

*A world-famous garden teeming with color every month of the year. Perhaps the most beautiful garden in the southeastern United States and one of America's top five.*

Mr. and Mrs. Walter D. Bellingrath began planting some of their excess azaleas here in 1928 to develop a family retreat. By 1932 the area had become famous locally, so much so that when the Bellingraths invited the citizens of Mobile to visit one weekend, a traffic jam of historic proportions ensued. Since then the crowds haven't stopped coming, but fortunately the roads have been improved.

From the beginning, Bellingrath was designed for visual

impact. Color is its mode, and anytime is its season. Indeed, the plantings were engineered to offer an unending progression of blossoms throughout the year: camellias, tulips, azaleas, roses, chrysanthemums, and poinsettias. And not just a few here and there. Bellingrath presents each of these groups as the star of a 65-acre outdoor "show" embellished by a cast of thousands. The azaleas, for example, number in the hundreds of thousands. The "Chrysanthemum Season," with over sixty thousand plants and millions of blossoms, is among the largest of its kind in the world.

LOCATION: 20 miles south of Mobile. Take U.S. 90 to Theodore, then Bellingrath Road to gardens.
ADDRESS: Bellingrath Rd., Rte. 1, Box 60, Theodore, AL 36582.
TELEPHONE: 205-973-2217.
HOURS: Daily, 7–sunset.
FEE: *Gardens:* $4/adult, $2/ages 6–11. *Mansion:* $5 per person. Group rates available.
TOURS: For groups by prearrangement. (All tours of mansion are guided.)
RESTAURANT: Cafeteria for breakfast and lunch.
SHOPS: Plants, film, books, mementos, gifts.
WHEELCHAIR ACCESS: Good; wheelchairs available.
SPECIAL ACTIVITIES: Boehm Gallery offers the world's largest public collection of the bird and flower porcelains created by Edward Marshall Boehm. A handsome chapel, next to the gallery, is available for meditation.

TIPS: 1. Don't miss any of the garden. See it all, then return at another time of year for a different show. Best shows: chrysanthemums, azaleas, poinsettias.
2. The Bellingrath Home possesses some outstanding antiques and artwork.

## EXCELLENT GARDENS

## BIRMINGHAM: ARLINGTON HOUSE AND GARDEN

This 1800s antebellum manor possesses 6 acres of lawns, stately oaks, and flowering trees (dogwoods, magnolias), azaleas, coleuses, and geraniums, as well as a rose garden and a boxwood garden.

Very colorful April to June. The eight-room manor contains period furnishings. Wheelchair access. Gift shop. Weddings and receptions by prearrangement. Open Tues.–Sat., 10–4, and Sun., 1–4. Fee: $2/adult, $1/ages 6–18; group rates. Located on the western side of downtown Birmingham. Address: 331 Cotton Ave. SW, Birmingham, AL 35211 Tel.: 205-780-5656.

## CULLMAN: AVE MARIA GROTTO

Set upon a hillside of pines and flowering shrubbery, this unusual garden consists of 125 miniature buildings and shrines from world history. Displays include Old Jerusalem, Rome's St. Peter's basilica, the Hanging Gardens of Babylon, and Rome's Pantheon—created with impressive authenticity. Open daily, 7–sunset. Fee: $2/adult, $1/child; group rates. Located at St. Bernard Abbey, 1 mile east of Cullman, on State Rte. 69. Address: St. Bernard Abbey, Cullman, AL 35055. Tel.: 205-734-4110.

## FORT PAYNE: DE SOTO STATE PARK

A tourist resort offering boating, swimming, tennis, and golf, as well as spectacular waterfalls and magnificent rhododendrons, mountain laurel, and wildflowers. Peak bloom mid-May. Open daily. Fee: None. Location: From Fort Payne, take State Rte. 35 east to State Rte. 89 north to the park. Address: Rte. 1, Box 210, Fort Payne, AL 35967. Tel.: 205-845-0051 (reservations: 800-ALA-PARK).

## GADSDEN: NOCCALULA FALLS PARK BOTANICAL GARDENS

Located along a rock gorge carved by Black Creek's 90-foot waterfall, Noccalula Falls Park is a tourist attraction (pioneer village, zoo, covered bridge, military museum, campground, souvenir shops, country store, western shows, entertainment, picnicking, and hiking) visited by over half a million people annually. In addition, there is a 10-acre botanical garden built amid unique rock formations and streams. Peak time is in spring when the garden's twenty-five thousand azaleas burst into bloom. Also of interest are the park's 240 acres of naturalized woodlands with trails. Gardens open daily, 8–sunset. Fee: In spring–summer, $1.50/adult, $.50/children; no fee in autumn and winter. Location: Off State Rte. 211, just north of Gadsden. For further information, write: P. O. Box 267, Gadsden, AL 35902. Tel.: 205-543-7412.

## MOBILE: MOBILE BOTANICAL GARDENS

Established in 1974 and created in cooperation with the South Alabama Botanical and Horticultural Society, the Mobile Botanical Gardens is still in the process of development. On its 64 acres it currently has collections of native azaleas, camellias, herbs, and ferns, as well as a fragrance and texture garden for the blind, and a woodland nature trail. Peak bloom is mid-March through May. Self-guided tour pamphlet available. Picnicking permitted. The botanical center hosts lectures, programs, and local garden club meetings and shows. Open daily, dawn to dusk. Fee: None. Located in Municipal Park, off Museum Drive. For further information, write to Mobile Botanical Gardens, P. O. Box 8382, Mobile, AL 36608. Tel.: 205-342-0555.

## MOBILE: OAKLEIGH

Built in 1833 and listed in the National Register of Historic Places, this impressive antebellum home is filled with antiques and artifacts and is surrounded by 3½ acres of stately oaks, masses of azaleas, a sunken floral garden (sunken because clay for the house's bricks was removed from this area), and an herb garden. Part of the Mobile Home and Garden Tour in spring, Oakleigh also hosts a Candlelight Christmas. Open Mon.–Sat., 10–4, and Sun., 2–4. Garden fee: None (guided tour of house requires small fee). Address: 350 Oakleigh Place, Mobile, AL 36604. Tel.: 205-432-1281.

## MONTGOMERY: JASMINE HILL GARDENS AND RESTAURANT

This garden is well known for both its sculpture and its azaleas, jasmines, and flowering cherry trees. Located in the Appalachian foothills, the garden was first developed in the late 1920s by Mr. and Mrs. Benjamin Fitzpatrick, who shared a penchant for Greek statuary. Making more than twenty trips to Greece for ideas and materials, the Fitzpatricks gradually filled Jasmine Hill with replicas of the Venus of Melos, Marathon Boy,

Mourning Athena, the Dying Gaul, and more than a score of other fine pieces. The centerpiece is the Temple of Hera, an exact replica of the remains of the oldest Olympian temple. The gardens are also home to the Jasmine Hill Arts Council, which provides a full schedule of entertainment, including an international folk festival, at the outdoor amphitheater. A wedding garden features an arch of jasmines and a lily pool. The Jasmine Hill Restaurant, built from the original 1830s settler's cottage, prides itself on its gourmet fare, hosts parties, balls, receptions, and dinners, and offers tour and dining packages. Garden tours available to groups. Open Tue.–Sat., 9–5. Garden fee: $2.50/adult, $1.00/ages 6–12. Location: Northeast of downtown Montgomery, on Jasmine Hill Road off U.S. 231. Mailing address: P.O. Box 6001, Montgomery, AL 36106. Tel.: gardens, 205-567-6463; restaurant, 205-567-6362; amphitheater, 205-567-9444.

# *Connecticut*

## EXCELLENT GARDENS

### BRISTOL: BRISTOL NURSERIES, INC.

Known as "Mum City, U.S.A.," this wholesale nursery contains 3 acres of outdoor gardens filled with chrysanthemums of all colors and kinds (seventy-eight varieties). The public is invited to visit, and in autumn a retail sale is held. Group tours by prearrangement. Open daily, 8–5. Fee: None. Location: Bristol is located in central Connecticut on State Rte. 10, approximately 15 miles southwest of Hartford. Address: 73 Pinehurst Rd., Bristol, CT 06010. Tel.: 203-582-3151.

### COVENTRY: CAPRILANDS HERB FARM

Caprilands offers thirty-one garden displays and greenhouses containing more than three hundred varieties of herbs. "Everything for the herb gardener," including plants, seeds, dried herbs, books, crafts, dolls, Christmas decorations—as well as a continual slate of programs and tours. One of America's most complete displays of herbs. Luncheon tours and programs by reservation. Shops offer books, baskets, plants and seeds. Programs and festivals scheduled year round. Open daily, 9–5; closed major holidays. Fee: None. Located approximately 8 miles north of Coventry and 40 miles east of Hartford; Silver St. is off U.S. Alt. Rte. 44, ½ mile west of the intersection with State Rte. 31. Address: 534 Silver St., Coventry, CT 06238. Tel.: 203-742-7244.

### DANIELSON: LOGEE'S GREENHOUSES

A retail mail-order business run by the same family since 1892, Logee's Greenhouses present a wonderland of rare and tropical plants, more than two thousand varieties in all. They feature the largest collection of begonias in the East, as well as an excellent selection of geraniums, African violets, herbs, ferns, and nearly every popular flowering house plant. Also on display are specimens of bougainvillea, jasmine, camellia, and angel's trumpet, each more than a half century old. Group tours by prearrangement. Logee's is a popular site for garden club tours. Wheelchair accessible. Open daily, 9–4. Fee: None. Location: Danielson

# *Connecticut*

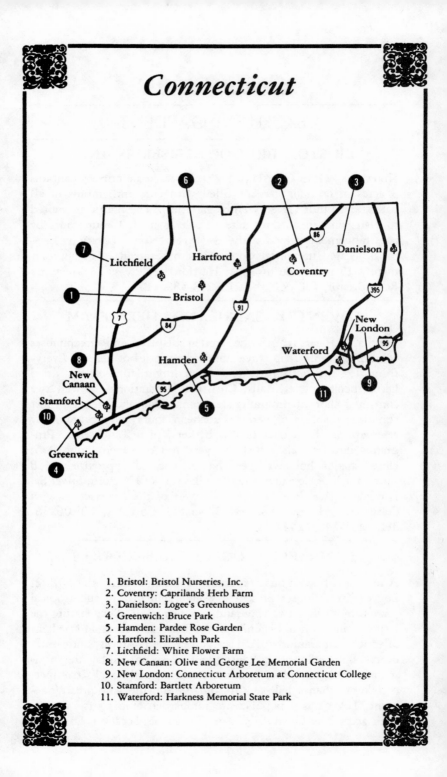

1. Bristol: Bristol Nurseries, Inc.
2. Coventry: Caprilands Herb Farm
3. Danielson: Logee's Greenhouses
4. Greenwich: Bruce Park
5. Hamden: Pardee Rose Garden
6. Hartford: Elizabeth Park
7. Litchfield: White Flower Farm
8. New Canaan: Olive and George Lee Memorial Garden
9. New London: Connecticut Arboretum at Connecticut College
10. Stamford: Bartlett Arboretum
11. Waterford: Harkness Memorial State Park

is located in east-central Connecticut, at the intersection of I-395 and U.S. 6; Logee's is 1 mile north of central Danielson—take U.S. 6 to Main St., then to North St. Address: 55 North St., Danielson, CT 06239. Tel.: 203-774-8083.

## GREENWICH: BRUCE PARK

This 61-acre all-purpose park contains plantings of azaleas, rhododendrons, and flowering trees, plus a rose garden covering 1 acre and containing more than five hundred shrubs. Peak color is in late spring and early summer, when guided tours are given. Bruce Park also offers picnicking, recreational facilities (tennis courts, playing fields, playground), and two lakes. Concerts are held in summer. The rose garden and landscaped areas are wheelchair accessible. Weddings held by prearrangement. Open daily, sunrise to sunset. Fee: None. Located on Bruce Park Dr., between Davis Ave. and Field Point Rd. For further information, contact Greenwich Dept. of Parks, Greenwich, CT. Tel.: 203-622-7814.

## HAMDEN: PARDEE ROSE GARDEN

Established in 1923 and located in East Rock Park, the 2-acre Pardee Rose Garden features 250 rose bushes set within formal gardens packed with annuals and perennials. The park also contains a conservatory offering permanent displays and seasonal shows. Free guided nature walks given on Friday afternoons. Weddings permitted by prearrangement. Open dawn to dusk. Fee: None. Location: East Rock Park is located approximately 6 miles south of central Hamden and 3 miles north of downtown New Haven, just off U.S. 5 (State St.). Address: 180 Park Rd., Hamden, CT 06518. Tel.: 203-787-8142.

## HARTFORD: ELIZABETH PARK

This municipal park is best known for one of America's largest and most spectacular rose gardens (fifteen thousand plants representing approximately one thousand species). Other attractions include a rock garden, beds of flowering annuals and perennials, an evergreen collection, and greenhouses where bedding plants are propagated and seasonal flower shows held (check for dates). In June an annual rose show is sponsored by the Connecticut Rose Society. In the Horticulture Center (across from the rose garden) classes are held for adults and children. In summer a series of performances from concerts to country dance are given. Wheelchair accessible. Gardens available for weddings. Open daily, dawn to dusk; greenhouse open daily, 9–4, except holidays. Fee: None. Located at Prospect and Asylum Aves., approximately 4 miles northwest of downtown Hartford. For further information, write Dept. of Parks and Recreation, 25 Stonington St., Hartford, CT 06106 Tel.: 203-722-6541.

## LITCHFIELD: WHITE FLOWER FARM

A retail and mail-order nursery, White Flower Farm has, in addition to its 40 working acres, 10 acres of display gardens. These contain hundreds of varieties of flowers, shrubs, and trees, including exhibits of azaleas, tree peonies, and dwarf conifers, and a 2-acre trial garden. One of the greenhouses, open to the public from July to September, holds an impressive collection of tuberous begonias. Retail shop. Guided tours by prearrangement. Open daily, mid-Apr. to late Oct., weekdays, 10–5, and Sat./Sun., 9–5. Fee: None. Located on Rte. 63, 3 miles south of historic Litchfield. Address: Litchfield, CT 06759. Tel.: 203-567-0801 for information or free consultation with a staff horticulturist.

## NEW CANAAN: OLIVE AND GEORGE LEE MEMORIAL GARDEN

This superb natural garden was begun by George Lee in 1940 after he was given a dozen azaleas by his brother, Frederic Lee, an azalea expert. Bequeathed in 1979 to the New Canaan Garden Center, this 3-acre garden now possesses nearly two thousand azaleas representing 175 varieties. Most notable is the extensive collection of hardy Gable azaleas (40 varieties). The garden also offers a rhododendron path with some 280 species and hybrids. Underplantings include a wide array of wildflowers and ground covers, ferns, primroses, phlox, ivies, iris, and daffodils. Peak bloom is in May. Plants are labeled. Cuttings can be purchased. Open daily, dawn to dusk. Fee: None. Location: New Canaan is located on State Rtes. 106 and 124 in the southeast tip of Connecticut, about 7 miles north of Stamford and Darien; from New Canaan take Rte. 124 north, turn left onto Greenley Rd., turn left onto Chichester. Address: 89 Chichester Rd., New Canaan, CT 06840.

# NEW LONDON: CONNECTICUT ARBORETUM AT CONNECTICUT COLLEGE

Established in 1931, this 425-acre arboretum is located on the Connecticut College campus and specializes in the collection of native woody plants from the eastern United States. Collections include hollies, heaths and viburnums, plus a native azalea garden and a laurel walk. Trails wind through 200 acres of woodland with wildflowers. Across the campus is the Caroline Black Botanical Garden with 4 acres of ornamental displays. Group tours by prearrangement. Picnicking permitted. Open daily, dawn to dusk. Fee: None. Location: New London is located along the Connecticut coast, 53 miles west of New Haven; the college is located on Williams St. For further information write to Connecticut Arboretum at Connecticut College, New London Hall, Rm. 209, New London, CT 06320. Tel.: 203-447-1911.

# STAMFORD: BARTLETT ARBORETUM

Operated by the University of Connecticut, this 62-acre arboretum contains trails through natural woodland and swamp areas. Of particular beauty are the collections of azaleas and rhododendrons, in bloom from April to June, and the daffodils in early spring. There is also a greenhouse with seasonal shows. The arboretum offers a full schedule of lectures, classes and workshops, plant sales, and trips to other northeastern gardens. Book shop and library. Group tours by prearrangement. Open daily, 8:30–sunset; administration building open Mon.–Fri., 8:30–4:00. Fee: None. Located just off State Rte. 137 (High Ridge Road), approximately 5 miles north of downtown Stamford and 1 mile north of the Merritt Pkwy. (Rte.15). Address: 151 Brookdale Rd., Stamford, CT 06903. Tel.: 203-322-6971.

# WATERFORD: HARKNESS MEMORIAL STATE PARK

Located on Goshen Point where the Thames River enters Long Island Sound, the park is actually a 234-acre estate built in 1902 and bequeathed to the public in 1950. The 42-room, vine-covered mansion ("Eolia") overlooks an Italian garden, an oriental garden, a rock garden, flower gardens and statuary, and a greenhouse. Peak bloom is May to June. The mansion holds a permanent collection of watercolors of bird species by Rex Brasher. Picnicking. Fishing. Garden open daily, 8–sunset; house open Memorial Day to Labor Day, 10–5. Garden fee: None (fee for parking). Located on State Rte. 213 (Great Neck Rd.), approximately 3 miles south of Waterford and 4 miles south of New London. Address: 275 Great Neck Rd., Waterford, CT 06385. Tel.: 203-443-5725.

# *Delaware*

## WILMINGTON: NEMOURS

*An estate of unique opulence, a miniature Versailles with a garden to match.*

From the moment you approach the imposing Nemours mansion, you feel you have somehow stepped out of modern-day Delaware and into seventeenth-century France. It isn't that North America doesn't possess many impressive estates (see Vizcaya, Castle Hill, and other listings in this book), but Nemours (pronounced nuh-MOOR) is something very special. The two marble sphinxes on the front terrace originally graced the gardens of Sceaux, the chateau of Colbert (1619–1683), the famous finance minister of Louis XIV and proponent of the theory of mercantilism. The sphinxes are actually portraits of Louise de La Valière, one of Louis XIV's favorite mistresses. Colbert received the sphinxes as a gift from Louis for caring for the mistress during each of her four pregnancies and seeing to the rearing of the four illegitimate princes. Sceaux was destroyed during the French Revolution, but the sphinxes survived.

Then notice the English gates on the way to the garden. These date back to 1488 when they were built for Wimbledon Manor. Fifty or so years later, Henry the Eighth gave Wimbledon Manor to his sixth wife, Catherine Parr. During the Puritan reign under Oliver Cromwell, royal estates became viewed as undesirable excesses, so in 1649 Wimbledon Manor was sold and later dismantled, yet the gates survived.

Nemours was built in 1909 by Alfred I. du Pont. The 300-acre garden was completed in 1932. Alfred and his son, Alfred Victor, wanted to create a garden decidedly different from their cousins' at Longwood and Winterthur, so they chose as their inspiration the ultimate of French gardens—Versailles. With its formal flower beds (parterres), fountains and tree-lined avenues (allees), this garden is strictly a design garden, which is best appreciated when viewed from the house or terraces. As mentioned, great care was exercised in every detail, from its statuary to the terrace's tree boxes, which are similar to those that held Versailles's three thousand orange trees. Over the

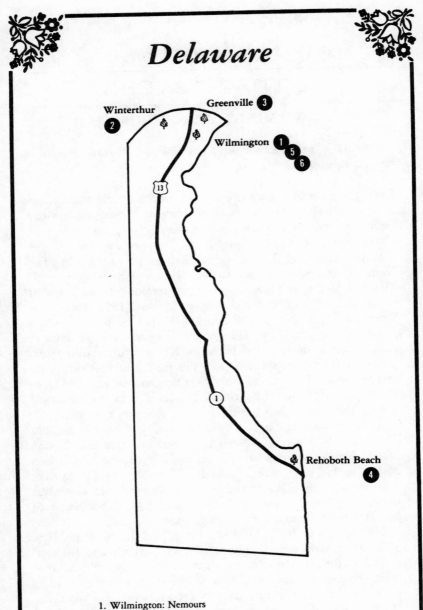

# Delaware

Winterthur

Greenville ③

② Winterthur

Wilmington ① ⑤ ⑥

⑬

①

Rehoboth Beach

④

1. Wilmington: Nemours
2. Winterthur: Winterthur
3. Greenville: Mt. Cuba Center for the Study of Piedmont Flora
4. Rehoboth Beach: The Homestead
5. Wilmington: Hagley Museum and Library
6. Wilmington: Rockwood Museum and Gardens

years, some color has been added, including twenty thousand tulips that glow in early spring.

---

LOCATION: Approximately 4 miles north of Wilmington on Rockland Rd.; take I-95 to the U.S. 202 exit, go north on U.S. 202, turn left onto State Rte. 141, then left onto Rockland Rd.

ADDRESS: Nemours Mansions and Gardens, P.O. Box 109, Wilmington, DE 19899.

TELEPHONE: 302-651-6912.

HOURS: Open May–Nov. only. All visits begin with a guided tour of the mansion. Tours are Tues.–Sat., at 9, 11, 1, and 3; and Sun., at 11 and 1. Visitors are requested to arrive at the reception center 15 minutes early. Reservations recommended.

FEE: $7/person. Visitors must be 16 or older.

TOURS: Garden bus tour available to all.

RESTAURANTS: Alfred I. Du Pont Institute cafeteria; for information call 302-651-4742.

SHOPS: None on grounds.

WHEELCHAIR ACCESS: Not permitted because of many stairways.

---

TIPS: 1. Don't miss:
   a. Sunken Gardens, with walls and stairs of travertine marble and a fascinating fountain display.
   b. Reflecting Pool, originally the swimming pool and over an acre in size, with 157 fountain jets.
   c. Southern Gardens, nearly a quarter acre of formal beds of annuals and perennials.
   d. The Temple of Love, containing a sculpture by Jean-Antoine Houdon, who befriended Benjamin Franklin in Paris during the American Revolution and later came to the United States. His works are also on exhibit at Mount Vernon and the Virginia State House in Richmond.
2. Open May to November only; each of these months offers something special in the gardens. Still, May and October stand out—May for its blossoms and fresh breezes, October for the brilliant colors of the estate's specimen trees and surrounding wooded hillsides.
3. For contrast, don't miss the gardens of Alfred's cousins at Longwood and Winterthur, as well as the restored

garden of his great grandfather, E. I. du Pont, at the Hagley Museum and Library.

## WINTERTHUR: WINTERTHUR

*One of North America's loveliest naturalized gardens, where native flora blend with cultivated species, especially azaleas and rhododendrons, to produce a handsome effect.*

"Naturalized gardens on a princely scale" is how the *New York Times* described Winterthur (pronounced Winter-TOUR). The description is deserved. Named after a town in Switzerland, the gardens were created by Henry Francis du Pont in the late 1920s. Mr. du Pont wanted to maintain the tranquil parklike essence of his 1,000 acres of rolling hills, forests, and streams, and yet enhance 200 of them by the addition of rare species from around the globe, especially from East Asia. With the assistance of the Arnold Arboretum, du Pont was able to obtain a vast assortment of azaleas and rhododendrons, carefully selected for quality of color. The author has walked through Winterthur with du Pont, who explained many of the unique and meticulous methods utilized here. For example, du Pont would have his gardener drive long stakes into the ground at the point where certain trees were to be planted. du Pont would leave the stakes for as long as a year, looking at them from all directions at all seasons, to make certain that the trees would harmonize with the existing flora. Another example: being fond of daffodils, he would have a limb of white pine cut and spread across the ground, using the outline of its irregular branch structure to shape a new daffodil bed.

LOCATION: On Delaware Highway 52, 6 miles northwest of Wilmington, 36 miles south of Philadelphia.
ADDRESS: Winterthur Museum and Gardens, Winterthur, DE 19735.
TELEPHONE: 302-654-1548.
HOURS: Tues.–Sat., 10–4; Sun., 12–4. Closed Mon., as well as Thanksgiving, Dec. 24 and 25, and Jan. 1.
FEE: $8/adult; discounts for students and senior citizens.
TOURS: 45-minute tram tours, narrated by guides, scheduled throughout the day; self-guided walking tours.
RESTAURANT: In visitors' pavilion, for breakfast, lunch and snacks;

Outdoor Gallery Cafe open April–Oct. for lunch and snacks, weather permitting. Picnicking in designated areas.

SHOPS: Book shop in visitors' pavilion; shops (plants, gifts, reproduction furniture) also located in Gallery.

WHEELCHAIR ACCESS: Generally accessible by wheelchair. Tour tram adapted for two wheelchairs.

SPECIAL ACTIVITIES: Winterthur maintains a regular schedule of interpretive programs and workshops. It is also actively engaged in the propagation and distribution of rare plants.

---

TIPS: 1. Don't miss:

    a. Azalea Woods with its excellent collection of azaleas in white, pink, mauve, salmon, and red, and the famous Dexter rhododendrons, noted for their pure colors.

    b. Oak Hill and March Bank offer the best views and bright color from March through October.

    c. Pinetum, possessing more than fifty species, one of North America's best collections of rare conifers.

    d. Chandler Woods, natural woodland magnificent in autumn. The 300-year-old William Penn Tree, the tallest in Delaware, is located here.

    e. Winterthur Museum, in the former du Pont mansion, displaying more than seventy thousand objects of decorative and fine art from the mid-seventeenth through the mid-nineteenth centuries.

2. Winterthur is best in spring, with its bulbs and flowering trees, peaking in May with azaleas and rhododendrons. Autumn is excellent for foliage and berries, further embellished by unexpected blossoms of fall crocuses, goldenrod, and asters. A calendar of blooms is available upon request.

3. It is helpful to take the tram tour through the garden to get an overview first, then proceed on foot to the areas that interest you.

4. For contrast, see the gardens of Henry's cousins at Nemours and Longwood, as well as the restored garden of his great-grandfather, E. I. du Pont, at the Hagley Museum and Library.

# EXCELLENT GARDENS

## GREENVILLE: MT. CUBA CENTER FOR THE STUDY OF PIEDMONT FLORA

The display gardens of Mt. Cuba, under development for twenty years, are a superb blend of a collector's garden with a sensitively developed naturalistic landscape. In 1985 Mrs. Lammot du Pont Copeland, owner and designer of these gardens, opened them for the first time to a limited number of visitors from late April to early June. The native plant gardens, featuring wildflowers and native trees and shrubs, occupy a slope clothed with young forest and open meadow. There are ponds, dry rocky hillsides, sunny sites and moist, densely shady areas. In spring, hundreds of wildflowers, native rhododendrons, flowering trees, and mountain laurel burst into bloom, leaving no doubt that plants from North America are at least equal in beauty to exotics from far-off lands. A limited number of days and tour times are available to organized horticultural groups of ten to fifteen members by prearrangement only. There are no restroom facilities, because of the rough terrain, and no wheelchair access. Fee: None. Location: About 5 miles northeast of Wilmington. For further information, write: Box 3570, Greenville, DE 19807. Tel.: 302-239-4244.

## REHOBOTH BEACH: THE HOMESTEAD

The Homestead and its gardens are owned and maintained by the Rehoboth Art League, Inc. Begun in 1930, the gardens today include Tea Terrace, Crown Garden (foxglove, begonia, columbine, topiary boxwood), Sundial Garden, Chain Garden (roses, sedums), Criss-Cross Garden (ground covers, bulbs, lilies), and Herb Garden (culinary and medicinal herbs). The Homestead, built in 1743, is in the National Register of Historic Places and is the oldest house in Rehoboth Beach. Studios, galleries, and classrooms of the Rehoboth Art League are also located on the grounds, and a full schedule of performances and exhibitions are held throughout the season. Guided tours of the gardens are available. Wheelchair access. Open mid-May to mid-Oct., Mon.–Sat., 10–4, and Sun., 12–4. Fee: None. Location: Rehoboth Beach is located in south Delaware, on the ocean. Address: 12 Dodds Lane, Henlopen Acres, Rehoboth Beach, DE 19971. Tel.: 302-227-8408.

## WILMINGTON: HAGLEY MUSEUM
## AND LIBRARY

Located on 230 scenic acres along the Brandywine River, Hagley Museum offers a fascinating glimpse into nineteenth-century industrial life via a diversity of restorations, exhibits, and live demonstrations. Among these is Eleutherian Mills, the house and garden of E. I. du Pont, who came to the United States in 1800 and here began his black powder mills and, later, textile mills. Nostalgic for his home and garden in France, he immediately sent for seeds and cuttings and started a 2-acre garden in the French style (thus inspiring such later du Pont masterpieces as Longwood, Nemours, and Winterthur). Today the garden has been faithfully restored according to the original plan. Flower and vegetable beds are laid out in geometric designs, and fruit trees trained as espaliers. Color is prominent in spring (hyacinths, crocuses, narcissuses, violets, tulips, lilacs) and summer (poppies—said to have been introduced into America by du Pont—zinnias, marigolds, lobelias, sunflowers, dahlias, scarlet sage). Flowering trees (magnolias, dogwoods) and shrubs (azaleas) add to the beauty. The Eleutherian Mills house, built in 1802 in the Georgian style, contains furnishings of five generations of du Ponts. Also on view is a small vegetable garden at Blacksmith's Hill, the restored workers' community adjacent to the mill area. Other Hagley Museum attractions include massive stone mills, an 1870s machine shop, powder mills, and a steam engine. The barn contains a collection of wagons, carriages, and two vintage automobiles including one manufactured by the Du Pont Automobile Company. The workshop displays Lammot du Pont's work as a chemist and inventor. The library contains manuscript collections and conference facilities. The Hagley store sells gifts and other items. Snacks and beverages available at several locations. Wheelchair access. Gift shop. Open daily, Apr.–Dec., 9:30–4:30; Sat. and Sun. only, Jan.–March, 9:30–4:30; a tour is provided on weekdays, Jan.–March, at 1:30; closed Thanksgiving, Christmas, and Jan. 1. Fee: $5/adult, $4/seniors and students, $2/children 6–14. Located on State Rte. 141, north of downtown Wilmington. For further information, write to Box 3630, Wilmington, DE 19807. Tel.: 302-658-2400.

## WILMINGTON: ROCKWOOD MUSEUM AND GARDENS

Listed in the National Register of Historic Places, Rockwood represents the Gothic-style estate of the mid-nineteenth century with gardens landscaped in the naturalistic tradition, emphasizing broad lawns, graceful trees, and sweeping vistas. Open Tues.–Sat., 11–3. Fee: None for garden; for mansion tour, $3/adult, $2.50/seniors, $1/children 5–16. Located north of downtown Wilmington, between I-895 and U.S. 13 (Market St.); take Washington St. north, turn left onto Shipley Rd. Address: 610 Shipley Road, Wilmington, DE 19809. Tel.: 302-571-7776.

# District of Columbia

## "DON'T MISS" GARDENS

### DUMBARTON OAKS

*Carefully conceived and embellished, this once private garden demonstrates the best of garden design in every detail. A garden not to be missed, especially by students of horticulture and garden architecture.*

Originally named after an area in Scotland, this farmland was purchased in 1920 by Mr. and Mrs. Robert Woods Bliss. The story of how they met is romantic—their parents, each widowed, married in 1894, thereby bringing Robert Bliss, age 18, and Mildred Barnes, age 14, together. Married in 1908, Robert and Mildred Bliss spent most of their time abroad because of his career in the foreign service. During these years Mildred Bliss toured many of the world's most famous gardens and conceived the idea of turning Dumbarton Oaks into a place of quiet elegance. Working closely with the renowned landscape architect Beatrix Farrand, she created a 16-acre garden, encompassing many features of Italian design. The garden was divided into several segments, or "garden rooms," designed to serve as extensions of the house itself. Secluded nooks provided privacy for reading, meditation, and conversation. There is also a small courtyard for family meals and a broad terrace for lavish parties. Each of these areas, including every bench, tile, fence, wall, stairway, and pergola, was individually detailed in Farrand's plan. For example, the broad stairway made of grass is a touch rarely seen elsewhere. Each item in the garden, no matter how small, was simulated by mock-up design, then submitted for approval by Mildred Bliss and by Beatrix Farrand herself, and finally permanently set. Every piece of Swedish wrought-iron furniture was designed by Farrand.

In 1940 the Blisses deeded the house and gardens to Harvard University. In 1944, the Dumbarton Oaks conferences were held here, during which the principles later incorporated into the United Nations charter were formulated.

LOCATION: The garden entrance is on R Street at 31st, in the Georgetown section of Washington.

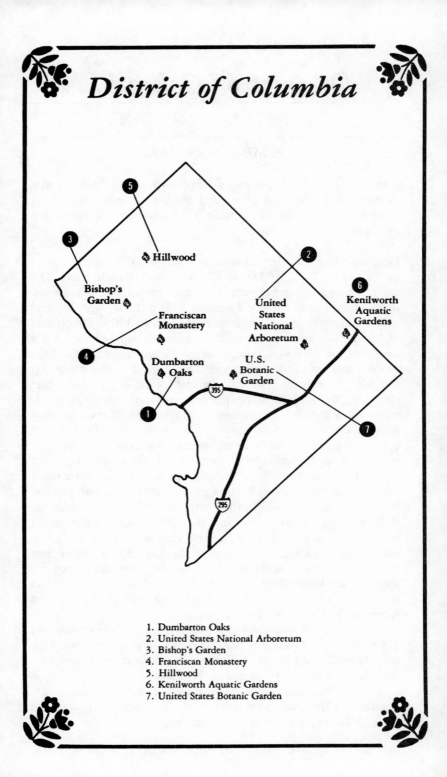

# District of Columbia

5

3

Hillwood

2

6

Bishop's
Garden

United
States
National
Arboretum

Kenilworth
Aquatic
Gardens

Franciscan
Monastery

4

Dumbarton
Oaks

U.S.
Botanic
Garden

395

1

7

295

1. Dumbarton Oaks
2. United States National Arboretum
3. Bishop's Garden
4. Franciscan Monastery
5. Hillwood
6. Kenilworth Aquatic Gardens
7. United States Botanic Garden

ADDRESS: 1703 32nd Street, NW, Washington, DC 20007.

TELEPHONE: 202-338-8278.

HOURS: Open daily, Apr.–Oct., 2–6, and Nov.–Mar., 2–5. Closed during inclement weather as well as on national holidays and Christmas Eve.

FEE: $1/Apr.–Oct.; free/Nov.–Mar. Senior citizens free on Wed.

TOURS: By prearrangement. Call 202-342-3212.

RESTAURANT: None on grounds.

SHOPS: A small shop in the museum sells cards, books, and pamphlets.

WHEELCHAIR ACCESS: Slopes and stairs make this garden inaccessible.

SPECIAL ACTIVITIES: Lectures and concerts throughout the year. Ask for schedule.

---

TIPS: 1. Don't miss:
   a. Pebble Garden, an imaginative design of greenery, pebbles, and a fountain.
   b. Fountain Terrace, Rose Garden, Green Garden—blossoms, stately trees, vistas.
   c. Cherry and Crabapple Hills, lovely in spring.
   d. Orangery, erected in 1810, a copy of those traditionally used in Europe to protect orange trees in winter.
2. Designed as a year-round garden, Dumbarton Oaks is worthy of a visit any time of year, but it's at its best in spring and autumn.
3. The neighboring Dumbarton Oaks Museum, with its world-famous collections of Byzantine and pre-Columbian art, is worth a tour. There is also an extensive collection of books on garden design and horticulture, some dating back to the sixteenth century. A music room is filled with antiques, tapestries, and paintings, including *The Visitation* by El Greco. Igor Stravinsky attended concerts here, and his well-known Concerto in E-flat ("Dumbarton Oaks Concerto") was commissioned in celebration of Mr. and Mrs. Bliss's thirtieth anniversary.

---

# UNITED STATES NATIONAL ARBORETUM

*A multipurpose garden with excellent collections of bonsai, herbs, flowering trees, dwarf conifers, and holly, as well as a wide range of educational programs.*

Established in 1927, the National Arboretum features 9 miles of paved roads through its 444 acres of floral displays, and includes several collections of national prominence. The National Bonsai Collection contains fifty-three plants ranging from 40 to 360 years of age—a bicentennial gift from the Japanese people to the United States. One bonsai is the first from the Imperial collection ever to leave Japan. Other bonsai represent a gift from the King of Morocco, and an American bonsai collection and a Chinese collection will be added soon. The 2-acre National Herb Garden is the largest designed herb garden in the United States. Flowering trees include crab apples, cherries, magnolias, and seventy kinds of dogwoods. Other displays include Fern Valley, Holly Walk, and the Gotelli Dwarf Conifer Collection (1500 specimens). The United States National Arboretum also serves as a center for plant introduction and study, research and breeding.

LOCATION: In northeast Washington, on New York Ave. (U.S. 50), just west of the intersection at Bladenburg Rd.
ADDRESS: 3501 New York Avenue, NE, Washington, DC 20002.
TELEPHONE: 202-475-4815
HOURS: Mon.–Fri., 8–5, and Sat.–Sun., 10–5; closed Christmas. Bonsai collection open daily, 10:00–2:30.
FEE: None.
TOURS: Group tours scheduled with three weeks advance notice.
RESTAURANT: None on grounds.
SHOPS: None on grounds.
WHEELCHAIR ACCESS: Most of garden is accessible.
SPECIAL ACTIVITIES: Full schedule of lectures, workshops, exhibitions, children's programs, and flower shows. Library.

TIPS: 1. Don't miss:
   a. Azaleas in bloom April to June (peak, late April to early May).
   b. Flowering cherries and dogwoods in April.
   c. Bonsai collection, National Herb Garden, Gotelli Dwarf Conifer Collection.
2. Newly constructed Latrobe Capitol Columns with reflecting pool and fountain.
3. Numerous flower shows sponsored by local garden societies throughout the year (check for dates).

# EXCELLENT GARDENS

## BISHOP'S GARDEN

Adjacent to the Gothic Washington Cathedral, this garden contains a variety of excellent medieval sections, a rose garden, an array of flowering trees (cherry, witch hazel, Washington thorn), pathways lined with bulbs in spring and chrysanthemums in autumn, and masonry and sculpture dating back to the ninth century. Of particular note is the stonework, which, in order to harmonize with the cathedral's fourteenth-century style of architecture, was taken from old walls, mills, ice houses, and chimneys. In the Hortulus (Latin for "Little Garden") is a ninth-century French baptismal font. The Perennial Border walkway is edged with curbstones originally laid in the streets of nearby Alexandria by Hessians captured during the American Revolution. Peak bloom is in April. Gifts can be purchased at the Herb Cottage and Museum Shop; live plants available at the Cathedral Greenhouse. Group tours or slide presentations by prearrangement. On the first Friday and Saturday of May, a flower mart is held offering spring blossoms, entertainment, crafts, food, music and films, and children's activities, including an antique carousel. In late September and early October there is an open house with demonstrations of stone carving, calligraphy, and bell ringing, as well as entertainment and garden tours. Garden open daily. Fee: None. Located in northwest Washington at Wisconsin (State Rte. 355) and Massachusetts Aves., NW. For further information, write All Hallows Guild, Washington Cathedral, Mt. Saint Alban, Washington, DC 20016. Tel.: 202-537-6200.

## FRANCISCAN MONASTERY

Established in 1900, the monastery covers 45 acres of which fifteen are landscaped into the secluded gardens well known to Washingtonians. From April into October the gardens offer blossoms in the form of daffodils, tulips (three thousand), azaleas, rhododendrons, roses (two thousand), and perennials. In addition, the church possesses interesting paintings and statuary, as well as actual-size replicas of many famous shrines and monuments (Holy Sepulchre, Grotto at Lourdes). The garden will be wheelchair accessible by late 1987. Tours of church (not garden) provided hourly, 9–4 daily. Grounds open 8–sunset. Fee: None. Located in northeast Washington, about a ten minute walk from Catholic University; take Rhode Island Ave. to 14th St., turn left and proceed to Quincy St. Address: 1400 Quincy St., N.E., Washington, DC 20017. Tel.: 202-526-6800.

## HILLWOOD

The residence of Marjorie Merriweather Post until 1973, the Hillwood mansion and the 25-acre grounds are now open to the public. The mansion contains Post's impressive collections of eighteenth- and nineteenth-century French and Russian art, while the grounds offer a rose garden, a Japanese garden, French parterres, seasonal flowers, azaleas, laurels and rhododendrons, broad lawns and natural woodlands, and a greenhouse containing an orchid collection. Gift shop. Tea room for breakfast or lunch (the food is excellent). Wheelchair access by special arrangement. Open Mon., Wed.–Sat., garden hours, 11–4, and mansion tours at 9:00, 10:30, 12:00, and 1:30. Fee: Gardens only, $2; 2-hour mansion tour, $7 (call for reservation). Located near Rock Creek Park; take Connecticut Ave. north to Upton St. to Linnean Ave. Address: 4155 Linnean Ave., NW, Washington, DC 20008. Tel.: 202-686-5807.

## KENILWORTH AQUATIC GARDENS

Located in the 703-acre Kenilworth Park and developed on tidal flats of the Anacostia River, these gardens started as a commercial business in 1882. What began for Walter Shaw as a hobby of raising and hybridizing waterlilies became the nation's largest aquatic garden business, shipping plants around the world. Now owned by the National Park Service, the gardens today offer nearly 14 acres of ponds containing thousands of lily plants and marshlands filled with native aquatic plants. There is a visitor center with displays and exhibits, and a greenhouse. Peak lily bloom: June to July. Open daily, 8–sunset. Fee: None. Located in northeast Washington off Kenilworth Avenue, directly across the Anacostia River from the National Arboretum (a ferry is planned to connect the two). For further information, write, National Capital Parks—East, 1900 Anacostia Drive, SE, Washington, DC 20020. Tel.: 202-426-6905.

# UNITED STATES BOTANIC GARDEN

The U.S. Botanic Garden Conservatory, an educational display garden under 29,000 square feet of glass, includes major collections of aroids, bromeliads, begonias, cacti, cycads (primitive palmlike plants), palms, and orchids (more than 250 plants). There are four annual shows: Spring Show (masses of spring flowers—Palm Sunday through Easter Sunday); Summer Terrace Display (hundreds of hanging baskets—late May through September); Chrysanthemum Show (mid-November through Thanksgiving); Holiday Show (poinsettias—mid-December through the holidays). The garden also hosts plant and flower shows held by local garden clubs. Adjacent to the conservatory is the 1-acre U.S. Botanic Park with its Bartholdi fountain (Bartholdi is best known in America as the sculptor of the Statue of Liberty), and its summer bulbs and annual and perennial flowers. Group tours of U.S. Botanic Garden by prearrangement. Wheelchair accessible. Classes and lectures scheduled year round. Plant information service available via letter or phone, Mon.–Fri., 1–4. Open daily, June–Aug., 9–9, and Sept.–May, 9–5. Fee: None. Located at Maryland Ave. and First St., SW. Address: 245 First St., SW, Washington, DC 20024. Tel.: 202-225-8333.

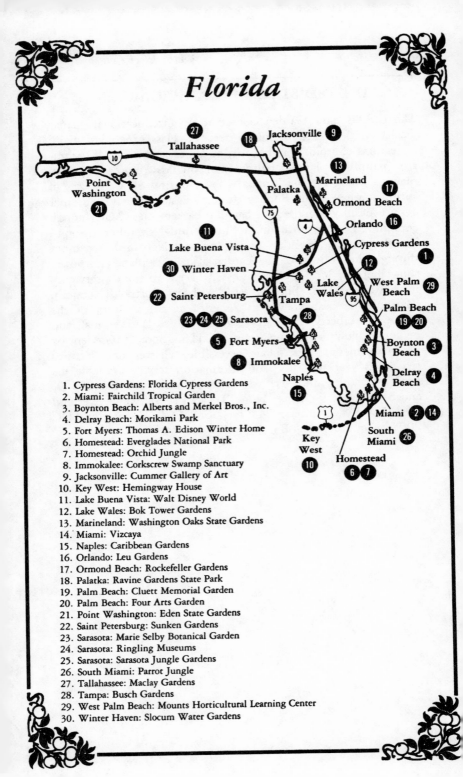

# Florida

1. Cypress Gardens: Florida Cypress Gardens
2. Miami: Fairchild Tropical Garden
3. Boynton Beach: Alberts and Merkel Bros., Inc.
4. Delray Beach: Morikami Park
5. Fort Myers: Thomas A. Edison Winter Home
6. Homestead: Everglades National Park
7. Homestead: Orchid Jungle
8. Immokalee: Corkscrew Swamp Sanctuary
9. Jacksonville: Cummer Gallery of Art
10. Key West: Hemingway House
11. Lake Buena Vista: Walt Disney World
12. Lake Wales: Bok Tower Gardens
13. Marineland: Washington Oaks State Gardens
14. Miami: Vizcaya
15. Naples: Caribbean Gardens
16. Orlando: Leu Gardens
17. Ormond Beach: Rockefeller Gardens
18. Palatka: Ravine Gardens State Park
19. Palm Beach: Cluett Memorial Garden
20. Palm Beach: Four Arts Garden
21. Point Washington: Eden State Gardens
22. Saint Petersburg: Sunken Gardens
23. Sarasota: Marie Selby Botanical Garden
24. Sarasota: Ringling Museums
25. Sarasota: Sarasota Jungle Gardens
26. South Miami: Parrot Jungle
27. Tallahassee: Maclay Gardens
28. Tampa: Busch Gardens
29. West Palm Beach: Mounts Horticultural Learning Center
30. Winter Haven: Slocum Water Gardens

# *Florida*

## "DON'T MISS" GARDENS

### CYPRESS GARDENS: FLORIDA CYPRESS GARDENS

*A well-known tourist attraction combining the beauty of magnificent flowering shrubbery with the fun of spectacular waterski shows, children's rides, a petting zoo, a walk-through aviary, and shops and snacks.*

Opened in 1936, Florida Cypress Gardens broke away from the tradition of planning gardens as remote cloisters of sanctuary and tranquillity. From the start it was devised by Richard and Julie Pope as an extravaganza meant to attract hordes of visitors from the Northeast. This is a lively, often noisy place, yet it is well-organized and impressive in its beauty.

After a successful career in advertising, Mr. Pope braved the Great Depression by returning in 1932 to Winter Haven, where he grew up, to build Cypress Gardens. He designed the area into what *Life Magazine* once called a "photographer's paradise." The Original Gardens, for example, contain stunning bougain-villea vines, so large that they require the support of telephone poles. Here, too, is an enormous glory bush with a breathtaking display of purple flowers, and a giant banyan, planted from a 5-gallon bucket about 50 years ago, now 200 feet in diameter.

By attracting the cameras of magazine photographers and moviemakers seeking to use Pope's 223-acre creation for their productions, Florida Cypress Gardens has earned itself invalu-able publicity, which has brought visitors by the thousands to its once unknown gates in central Florida. Over the years, more than 30 million have come—nearly 1.5 million last year alone. Florida Cypress Gardens remains one of Florida's best-known and most-loved attractions, a worthy neighbor to Disney World 30 miles up the road. Indeed, Mr. Pope told the author that more film is sold in his shops than anywhere else in Florida.

LOCATION: In central Florida, 4 miles southeast of Winter Haven on State Rte. 540; 30 miles from Disney World.
ADDRESS: Box 1, Cypress Gardens, FL 33880.

TELEPHONE: 813-324-2111.
HOURS: Open daily, 8–sunset.
FEE: $14.95/adult, $9.95/child.
TOURS: For groups by prearrangement.
RESTAURANTS: Snack bar and restaurant.
SHOPS: Film, plants, mementos, books.
WHEELCHAIR ACCESS: Access to most areas. Wheelchairs available free of charge.

---

TIPS: 1. Don't miss:
  a. Original Gardens, already mentioned, with their incredible color (eight hundred varieties of plants). The chrysanthemum display (over one million flowers), for example, is equalled only at Longwood Gardens. This area can be viewed by an electric boat tour, a good way to get an overview before setting out on foot.
  b. Gardens of the World offers examples of various cultures, including the lush Mediterranean Water Falls, Greek Stage, and Italian Fountains.
  c. Cypress Point Pier, via a boardwalk, provides an excursion into "old" Florida with its primeval swamps and moss-hung cypress trees.

  2. Peak color is November through May.

  3. Especially renowned for its waterskiing shows, Florida Cypress Gardens is a first-class family attraction offering shows, rides, restaurants and snacks, a walk-through aviary, a sky ride, an animal forest, and a petting zoo. Southern belles dressed in 9-foot hoop skirts are strategically stationed among the flora to add to the over-all ambience. Special tourist services include strollers for infants, kennels, and a first-aid station. If there was ever a garden, holding something for the whole family, this is it. With Disney World just down the road, the area is perhaps the world's foremost family vacation spot.

---

## MIAMI: FAIRCHILD TROPICAL GARDEN

*Primarily an educational and scientific garden, Fairchild Tropical Garden is the largest tropical garden in the United States with extensive collections of palms and cycads and superior collections of orchids and flowering vines.*

Named after the famous plant explorer, David Fairchild, this is a prime example of a botanical garden designed with consideration for aesthetics. For the expert it offers excellent tropical flora, palms, and cycads, and for all visitors it provides winding paths, eight lakes, and fine vistas embellished by wild waterbirds and lush vegetation.

The palm collection, one of the world's finest, has more than five hundred species, many collected by David Fairchild. Because palms grow only in tropical and subtropical areas, many Americans aren't acquainted with this highly useful family. Among its products are fruits, nuts, oil, sugar, milk, coconut, sago—over five hundred in all.

Complementing the palms are the cycads, the first seed plants on earth. The cycads lived with the dinosaur. These plants once represented a major evolutionary step—the first employment of seed, a more durable form of propagation than the primitive and vulnerable spore.

Also found here are aroids, ferns, orchids, bromeliads, flowering trees, and plants indigenous to south Florida, the Everglades, and the Bahamas. The tropical tree collection is first-rate. Tropical trees often have thin barks (drying out is a rare concern), subsidiary trunks, and air roots. A good example is the banyan tree, one of which can create a small forest of its own with its innumerable secondary trunks and outreaching limbs. Also here is the baobab, whose trunk is so large that in Africa it's sometimes hollowed out to make a small house. The tree is pollinated by a rarely considered agent—the bat.

---

LOCATION: On Biscayne Bay, 10 miles south of downtown Miami, in southeast Coral Gables.

ADDRESS: 10901 Old Cutler Rd., Miami, FL 33156.

TELEPHONE: 305-667-1651.

HOURS: Open daily, 9:30–4:30; closed Christmas.

FEE: $3.00/ages 13 and older.

TOURS: Guided tours available via tram or on foot. Group tours by prearrangement.

RESTAURANTS: Snack bar.

SHOPS: Book shop.

WHEELCHAIR ACCESS: Some displays accessible.

SPECIAL ACTIVITIES: Educational programs on a wide variety of subjects. Auditorium for lectures and shows. Palm Museum and Library.

---

TIPS: 1. In addition to the palms, cycads, and tropical trees, don't miss:
   a. The Sunken Garden, a cool expedition along a tropical forest floor.
   b. Rare Plant House filled with orchids, bromeliads, and jade vine.
   c. Semple Vine Pergola and its incredible bougainvillea.
   d. The Rain Forest, displaying the lush, layer-upon-layer growth of plants climbing and competing for light. Probably the best replica of a tropical rain forest in the United States.
2. Peak blossoming periods are March and October.
3. Bring insect repellant in summer.

# EXCELLENT GARDENS

## BOYNTON BEACH: ALBERTS AND MERKEL BROS., INC.

Opened in 1890, this private nursery specializes in orchids and other tropical foliage. Greenhouses offer continually blooming orchid displays. Open Mon.–Sat., 8:00–4:30. Free: None. Located on U.S. 1 between West Palm Beach and Boca Raton. Address: 2210 S. Federal Hwy., Boynton Beach, FL 33435. Tel.: 305-732-2071.

## DELRAY BEACH: MORIKAMI PARK

Morikami Park contains a Japanese garden with a bonsai collection and a 1-mile self-guided nature trail. There is also a museum that offers exhibits, lectures, concerts, and plays relevant to Japanese culture, with Children's Activities Days in June, July, and August. Picnicking facilities. Open Tues.–Sun., 10–5, closed most holidays. Fee: None. Located off Carter Rd. in west Delray Beach, between I-95 and the Florida Tpk. Address: 4000 Morikami Park Rd., Delray Beach, FL 33446. Tel.: 305-499-0631 (recording) or 305-495-0233.

## FORT MYERS: THOMAS A. EDISON WINTER HOME

Known more for his technological inventions, Edison had an indefatigable curiosity that also encompassed the world of flora.

His winter home with its 13-acre garden on the bank of the Caloosahatchee River is where he conducted most of his botanical experiments. Rare trees predominate—a lovely South American rain tree, a 100-foot hibiscus, a sloth tree of the West Indies, a sausage tree (whose fruit look like large potatoes dangling from long vines), a fried egg tree, a dynamite tree, mangoes, sapodillas (which produce chicle for chewing gum), and a banyan tree that was 2 inches high when given to Edison by Harvey Firestone (Firestone Rubber) and now measures 400 feet around. Aerial orchids and flowering vines also abound. In addition, there are tours of the great man's laboratory, his antique car collection (including several personal gifts from Henry Ford), a swimming pool made with reinforced bamboo, and an exhibit detailing Edison's investigations into producing synthetic rubber from goldenrod, a process of crucial importance during World War II. Tours are guided. Wheelchairs available. Open daily, Mon.–Sat., 9–4, and Sun., 12:30–4:00. Fee: $4/adult, $1/children ages 6–12. Located 2 miles southwest of downtown Fort Myers. Address: 2350 McGregor Blvd., Fort Myers, FL 33901. Tel.: 813-334-3614.

## HOMESTEAD: EVERGLADES NATIONAL PARK

One of the world's great natural botanical gardens, with a particularly wide and unusual array of bog and water plants. Viewable by car or boat. Open daily, all hours; interpretive center open daily, 8–5. Fee: $2/car. Location: entrance to park is off U.S. 1, near Florida City, about 26 miles south of Miami. For further information write to P.O. Box 279, Homestead, FL 33030. Tel.: 305-247-6211.

## HOMESTEAD: ORCHID JUNGLE

Billing itself as the world's largest orchid garden, Orchid Jungle consists of 23 acres of natural forest with exotic plants covering the trees and ground. There are small greenhouses and a lath house filled with many colorful and interesting orchid species. An orchid show is offered daily (check for time), and selected specimens are for sale. Open daily, 8:30–5:30. Fee: $3.50/adult, $2.80/ages 13–17, $1.25/ages 6–12. Located just off U.S. 1 at 272nd St., 25 miles south of Miami. Address: 26715 S.W. 157th Ave., Homestead, FL 33030. Tel.: 305-247-4824.

## IMMOKALEE: CORKSCREW SWAMP SANCTUARY

Corkscrew Swamp Sanctuary provides a fascinating experience, made possible by a mile-long boardwalk through a swamp as impenetrable and mysterious as the Everglades. This is the old Florida, the natural Florida—ancient trees, shrubs, vines, and air plants in a lush tangle that gives sanctuary to innumerable waterfowl and reptiles. Immaculately designed and maintained by the National Audubon Society, this is perhaps the best display of its type in North America. A must for anyone wanting to view the real thing from closer than a car seat. Wheelchairs available. Open daily, 9–5. Fee: $4/adult, $2/students and children over age 12. Located near Rte. 846, 30 miles northeast of Naples. For further information, write to the Corkscrew Swamp Sanctuary, Rte. 6, Box 1875, Sanctuary Rd., Naples, FL 33939. Tel.: 813-657-3771.

## JACKSONVILLE: CUMMER GALLERY OF ART

Begun in 1903, this 2½-acre garden is styled upon English and Italian prototypes and contains the appropriate shrubs, bulbs, and evergreens along the banks of the Saint Johns River. Peak bloom is in spring. The gallery contains works from the times of ancient Greece to the twentieth century. Open Tues.–Fri., 10–4; Sat., 12–5; Sun., 2–5. Fee: None. Located south of downtown Jacksonville, just off U.S 17. Address: 829 Riverside Dr., Jacksonville, FL 32204. Tel.: 904-356-6857.

## KEY WEST: HEMINGWAY HOUSE

The Spanish-Colonial-style home of Ernest Hemingway is located upon an acre of lushly landscaped grounds. Hemingway wrote many of his best works here (*The Snows of Kilimanjaro, For Whom the Bell Tolls*). The grounds are packed with tropical plants (as well as several offspring of Hemingway's fifty cats), and the house is filled with furnishings and mementos obtained by the Nobel Prize-winning author in Spain and Africa. Open daily, 9–5. Fee: $3/adult, $1/children 6–12. Located in western Key West at the intersection of Whitehead and Oliva, near the Lighthouse and Military Museum. Address: 907 Whitehead St., Key West, FL 33040. Tel.: 305-294-1575.

# LAKE BUENA VISTA: WALT DISNEY WORLD

The new home of the world-famous Magic Kingdom, Epcot Center, and Walt Disney World Village is also well known to horticulturists as one of North America's finest landscaped theme parks. Almost every day of the year gardeners plant and replant flower beds and borders, maintaining an unspoiled display of color and greenery despite changing weather conditions and daily crowds. At Disney World the flora is intended only to augment the various displays, attractions, and rides, but it is worth taking a moment to notice the degree of perfection with which the gardens and beds are kept. In addition, nine diverse gardens are presented at the the Garden of the World Showcase. Walt Disney World is also a first-class resort as well as a tourist attraction. Entertainment, sports, boat rides, beaches, and baby-sitting are just a few of the amenities offered to visitors of all ages. Hours and fees vary—check for specifics. Located off U.S. 192 in central Florida, near the intersection of I-4 and the Florida Tpk. For further information, write to Walt Disney World, P.O. Box 40, Dept GL, Lake Buena Vista, FL 32830. Tel.: 305-824-8000.

# LAKE WALES: BOK TOWER GARDENS

This 128-acre garden of dense greenery and flowering trees is the setting for the famous Bok Tower. The tower holds one of the world's largest carillons (fifty-three bells, ranging from 17 pounds to 12 tons) and may be heard every hour and half hour as well as at the daily 3:00 P.M. recital. Bok Tower Gardens is a lovely and peaceful place, carefully designed and caringly maintained. Even the ducks are friendly, and children adore feeding them. Azaleas in bloom December through April; camellias in bloom November through March. Picnicking. Garden cafe and gift shop. Wheelchairs and strollers available. Special activities include the Moonlight Recitals, the Easter Sunrise Service, Christmas programs, and the Pinewood Concert and Lecture Series. Open daily, 8:00–5:30. Fee: $2/ages 12 and over; group rates. Located 3 miles north of Lake Wales in central Florida, off Burns Ave. (County Rd. 17A). For further information, write to Bok Tower Gardens, P.O. Drawer 3810, Lake Wales, FL 33853. Tel.: 813-676-1408.

## MARINELAND: WASHINGTON OAKS STATE GARDENS

Bordered by the Altantic Ocean and the Matangas River, these 390 acres contain a boardwalk along beach rock formations, a native hardwood hammock forest, and, unusual for this area, formal gardens featuring azaleas, camellias, roses, and exotic species from around the world. Tours by prearrangement. Picnicking. Pavilion available for weddings. Open daily, 8–sunset. Fee: $.50 per person. Located in northern Florida on State Rte. A1A, 2 miles south of Marineland. For further information, write to the State of Florida, Dept. of Natural Resources, 3900 Commonwealth Blvd., Tallahassee, FL 32303. Tel.: 904-488-1234.

## MIAMI: VIZCAYA

The garden at Vizcaya is an excellent replica of an Italian Renaissance hillside garden. The Vizcaya mansion, called "America's most beautiful home," is a 10-acre estate begun in 1914. The project employed a thousand workers for a period of 2 years (at a time when Miami's total population was ten thousand). The garden, which took 9 years to develop, was designed in the classical Italian manner as an extension of the villa itself—an outdoor "room" offering tranquillity and cool shade in the warm climate. Hence the grottoes (shell-lined nooks or caves) that remain cool in summer. The Italian soil does not favor profuse and colorful growth, so Italian Renaissance gardens were evergreen gardens—all-season sanctuaries of greenery, water, and stone. Fountains are frequently utilized, and Vizcaya's Bassani di Sutri Fountain is an original from the town of the same name (it's said the town demanded reconstruction of its water system before parting with the fountain). The best view of this garden, which is designed like a tapestry, is from the mansion's second floor. Peak season is November through May. Guided tours of the mansion; group garden tours by prearrangement. "Sound and Light at Vizcaya," an evening presentation of music, dancing fountains, and narration, is presented regularly. Gift shop. Restaurant on premises. Open daily, 9:30–5:00; closed Christmas. Fee: $4. Located on Biscayne Bay, south of downtown Miami. Address: 3251 S. Miami Ave., Miami, FL 33129. Tel.: 305-854-6559.

## NAPLES: CARIBBEAN GARDENS

Also known as Jungle Larry's Safari, Caribbean Gardens contains tropical animals and birds throughout the garden's 52 acres of towering palms and dense cypress groves, which can be viewed by foot or tram tour. Greenhouses contain singular displays of orchids and bromeliads. There is an adjacent zoo. Animal shows at 11, 2, and 4. Open 9:30–5:30; closed Mondays. Fee: $6.95/adult, $5.95/juniors, $4.95/children. Location: Naples is located in southwestern Florida, 104 miles due west of Miami and 36 miles south of Fort Myers; Caribbean Gardens can be found 2 miles north of Naples. Address: 1590 Goodlette Rd., Naples, FL 33940. Tel.: 813-262-4053.

## ORLANDO: LEU GARDENS

This beautiful 56-acre garden holds over two thousand varieties of plants and features central Florida's largest collection of camellias. Displays also include an acre of roses, an azalea garden, a lily circle, a ravine garden, a floral clock, and a conservatory with tropicals and orchids. Paths meander under arching oaks and camphor trees, within view of Lake Rowena. Festivals are held in March (Strawberry Spring—a weekend of visual and performing arts), October (Central Florida Lawn and Garden Show), and December (Holidays at Leu Gardens). Scheduled events include concerts, art shows, classes, workshops, and lectures. Tours on weekends; group tours by prearrangement. Leu House open for tours and available for weddings, receptions, or meetings. Open daily, 9–5; closed Christmas. Fee for house and garden: $3/ages 12 and over; $.50/ages 5–11. Located in central Orlando; take U.S. 17 (State 92) to Nebraska to Forest. Address: 1730 Forest Ave., Orlando, FL 32803. Tel.: 305-894-6021.

## ORMOND BEACH: ROCKEFELLER GARDENS

Seasonal flowers, a natural woodland with pools and footbridges, a grand promenade, and a citrus garden along the riverfront, represent the outdoor displays at John D.'s winter home, The Casements, constructed in the 1920s. Garden open daily; mansion open Mon.–Thurs., 9–9; Fri., 9–5; and Sat., 9–12.

Garden fee: None; free tours of mansion conducted Mon.–Fri., 10–3. Located 6 miles north of Daytona Beach. Address: 25 Riverside Dr., Ormond Beach, FL 32074. Tel.: 904-673-4701.

## PALATKA: RAVINE GARDENS STATE PARK

An unusual setting results in a particularly effective display: a steep, water-carved ravine, filled with masses of native azaleas. These colorful plants—over a hundred thousand of them—create a dazzling spectacle every year from late February to early March, at which time an azalea festival is held. By May, three hundred thousand flowering annuals start to take over, carpeting the park with drifts of multicolored blossoms. Created in 1933 by the Federal WPA program, the park and its buildings are available for weddings, meetings, receptions, or dances. Group tours by prearrangement. Open daily, 8–sunset. Fee: None. Located on Twigg St., south of Palatka, just off State Rte. 20 in northern Florida. Address: P.O. Box 1096, Palatka, FL 32077. Tel.: 904-328-4366.

## PALM BEACH: CLUETT MEMORIAL GARDEN

Part of the Episcopal Church of Bethesda-By-The-Sea, which was built in 1925, the Cluett Memorial Garden consists of terraces containing pools, pergolas, fountains, and colorful flowering and tropical plants. Open daily, 9–5. Fee: None. Address: S. County Rd. and Barton Ave., Palm Beach, FL 33480. Tel.: 305-655-4554.

## PALM BEACH: FOUR ARTS GARDEN

A splendid collection of demonstration gardens, especially for the horticultural enthusiast, created through the efforts of the Palm Beach Garden Club. The "four arts" pertain not to the garden per se, but to the Society of Four Arts, which produces concerts, lectures, and exhibits. The gardens were added in 1938. The blend of small gardens includes a formal flower garden, rose garden, jungle garden, rock garden, herb garden, moonlight garden (containing white-blossoming shrubs and vines), and an authentic Chinese garden noted for its sculpture and plantings. Open: weekdays, 10–5. Fee: None. Address: Four Arts Plaza, Royal Palm Way, Palm Beach, FL 33480. Tip: In order to raise funds, once a year the Palm Beach Garden Club promotes a tour of the luxuriant homes and gardens of fabled Palm Beach. Tel.: 305-655-7226.

## POINT WASHINGTON: EDEN STATE GARDENS

Originally built in 1895, this restored white-columned Greek Revival mansion reflects the opulent life-style of Florida's Gold Coast at the turn of the century. Complementing the house are 11 beautifully landscaped acres with sprawling, moss-covered oaks, and masses of azaleas and camellias. Tours of the mansion on the hour. Open 8–sunset daily, May 1–Sept. 15; Fri.–Tues. only, Sept. 16–Apr. 30. Fee: None for garden; $1 for mansion. Located on U.S. 98 in the Florida panhandle, 1 mile west of Point Washington and 30 miles west of Panama City. Address: Point Washington, FL. Tel.: 904-231-4214.

## SAINT PETERSBURG: SUNKEN GARDENS

This family-oriented attraction in downtown Saint Petersburg draws half a million visitors a year. Its paths wind through 8 lush acres of colorful vines and flowering plants. Over five thousand varieties of tropical and subtropical species are featured, including orchids, bromeliads, ferns, and African violets. A huge, walk-through aviary offers hundreds of exotic and rare birds, including peacocks, flamingos, macaws, parrots, and hornbills. You can see Australian wallabies, African Pygmy goats, or alligators lurking in their lagoons. Or you can shake hands with the friendly monkeys or pluck a pearl from an oyster. Something for every member of the family. Wheelchair accessible. Open daily, 9:00–5:30. Fee: $5/adult, $3/children ages 6–12; group rates. Located on Tampa Bay, on 4th St. north between Central and 22nd Ave. Address: 1825 Fourth St. North, St. Petersburg, FL 33704. Tel.: 813-896-3186.

## SARASOTA: MARIE SELBY BOTANICAL GARDEN

This garden of 14 acres occupies a beautiful bayfront peninsula on Sarasota Bay. A botanical garden as well as a tourist attraction, the Marie Selby has one of the world's most complete collections of epiphytes—orchids, bromeliads, and related plants. Epiphytes are not parasitic—they obtain all of their nutrients from the air and precipitation—and scores of them are grown here on twelve ancient oaks. This garden also boasts the world's largest collection of African violets. Nearly half an acre of greenhouses is devoted to outstanding tropical displays. Open daily, 10–5. Fee: $3.50/ages 12 and over. Location: In downtown Sarasota, on U.S. 41. Address: 811 S. Palm Ave., Sarasota, FL 33577. Tel.: 813-366-5730.

## SARASOTA: RINGLING MUSEUMS

Reminiscent of Vizcaya in style and tone, the Ringling Mansion, also known as Ca'd'Zan, was designed after the famous doge's palace in Venice. In addition to the mansion, this richly landscaped 38-acre estate on Sarasota Bay offers the following: the Ringling Museum of Art, which holds classical and contemporary art works; the Museum of the Circus, with a fascinating collection of posters, photographs, and memorabilia; and the Asolo Theater, which was built in Italy in 1798 and restored here in 1948 and now offers regular performances. As at Vizcaya, the grounds here are meant to complement the mansion and other structures, and they do so admirably. Formal gardens include a rose garden, parterre garden, and a "secret" garden. Many rare trees and other plantings can be found, and the 350-foot garden court of the museum is a wonder of stone and bronze statues, fountains, columns, and arches. Open 10–6 daily, except Thurs. open 10–10. Fee: $4.50/adult, $1.75/children ages 6–12. Located on U.S. 41, three miles north of Sarasota. For further information, write to Ringling Museums, P.O. Box 1838, Sarasota, FL 33578. Tel.: 813-355-5101.

## SARASOTA: SARASOTA JUNGLE GARDENS

Here brick trails wind through banana groves, fern gardens, hibiscus gardens, and lush plantings of bougainvilleas, roses, gardenias, and palms, amid which flamingos, cranes, peacocks, and parrots stroll. Situated on a lake at the center of all this is a beautifully designed, colorful formal garden. Over thirty-five thousand different plants can be seen here. Other attractions include a reptile show, the Jungle Bird Circus, animal displays (monkeys, leopards, iguanas), a petting zoo, and the Shell and Butterfly Museum. Snack bar. Gift shop. Open daily, 9–5. Fee: $4.95/adult, $2.95/children ages 6–16. Located at Myrtle (37th) St. and Bayshore Rd., 2 blocks west of U.S. 41, 2 miles south of the Sarasota-Bradenton Airport. Address: 3701 Bayshore Rd., Sarasota, FL. Tel.: 813-355-5305.

## SOUTH MIAMI: PARROT JUNGLE

Primarily known for its collection of parrots of all sizes, types, and colors, the garden also has trails, pools, and grounds lush with orchids and native plants. Open daily, 9:30–5:00. Fee: $6.75/adult, 3.75/child. Located on S.W. 57th Ave. at Kilian Dr., approximately 2 miles south of downtown South Miami. Address: 11000 S.W. 57th Ave., South Miami, FL 33156. Tel.: 305-666-7834.

## TALLAHASSEE: MACLAY GARDENS

This magnificent 28-acre garden possesses one of the South's most extensive plantings of azaleas and camellias. Perched on a hill over Lake Hall and against a backdrop of towering oaks and pines, Maclay Gardens makes a dramatic setting for the flowering trees (dogwoods, cherry, redbud, magnolia) and extensive plantings of irises, pansies, and various bulbs. Display gardens include the Camellia Walk, the Walled Garden (a brick-walled courtyard with a pool surrounded by flowers), Lake Vista (view across a reflecting pool bordered by white azaleas, native palms, Italian cypress), the Pond Walk (a spectacular hillside of azaleas, daylilies, irises, bulbs mirrored by a pond), and the Lake Walk (across Azalea Hillside and down to the lake). Peak bloom is in mid-March; good color from January through April. Wheelchair access to some areas. Group tours by prearrangement. Open daily, Jan.1–Apr. 30, 8–5. Fee: $2/ages 12 and over, $1/ages 6–12. The garden is closed May 1 through December 31, but the park remains open (8–sunset) as a recreational area (picnic area, fishing, swimming—$.50/ages 12 and up). Located approximately 6 miles north of Tallahassee on U.S. 319, just past I-10. For further information, write to Florida Dept. of Natural Resources, 3900 Commonwealth Blvd., Tallahassee, FL 32303. Tel.: 904-488-1234.

## TAMPA: BUSCH GARDENS

Better known for the amusement park and wild animal kingdom adjacent to its famous brewery, Busch Gardens includes a 48-acre expanse of tropical trees, shrubs, and vines. Winding footpaths meander around sparkling lakes and through thousands of flowering plants. Lovely to look at and a great family excursion. Open daily, 9–5 in winter, 9–6 in summer. Fees vary—check for specifics. Located on Busch Blvd. at 40th St., approximately 6 miles north of downtown Tampa. Address: 3000 Busch Blvd., Tampa, FL 33612. Tel.: 813-971-8282.

# WEST PALM BEACH: MOUNTS HORTICULTURAL LEARNING CENTER

In the 1950s, several fruit trees were planted here by Marvin "Red" Mounts to demonstrate the usefulness of these species. Owned by the County of Palm Beach and maintained by the Friends of the Mounts Horticultural Learning Center, since 1978 the original 3 acres of this garden have been developed and another 10 acres added. Today, exhibits include a wide assortment of citrus and tropical fruit trees, the Hibiscus Garden, the Rose Garden, the Fern House, the Lily Pond, the Herb Garden, the Touch Garden, and displays of hedge materials, native plants, and salt-tolerant plants. Plant sales, workshops, and seminars are held throughout the year at the Valerie Delacorte Pavilion. A free guided tour starts at 2:30 on Sundays; group tours by prearrangement. Picnicking permitted. Open Mon.–Sat., 8:30–5:00, and Sun., 1–5. Fee: None. Address: 531 North Military Trail, West Palm Beach, FL 33415. Tel.: 305-683-1777.

# WINTER HAVEN: SLOCUM WATER GARDENS

Slocum Water Gardens is a retail and mail-order nursery specializing in waterlilies. Over one hundred varieties of every color and fragrance are displayed across 5 acres of lakes and pools. Peak bloom is in summer. Open Mon.–Fri., 8–4, and Sat., 8–12. Fee: None. Located east of Winter Haven, on State Route 540 in central Florida. Address: 1101 Cypress Gardens Blvd., Winter Haven, FL 33880. Tel.: 813-293-7151.

# *Georgia*

## "DON'T MISS" GARDENS

### PINE MOUNTAIN: CALLAWAY GARDENS

*A magnificent garden covering 2,500 acres and offering over 10 miles of trails, it includes one of the largest azalea collections in North America (over seven hundred varieties) and the world's largest public holly collection (nearly five hundred varieties). Adjacent to the garden, this famous resort offers activities and entertainment for the entire family.*

When presenting Callaway Gardens, it's difficult to limit the description to its gardens, which form merely one aspect of this beautifully developed and incredibly diverse resort. During the 1930s, Cason and Virginia Callaway acquired a large tract of agriculturally depleted land in southwestern Georgia. Initially intended as a quiet retreat of lakeside homes, the Callaways' success in improving the land spurred them on to create "gardens prettier than anything since the Garden of Eden." Forests were restored, lakes formed, roads and trails constructed. Plants of all kinds were dispersed throughout the grounds: azaleas, rhododendrons (approximately seventy varieties), daffodils (over a hundred varieties), laurels, magnolias (five thousand trees), dogwoods, and hollies. Opened in 1952, Callaway Gardens was dedicated to preserving and enhancing the natural beauty of the area and to increasing the public's awareness of nature through its scientific, horticultural, and educational displays and activities. Along the winding scenic drives, Callaway Gardens' success in the preservation of the native southeastern flora can be readily appreciated.

Today Callaway Gardens is universally considered one of North America's finest gardens. It is ranked as one of the ten best family resorts and among the top fifty tennis resorts in the United States. Amenities include golf courses, a 175-acre lake stocked for fishing, a hunting preserve, the largest inland man-made beach in the world (1 mile around), water sports, horseback riding, children's activities plus a year-round schedule of symposia and workshops offered by the Callaway Gardens Education Department.

# *Georgia*

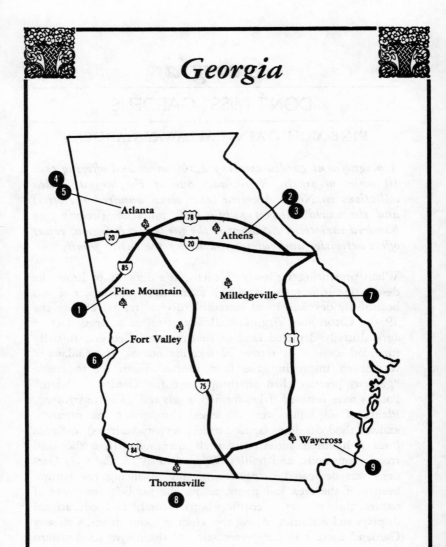

1. Pine Mountain: Callaway Gardens
2. Athens: Founders Memorial Garden
3. Athens: State Botanical Garden of Georgia
4. Atlanta: Atlanta Botanical Garden
5. Atlanta: Cator Woolford Memorial Garden
6. Fort Valley: Massee Lane
7. Milledgeville: Lockerly Arboretum
8. Thomasville: Thomasville Nurseries, Inc.
9. Waycross: Okefenokee Swamp Park

LOCATION: In western Georgia, just off U.S. 27 near the junction with State Rte. 18, about 70 miles south of Atlanta and 28 miles north of Columbus.

ADDRESS: Pine Mountain, GA 31822.

TELEPHONE: 404-663-2281. For hotel and restaurant information, call 800-282-8181.

HOURS: Feb.–Nov., daily, 7–6. In Dec. and Jan., daily, 8–6.

FEE: Garden, $4/ages 12 and up; $1.00/ages 6–11. Beach (in season, includes waterski shows, miniature golf, canoeing, Ping-Pong, paddleboats), $9/ages 12 and up, $4.00/ages 6–11. Group rates and season passes are available.

TOURS: A garden tour is scheduled daily—check for time. Group tours by prearrangement.

RESTAURANT: Six restaurants from casual to formal.

SHOPS: Book, gift, and plant shops.

WHEELCHAIR ACCESS: Trails not suitable for wheelchairs, but the new John A. Sibley Horticultural Center is. In addition, the resort offers rooms specifically designed for handicapped visitors.

SPECIAL ACTIVITIES: Azalea Festival in spring, arts and crafts fairs, Chrysanthemum Festival every October through November, Symphony in the Gardens series, July 4th program and fireworks, summer recreation program geared to family vacations, and the marathon through the gardens every January, which serves as a qualifier for the Boston Marathon.

TIPS: 1. Don't miss:
   a. The azalea collection, one of the most extensive in North America, in bloom April through August, including the plumleaf azalea indigenous to this area of Georgia and rescued from extinction by Cason Callaway.
   b. Meadowlark Gardens: Five trails through the superb holly collection, camellias, magnolias, daffodils, and wildflowers in spring.
   c. Mr. Cason's Vegetable Garden: 7½ acres devoted to fruit and vegetable culture. All produce of the garden is used by the Callaway Gardens restaurants or sold to the public. This garden may seem familiar—

"Victory Garden South," a feature of PBS's "Victory Garden," is photographed here.

d. The John A. Sibley Horticultural Center: a bold new greenhouse/garden complex offering year-round indoor/outdoor displays such as seasonal flower shows, a two-story waterfall, and movable walls of glass, which are open during mild weather.

2. Best color is in spring and fall, with April being perhaps the peak month.

3. Before touring the garden, it's worth viewing the brief orientation film at the Information Center.

4. The John A. Sibley Horticultural Center presents magnificent flower shows around major holidays. The crowds are large, so arrive early.

# EXCELLENT GARDENS

## ATHENS: FOUNDERS MEMORIAL GARDEN

Opened in 1946 through the joint efforts of the University of Georgia School of Environmental Design and the Garden Club of Georgia, Inc., this charming 2 ½-acre garden honors those who established the United States' first garden club—the Ladies Garden Club of Athens. The garden (and its historic headquarters, built in 1857) is located on the university campus and serves both as a museum of landscape design and as a natural laboratory for students of horticulture and related disciplines. The garden contains definitive collections of the flora of Georgia and the Piedmont, with displays including a perennial garden, a boxwood garden, flower terraces, two courtyard gardens, and an arboretum. Group tours by prearrangement. Wheelchair accessible. Open Mon.–Fri., 9–12 and 1–4. Fee: $1 donation requested. Located on the University of Georgia campus. Address: 325 S. Lumpkin St., Athens, GA 30602.

## ATHENS: STATE BOTANICAL GARDEN OF GEORGIA

This 293-acre garden contains over 5 miles of trails through rolling hills, meadows, and hardwood forest. Collections (several sponsored by the Garden Club of Georgia) include roses, wildflowers, spring bulbs, (crocuses, daffodils), azaleas, camellias, laurels, dogwoods, and magnolias, as well as beds of annual and perennial flowers from May to November. This garden is still being enlarged, with several new gardens (herb, fragrance, boxwood, rock, water, sculpture, and azalea gardens) in the process of development. Newly built is the spacious, glass-and-steel Visitor Center/Conservatory Complex, offering tropical plant displays, slide shows, a gift shop, and a very pleasant tea room that serves lunch. Conservatory and grounds are available for meetings, receptions, weddings, and dinners. The garden offers a full schedule of classes for all ages on garden topics, Christmas wreath and ornament demonstrations, and a story hour for children. Activities include the All-in-the-Garden series of concerts and art exhibits. Group tours by prearrangement. Garden open daily, May–Sept., 8–8, and Oct.–Apr., 8–5. Conservatory Complex open daily, Mon.–Sat., 9:00–4:30, and Sun., 11:30–4:30. Fee: None. Located off U.S. 129 and 441, 1 mile south of Athens. Address: 2450 S. Milledge Ave., Athens, GA 30605. Tel.: 404-542-1244.

## ATLANTA: ATLANTA BOTANICAL GARDEN

In the process of development, this 57-acre garden at present offers Japanese, rose, herb, and vegetable gardens, along with an array of seasonal flowers. Collections include azaleas, iris, hollies, and maples, as well as a fragrance garden for the visually impaired. Future additions will include an exhibition hall, a gift shop, classrooms, and an expansion of azalea and camellia collections. Open daily except holidays. Fee: None. Located at the north end of Piedmont Park. For further information, write to the Atlanta Botanical Garden, P.O. Box 77246, Atlanta, GA 30357. Tel.: 404-876-5858.

## ATLANTA: CATOR WOOLFORD MEMORIAL GARDEN

This colorful garden is located on the grounds of the Children's Rehabilitation Center, next to the Cerebral Palsy Center of Atlanta, and is maintained by special education high school students. The garden was originally developed in the 1920s as a private garden, then came into public domain in 1944. The centerpiece of the garden is a broad lawn surrounded by massed plantings of azaleas and bulbs and a border of dogwoods. There are also several smaller gardens, a wildflower trail, and an educational greenhouse. Peak bloom is in April, but blossoms can be seen into fall. Wheelchair accessible. The garden is available for weddings, social gatherings, or meetings. Open daily, sunrise to sunset. Fee: None. Address: 1815 Ponce de Leon Avenue, NE, Atlanta, GA 30307. Tel.: 404-377-3836.

## FORT VALLEY: MASSEE LANE

As headquarters of the American Camellia Society, this 9-acre garden offers one of the largest camellia gardens in the world. Cultivated in China as early as 4,000 years ago, camellias were introduced into the United States in 1797. Noted for their evergreen foliage and perfectly formed flowers, camellias are winter (October to April) bloomers with a peak in February and March. Massee Lane offers several other small gardens featuring roses, daylilies, and herbs. A camellia show is held the second weekend in November, attracting the finest specimens from growers throughout the southeastern states. A Christmas display is held in the greenhouse. There is a gift shop and a horticultural library containing books dating from 1669. A separate building holds a large collection of rare Edward Marshall Boehm procelain bird sculptures. Guided tours of the gardens are provided on request. Gardens open daily; buildings open Mon.–Fri., 8:30–4:00. Fee: None (donations greatly appreciated). Location: On State Rte. 49, 6 miles south of central Fort Valley and 25 miles south of Macon. For further information, write to the American Camellia Society, P.O. Box 1217, Fort Valley, GA 31030. Tel.: 912-967-2358.

## MILLEDGEVILLE: LOCKERLY ARBORETUM

Located on 47 acres at the south end of Milledgeville, Lockerly Arboretum is dedicated to the promotion of conservation and beautification. It is not a showcase garden, but instead a laboratory for the edification of those interested in plant life. Specialty beds include herbs, iris, daylilies, bulbs, and perennials. There is a rhododendron garden and tropical and desert greenhouses. Trails through the garden are well marked. Group tours by prearrangement. Grounds available for meetings of horticulturally oriented groups. Open daily, 8–4. Fee: None. Location: Milledgeville is located in central Georgia, at the junction of U.S. 441 and State Rtes. 49 and 22, about 30 miles northeast of Macon. Address: 1534 Irwinton Rd., Milledgeville, GA 31061. Tel.: 912-452-2112.

# THOMASVILLE: THOMASVILLE NURSERIES, INC.

Owned and operated by the Hjort family since 1898, this retail and mail-order nursery specializes in five groups of plants: azaleas, camellias, daylilies, liriope, and especially roses. An official test garden for All-America Rose Selections, the nearly ½-acre Thomasville rose garden is located next to the nursery. Over two thousand plants, including most varieties available in the Southeast, can always be seen here in top condition. The city of Thomasville holds an annual rose festival in late April. Wheelchair accessible. The nursery is open daily; the rose garden can be seen April through October. Hours: Mon.–Fri., 8:30–12:30 and 1:30–5:30; Sat., Sun., and holiday hours vary with the season. Fee: None. Location: Thomasville is located in south-central Georgia at the intersection of U.S. 19, 84, and 319, about 15 miles from the Florida state line. Address: 1840-42 Smith Ave., Thomasville, GA 31799. Tel.: 912-226-5568.

# WAYCROSS: OKEFENOKEE SWAMP PARK

Called "America's greatest natural botanical garden," this National Wildlife Refuge is filled with unusual and fascinating flora and fauna. The park offers walking trails, displays, and exhibitions, as well as a boat tour (recommended) into the swamp. Open daily, spring/summer, 9:00–6:30, and fall/winter, 9:00–5:30. Located in southeastern Georgia on U.S. 1 and 23, approximately 8 miles south of Waycross. Fee: $6/adult, $4/children 6–11. Address: Waycross, GA 31501. Tel.: 912-283-0583.

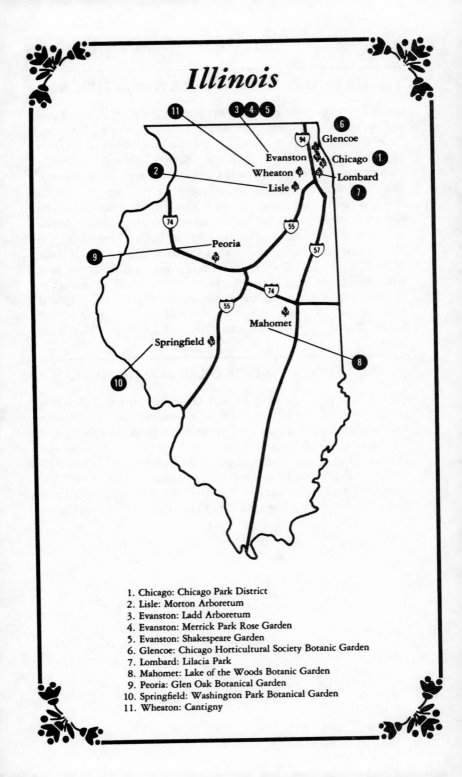

# Illinois

1. Chicago: Chicago Park District
2. Lisle: Morton Arboretum
3. Evanston: Ladd Arboretum
4. Evanston: Merrick Park Rose Garden
5. Evanston: Shakespeare Garden
6. Glencoe: Chicago Horticultural Society Botanic Garden
7. Lombard: Lilacia Park
8. Mahomet: Lake of the Woods Botanic Garden
9. Peoria: Glen Oak Botanical Garden
10. Springfield: Washington Park Botanical Garden
11. Wheaton: Cantigny

# *Illinois*

## CHICAGO: CHICAGO PARK DISTRICT

*Eleven distinct outdoor gardens with hundreds of thousands of flowering plants and two excellent conservatories make the Chicago Park District one of North America's foremost municipal horticultural attractions.*

The Chicago Park District gardens and conservatories are spread across eight separate city parks. The oldest garden is the Lincoln Park Grandmother's Garden, begun in 1893. This 3-acre garden with its broad lawns and shade trees contains a charming collection of old-fashioned plants, with over forty thousand annuals and perennials providing color, spring to fall. Lincoln Park also possesses an excellent conservatory (2400 N. Stockton Dr.). Erected in 1891, it now consists of four huge glass buildings and eighteen propagating houses—3 acres in all. Displays include the Palm House, the Fernery, the Tropical House, and the Show House, where four major shows are held each year. The conservatory also has a permanent orchid collection. Just south of the conservatory is the Lincoln Park Main Garden, more than 7 acres of formal gardens (some twenty-five thousand bedding plants), lawns, fountains, and statuary.

Garfield Park holds Chicago's other famous conservatory. Built in 1893, the 4½-acre Garfield Park Conservatory (300 N. Central Park Blvd.) represents one of the largest and finest publicly owned conservatories in the world. Its enormous collections contain over five thousand varieties and species, and its propagating houses grow nearly three hundred thousand plants each year. Displays include the Palm House, the Fernery (over a hundred kinds of ferns), the Aroid House (tropicals), the Cactus House, the Warm and Economic Plant Houses (tropicals, citrus, spices), and the main Horticultural Hall and the Show House, where massive floral exhibitions are held four times yearly. Near the conservatory is the large Garfield Park Garden, 4 acres containing over twenty-four formal flower beds (fifteen thousand annuals), and a pool containing the best waterlily collection (fifty varieties) in the Midwest.

Grant Park's Rose Garden (lakefront area) is one of the Midwest's largest, with over six thousand shrubs representing 260 varieties. Night viewing is made possible by a lighting system, which also features a spectrum-of-colors display at the elegant Buckingham Fountain bordering the garden. Grant Park also offers the Court of Presidents Garden (twelve thousand bedding plants) coupled with an excellent view of the Chicago skyline.

Other Chicago Park District gardens include the Douglas Park Formal Garden (near Ogden Ave. and Sacramento Blvd. —formal beds with sixteen thousand annuals, a waterlily pool, and a natural lagoon), Humboldt Park Flower Garden (near Division St. and Sacramento Blvd.—a sunken garden containing circular beds of flowers), Jackson Park Perennial Garden (at 59th St. and Stony Island Ave.—a unique sunken garden with concentric flower beds), Marquette Park Rose Garden and Trial Garden (at 3540 W. 71st St.—four thousand roses, eighty varieties, extensive trial gardens of annuals and perennials, shade trees, topiary), Washington Park Formal Garden (at 55th and Cottage Grove Ave.—flower displays in geometrically designed beds), Rainbow Park Garden (at the lakefront between 77th St. and 78th St. east of S. Shore Dr.—large beds of flowers, spring to fall), and the Japanese Garden (south of the Museum of Science and Industry—built in 1892 with a tea house, a moon bridge, waterfalls, and lanterns).

---

ADDRESS: Listed in text above. For further information, write to the Chicago Park District, Dept. of Public Information, 425 E. McFetridge Dr., Chicago, IL 60605.

TELEPHONE: Chicago Park District: 312-294-2493. Garfield Park Conservatory: 312-533-1281. Lincoln Park Conservatory: 312-294-4770.

HOURS: Outdoor gardens, open all day, every day. Conservatories: daily, 9–5; during major flower shows, open Sat.–Thurs., 10–6, and Fri., 9–9.

FEE: None.

TOURS: Free guided tours available at conservatories for schools and organizations by appointment.

RESTAURANT: None.

SHOPS: None.

WHEELCHAIR ACCESS: To most gardens and conservatories.

---

TIPS:
1. Don't miss the superb flower shows at the Garfield Park and Lincoln Park conservatories. Regular shows are the Azalea Show (February to March), the Spring and Easter Show (April), the Chrysanthemum Show (November), and the Christmas Show (December to January). Shows run approximately one month each. In addition there is a summer-long display of foliage plants (May through August).
2. Lincoln Park is also home to the Lincoln Park Zoo, the Historical Society, and the Academy of Sciences. The park also contains famous statuary, a nine-hole golf course, miles of protected beaches, recreational fields, and a fieldhouse, and the summer Theater On The Lake.
3. Conservatory personnel will answer questions on house plants and gardening in general. Call 312-533-1281.
4. Weddings can he held in several of the outdoor gardens (call 312-294-2493).

---

## LISLE: MORTON ARBORETUM

*One of North America's leading arboreta, famous for its collection of woody plants as well as for the spring flowering crab apples and lilacs.*

Morton Arboretum was established in 1922 on the estate of Joy Morton, the founder of the Morton Salt Company. Mr. Morton had a keen interest in trees, a trait inherited from his father, who, as a Nebraska statesman, originated Arbor Day. Today the arboretum's 1,500 acres serve as a public garden and research institution. Along its 30 miles of trails through dense forest and open prairie and beside placid lakes nearly five thousand types of plants can be found. Its most popular collections include the Hedge Garden (over one hundred hedges of unusual shapes and sizes), the Rose Garden, the Outpost Wild Garden (wildflowers and other native plants), the Fragrance Garden, the Ground Cover Garden (more than fifty kinds), and fine collections of lilacs, rhododendrons, and flowering trees (especially crab apples and magnolias). The extensive research facilities include a herbarium of dried plant specimens and a library open to the public. The arboretum can be toured by foot or automobile— the main auto route is 8 miles.

LOCATION: 12 miles west of Chicago on State Rte. 53, just off the East-West Tollway (State Rte. 5).

ADDRESS: Lisle, IL 60532.

TELEPHONE: 312-968-0074.

HOURS: Daily, 9–dusk.

FEE: $3/car.

TOURS: May–Oct., there is an open-air bus tour (fee) weekdays at 1 and 2, and Sat. and Sun. at 12, 1, 2, and 3. Tours for groups by prearrangement.

RESTAURANT: The Ginkgo Restaurant, overlooking Meadow Lake, offers a full menu. There is also a coffee shop for sandwiches and drinks.

SHOPS: Ginkgo Gift Shop on lower level of Information Building.

WHEELCHAIR ACCESS: The grounds can be toured by car.

SPECIAL ACTIVITIES: A full range of classes, lectures, workshops, field trips, and guided walks. In addition, there are programs on nature photography, maple syrup production, bird watching, and ski and travel programs. Special events include the Arbor Day Celebration, the Yuletide Celebration, the Bonsai Show, summer concerts, and others.

---

TIPS: 1. Don't miss:
   a. Flowering crab apples, lilacs, and rhododendrons, April through May.
   b. Autumn color along nature trails in October.
2. Before touring, catch the slide show in the theater. It's helpful to know what to look for in a garden of this size.
3. Morton Arboretum recommends visiting on weekdays from May through October; the weekends tend to be quite crowded.
4. For plant enthusiasts, there is a plant clinic offering advice on plant selection, landscaping, and plant care. Call 312-719-2424 for further information.

# EXCELLENT GARDENS

## EVANSTON: LADD ARBORETUM

A 23-acre strip of reclaimed land, best known for its cherry tree lane (lovely in spring), Ladd Arboretum also has attractive paths through forests and meadows, enjoyed by joggers, hikers, and in winter, cross-county skiers. Within the arboretum is the Evanston Ecology Center, which offers a solar greenhouse, a bird sanctuary, a prairie restoration site, a bookstore, as well as programs and classes (write for schedules and fees). Group tours of arboretum by prearrangement. Arboretum open daily, all day; Ecology Center open Tues.–Sun., 9:00–4:30. Fee: None. Address: 2024 McCormick Blvd., Evanston, IL 60201. Tel.: 312-864-5181.

## EVANSTON: MERRICK PARK ROSE GARDEN

This All-America Rose Selections accredited public rose garden consists of ½ acre of roses terraced around a Victorian fountain. The garden contains twelve hundred plants representing ninety varieties. Group tours by prearrangement. Garden available for weddings. Open daily, June–Oct. Fee: None. Located at the southwest corner of Lake Ave. and Oak St. For further information, write to the Evanston Parks Dept., 2100 Ridge Ave., Evanston, IL 60204. Tel.: 312-866-2910.

## EVANSTON: SHAKESPEARE GARDEN

Located on the Northwestern University campus, this award-winning garden was established by the Garden Club of Evanston. Designed by landscape architect Jens Jensen (Chicago Forest Reserves and Lakefront Parks), it contains only those plants mentioned in Shakespeare's plays and poems. A wide variety of attractive flowers and herbs can be seen here, bordered by trees and shaped hedges. Group tours by prearrangement. Garden available for weddings. Open daily, dawn to dusk. Fee: None. Located on Sheridan Rd. at the east end of Garrett Place, behind Garrett Evangelical Seminary. For further information, write to the Garden Club of Evanston, 2703 Euclid Park Place, Evanston, IL 60201. Tel.: 312-864-0655.

## GLENCOE: CHICAGO HORTICULTURAL SOCIETY BOTANIC GARDEN

This impressive garden consists of 300 acres, 60 acres landscaped, all of which can be viewed by foot or tram. Emphasizing plants usable in the Chicago climatic area, there is perhaps the finest array of demonstration gardens in the Midwest, as well as a Japanese island, a rose garden, a trial garden of annuals, a fruit and vegetable garden, and a landscape demonstration garden. The remaining 240 acres consist of natural woodland and prairie, including the Turnbill Woodland Trail. In addition, there are ten greenhouses full of tropical and desert plants where a succession of plant shows (orchid, bonsai, and others) are sponsored by local societies. The garden promotes classes and lectures on a wide variety of topics, as well as concerts and other activities. Wheelchair access to most areas. Group tours by prearrangement. Open daily, 8–sunset; closed Christmas. Fee: None ($1 parking fee per car). Location: Glencoe is located on Lake Michigan about 12 miles north of downtown Chicago; the garden can be found just east of the Edens Expressway (I-94). Address: Lake Cook Rd., Glencoe, IL 60022. Tel.: 312-835-5440.

## LOMBARD: LILACIA PARK

Begun in the 1870s as the private garden of Col. William Plum, today this 8½-acre public park offers winding paths amid spring bulbs and flowering trees, plus a pond and waterfall. Not to be missed, however, are the twelve hundred lilac bushes (275 varieties) and forty thousand tulips, which provide a grand spectacle in early May. During this time the park holds its "Lilac Time," which includes a Lilac Ball, a parade, and the coronation of a Lilac Queen. The Lombard Park District also offers a wide variety of programs and activities year round. Located in the park is the Coach House, which sells postcards, books and other items. The park is open daily, 9–9. Fee: None, except during Lilac Time ($1.50/adults, $1/seniors; children, military and clergy, free). Location: Lombard is located about 15 miles west of downtown Chicago; Lilacia Park can be found along Parkside and Park Aves. For further information write to Lombard Park District, 150 S. Park Ave., Lombard, IL 60148. Tel.: 312-627-1281.

## MAHOMET: LAKE OF THE WOODS
## BOTANIC GARDEN

Complementing a pioneer life museum, the 10-acre Lake of the Woods Botanic Garden offers collections of daylilies, peonies (250 cultivars), irises (250 cultivars), and wildflowers. Specialty gardens include an antique rose garden, an herb garden, a dye plant garden, and a half-acre conservatory with a tropical collection. The museum possesses over five thousand pieces from early American life (pre-1900) such as firearms, antiques, and housewares. Peak bloom is from late May to mid-August. Wheelchair accessible. Adjacent to the garden is Lake of the Woods Park with picnicking, recreational activities, and a lake. The garden and museum are open daily, 10–5, Memorial Day to Labor Day; open weekends, 10–5, in May and from Labor Day to Oct. 10. Fee: $2. Location: Mahomet is located in east-central Illinois at the junction of I-74 and State Rte. 47, about 75 miles south of Chicago and 10 miles west of Champaign; the garden can be found on State Rte. 47, ½ mile from I-74. For further information, write to P.O. Box 336, Mahomet, IL 61853. Tel.: 217-586-3360.

## PEORIA: GLEN OAK BOTANICAL GARDEN

The 4-acre Glen Oak Botanical Garden offers attractive indoor and outdoor floral displays year-round. The conservatory has a permanent display of tropical plants and six rotating flower shows (Spring, Easter Lily, Summer, Fall Harvest, Chrysanthemum, Poinsettia). Outdoor gardens include an herb garden and an extensive woody plant collection, plus a ½-acre (eight-hundred-bush) rose garden, which received the 1984 All-America Rose Selections Public Rose Garden of the Year Award. There is also a Crab Apple Cove Garden in which weddings and receptions are held (small weddings also held in the conservatory). Special events include the Spring Plant Sale and Arborfest (last weekend in April), the Rose Sunday in September (workshops, crafts, entertainment), the Harvest Fair in October (dried herbs, wreaths, plants, fragrances, potpourri), the Witches Walk through the Haunted Conservatory (Oct. 30), and Christmas Candlelight Tours through the poinsettia-filled conservatory. Local plant societies (orchid, bonsai, rose) also hold shows here. Workshops and classes held year-round. Facilities available for receptions and meetings. Wheelchair accessible. Gift shop. Outdoor gardens open daily, dawn to dusk. Conservatory open Mon.–Fri., 8–4, and Sat.–Sun., 12–4; hours extended to 8 P.M. in July and Aug. Fee: None. Located on the western side of Glen Oak Park. Address: 2218 N. Prospect Rd., Peoria, IL 61603. Tel.: 309-685-4321.

## SPRINGFIELD: WASHINGTON PARK BOTANICAL GARDEN

Washington Park Botanical Garden has a conservatory with four greenhouses and several excellent outdoor gardens, including a rose garden (approximately three thousand plants), an iris garden, and a perennial flower garden, a chrysanthemum garden, a shade garden, and a nature trail. Special shows held throughout the year include the Easter, Spring, Thanksgiving (Chrysanthemum), and Christmas (over six thousand poinsettias) shows. In May there is the Bonsai Society Display, and in June the Annual Rose Walk. Group tours. Weddings in gardens by prearrangement. Wheelchair accessible (call first). Open Mon.–Fri., 12–4, and Sat.–Sun., 12–5. Fee: None. Located in Washington Park, west of downtown Springfield. For further information, write to the Springfield Park District, P.O. Box 5052, Springfield, IL 62704. Tel.: 217-787-2540.

## WHEATON: CANTIGNY

This 500-acre estate, once the home of Chicago *Tribune* publisher Robert McCormick, contains 10 acres of landscaped gardens divided into seventeen areas and collections including roses, rock plants, flowering trees, and a profusion of annual and perennial flowers in blossom from April to November. The 1896 Georgian mansion houses the McCormick Museum as well as art exhibits, Sunday afternoon concerts, and documentary movies in summer. The First Division Museum, a military museum, is also located here. Picnic area. Group garden tours by prearrangement. Wheelchairs available. Garden open daily, sunrise to sunset (check for museum hours). Fee: None. Location: Wheaton is located 30 miles west of central Chicago; take East-West Tollway to Naperville Rd., go ½ mile north to Warrenville Rd., then 3 miles west to Winfield Rd., then 2 miles north to Cantigny. Address: 1 S. 151 Winfield Rd., Wheaton, IL 60187. Tel.: 312-668-5161.

# *Indiana*

## EXCELLENT GARDENS

### COLUMBUS: IRWIN HOME AND GARDENS

This historical home was originally built in 1864. Additions and renovations were made around 1910 and included an Italian walled garden designed after the Casa degli Innamorati in Pompeii. The formal garden is filled with interesting statuary, murals, pergolas, and a fountain copied after one in the Vatican Gardens in Rome. A private residence, the Irwin Home and Gardens are open to the public Sat., Sun., and holidays, 9–4. Fee: None. Located at 608 5th St. For further information, write to the Columbus Visitors Center, 506 5th St., Columbus, IN 47201. Tel.: 812-372-1954.

### FORT WAYNE: FOELLINGER-FREIMANN BOTANICAL CONSERVATORY

Covering over an acre in the heart of downtown Fort Wayne, the Foellinger-Freimann Botanical Conservatory contains three major display houses. The Tropical House holds a forest of 55-foot trees, more than two hundred species of plants, and a waterfall. The Arid House contains cacti and succulents from the Sonoran Desert of Mexico and southern Arizona. The Showcase (more than 10,000 square feet) exhibits six dramatic seasonal shows of vibrant color and foliage. Completed in 1984, this conservatory was designed as a solar energy collector, using the warmth of the sun to supply its energy needs. The Tulip Tree Gift Shop sells gifts, plants, and materials. Jungle Garden Halloween is held on October 31. Conservatory available during daytime or under the stars at night for weddings, dances, meetings, and special functions. The conservatory also hosts a wide variety of exhibitions and plant society shows. Open daily, Mon.–Sat., 10–5, and Sun. and holidays, 12–4. Fee: $1.50/adult, $.75/ages 12 and under. Located on Calhoun St., between Douglas St. and U.S. 24 (Jefferson Blvd.). Address: 1100 S. Calhoun St., Fort Wayne, IN 46802. Tel.: 219-422-3696. Also of note in Fort Wayne is Lakeside Park, which possesses a 3-acre rose garden with several thousand bushes (open dawn to dusk, no fee).

# *Indiana*

1. Columbus: Irwin Home and Gardens
2. Fort Wayne: Foellinger-Freimann Botanical Conservatory
3. Indianapolis: Garfield Park Conservatory and Sunken Gardens
4. Indianapolis: Hillsdale Gardens
5. Muncie: Christy Woods
6. West Lafayette: Purdue Horticulture Gardens

## INDIANAPOLIS: GARFIELD PARK CONSERVATORY AND SUNKEN GARDENS

Renovated in 1983, the conservatory presents seasonal shows (Spring Bulb Show in early April, Array of Annuals in summer, Haunted Conservatory on October 31, Chrysanthemum Exhibit in late November, Poinsettia Show in December), as well as permanent displays of arid and carnivorous plants, and a tropical plant collection, embellished by tropical birds and a 15-foot waterfall. The Sunken Gardens are located in front of the conservatory and consist of brick walkways among beds of summer flowers, urns, and fountains. Conservatory ("Wedding in Paradise") and gardens available for weddings, receptions, and social functions. Tours of conservatory held Tues.–Fri., 10–2; group tours by prearrangement. Wheelchair access to both conservatory and Sunken Gardens. Gift shop in conservatory. Hours: Conservatory, open Tues.–Sat., 10–5, and Sun., 12–5, closed major holidays; Sunken Gardens open daily, dawn to dusk. Fee: Conservatory, $.75/ages 18–54, $.50/ages 6–17, $.25/ages 5 and under or 55 and above; Sunken Gardens, free. Located in Garfield Park on Shelby St., just below intersection with Raymond St. Address: 2450 Shelby St., Indianapolis, IN 46203. Tel.: 317-784-3044.

## INDIANAPOLIS: HILLSDALE GARDENS

One of the largest and loveliest rose gardens in the Midwest, Hillsdale's rose displays include the Formal Rose Garden (designed after an estate near Sienno, Poland), the Rose Display and Test Garden, and the Formal Rose Sales Garden from which potted plants can be purchased. Other plantings include lilacs, tulips, and bulbs in spring, annuals and perennials in summer, and chrysanthemums in fall, as well as a rock garden and a lily pond. Groupings of magnolias, cherry trees, and crab apple trees add color in spring. The Annual Indiana Rose Festival, begun in 1937, is held on the second weekend in June. This festival attracts some sixty-thousand visitors with its Rose Show, band concerts, modern dance and ballet, and musical entertainment. Peak garden bloom is April through May for spring flowers, June through August for roses. Group tours available by prearrangement, as is the use of the Rose Room and picnic area. Plants and garden materials are sold in the Hillsdale Garden Centre. Open daily, 9 to sundown. Fee: None. Located at 7800

Shadeland Ave., 8 miles northeast of downtown Indianapolis and ¼ mile south of Castleton. Mailing address: Hillsdale Landscape Co., 7845 Johnson Rd., Indianapolis, IN 46250. Tel.: 317-849-2810.

## MUNCIE: CHRISTY WOODS

Located on the campus of Ball State University, Christy Woods consists of a 3-acre botanical garden and a 13-acre nature preserve. The botanical garden contains outdoor flower beds, an arboretum, and an orchid garden with a collection of seven thousand orchids representing over three thousand different species. Trails have been created through the nature preserve amid natural woodland and a broad array of wildflowers. Group tours by prearrangement. Open Mon.–Fri., 7:30–4:30; Sat., 8–4; Sun. (Apr. 15–Oct. 15 only), 1–5. Fee: None. Location: Muncie is located in east-central Indiana; Ball State is northwest of downtown Muncie. For further information, write to the Dept. of Biology, Ball State University, Muncie, IN 47306. Tel.: 317-285-8839.

## WEST LAFAYETTE: PURDUE HORTICULTURE GARDENS

Part of the Urban Horticulture Program of Purdue University, this 1-acre garden is composed of the very colorful Ornamentals Display Garden and the smaller Vegetable Display Garden. The Ornamentals Display Garden contains a broad collection of perennials (delphinium, dianthus, phlox), annuals (aster, impatiens, marigold, petunia, poppy, verbena, zinnia), and special collections of iris, daylilies, and daffodils. The Vegetable Display Garden is an intensive propagation garden, containing over one hundred different cultivars. Also on campus is the Horticulture Park consisting of 24 acres of lawns, flowering shrubs and trees, and woodlands. Wheelchair accessible. Group tours, weddings, picnics, and other gatherings by prearrangement. Gardens open daily, sunrise to sunset. Fee: None. Purdue Horticulture Gardens is located on the university campus between Marstellar St. and Horticulture Dr., adjacent to the Horticulture Bldg. For further information, write to the Purdue University Home and Urban Horticulture Extension, Horticulture Bldg., West Lafayette, IN 47907. Tel.: 317-749-2261.

# *Kentucky*

## EXCELLENT GARDENS

### CLERMONT: BERNHEIM FOREST, ARBORETUM AND NATURE CENTER

The forest consists of 8,000 reclaimed acres of combined wood-land and wildlife refuge. The 240 acres of arboretum and ornamental gardens contain collections of azaleas, rhododen-drons, viburnums, flowering trees (dogwoods, crab apples), hollies, and others—twelve hundred varieties in all. Displays include the Sun and Shade Trail, the Big Meadow, and the Quiet Garden. The Nature Center gives exhibits of flora and wildlife, as well as regularly scheduled classes, workshops, and seminars. Picnicking, fishing on Cedar Lake (requires license), horse trails. Open daily, Mar. 15–Nov. 15, 9 to one hour before sundown. Fee: None. Located on State Rte. 245, 5 miles east of I-65, approximately 30 miles south of Louisville. Address: Clermont, KY 40110. Tel.: 502-543-2451.

### LEXINGTON: LEXINGTON CEMETERY

One of North America's most beautiful cemeteries, this garden cemetery offers a 2½-acre display of flowering bulbs and annu-als, as well as a fine collection of trees including dogwoods, magnolias, cherries, redbuds, and panicle hydrangeas. There is also a rose garden, perennial garden, iris garden, and lily ponds. Established in 1848, the cemetery also possesses numerous historic monuments and other statuary. A tour-guide pamphlet for children is available on request. Grounds open daily, day-light hours; office open Mon.–Fri., 8–4, and Sat., 8–12. Fee: None. Address: 833 W. Main St. (U.S. Bus. Rte. 421), Lexington, KY 40508. Tel.: 606-255-5522.

### LOUISVILLE: KENTUCKY BOTANICAL GARDENS

Occupying temporary quarters since its inception in 1980, the Kentucky Botanical Gardens greenhouses currently possess col-lections of orchids (four hundred species), ferns (two hundred varieties), tropical plants (thirteen hundred species), cacti and succulents (nine hundred species), as well as displays of bromeliads, aroids, and carnivorous plants. The 35-acre outdoor garden offers woodland walks through native forest. Guided tours by prearrangement. Wheelchair accessible. The garden plans to move to its permanent 123-acre location (including a wedding garden) in 1987–88. Open Mon., Wed., and Thurs., 11–3; Sat. and Sun., 12:30–4:30. Fee: None. Address: 814 Cherokee Rd., Louisville, KY 40204. Tel.: 502-452-1121.

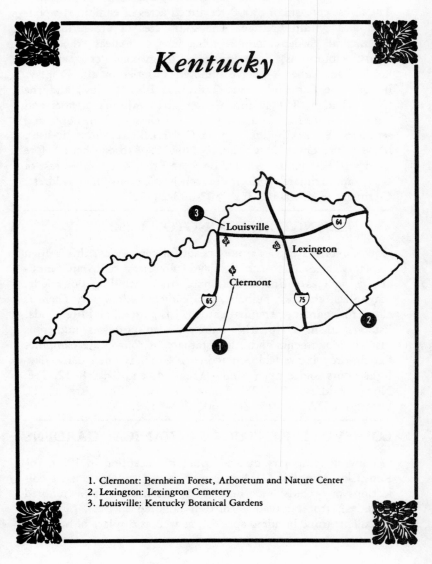

# *Kentucky*

1. Clermont: Bernheim Forest, Arboretum and Nature Center
2. Lexington: Lexington Cemetery
3. Louisville: Kentucky Botanical Gardens

# *Maine*

## EXCELLENT GARDENS

### BAR HARBOR: WILD GARDENS OF ACADIA

This award-winning garden offers a display of plants native to Mount Desert Island in Acadia National Park, including one of the East's best wildflower collections. Display areas include ferns, edible berries, mountain and bog habitats, heath, and wildflowers from May through September. Open daily, 8–8. Fee: None. Address: Acadia National Park, Sieur de Monts Spring, Bar Harbor, ME 04609. Tel.: 207-288-3338.

### CAMDEN: MERRY GARDENS

Merry Gardens is a mail-order nursery specializing in rare plants. Fifteen acres and three greenhouses hold over two thousand varieties of flowering and foliage plants, including excellent collections of herbs, geraniums, ivies, fuschias, cacti, and succulents. Open Mon.–Fri., 9–4. Fee: None. Location: Camden is located on U.S. 1 along the central coast of Maine; Merry Gardens can be found west of downtown Camden on Mechanic St. Address: Camden, ME 04843. Tel.: 207-236-9046.

### CAMDEN: MERRYSPRING

This 66-acre horticultural center emphasizes flowers, trees, and shrubs indigenous to Maine. There are nature trails, wildflowers, scenic lookouts, an herb garden, and a 10-acre arboretum. Workshops and exhibitions held regularly. Open daily, dawn to dusk. Fee: None. Location: Camden is located on U.S. 1 along the central coast of Maine; Merryspring can be found at the end of Conway Rd., just off of U.S. Rte.1, between Rockport and Camden. Address: Merryspring Foundation, P.O. Box 893, Camden, ME 04843. Tel.: 207-236-9046.

### NORTHEAST HARBOR: ASTICOU AZALEA GARDEN

Located adjacent to the Asticou Inn, this 2-acre garden is locally renowned for its masses of azaleas and rhododendrons, brilliant in late spring. There is also a Japanese sand garden with cherry

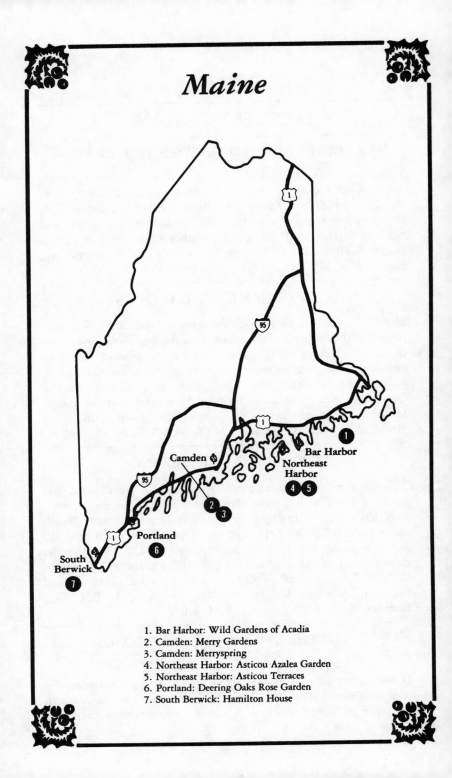

# Maine

1. Bar Harbor: Wild Gardens of Acadia
2. Camden: Merry Gardens
3. Camden: Merryspring
4. Northeast Harbor: Asticou Azalea Garden
5. Northeast Harbor: Asticou Terraces
6. Portland: Deering Oaks Rose Garden
7. South Berwick: Hamilton House

trees and a pond. Wheelchair accessible. Weddings by prearrangement. Open dawn to dusk, spring to fall. Fee: None. Located at the corner of Seal Harbor Dr. and Peabody Dr. in central Northeast Harbor. Tel. (Asticou Inn): 207-276-3344.

## NORTHEAST HARBOR: ASTICOU TERRACES

This 1½-acre garden offers winding paths amid beds of local flowers, rhododendrons, and exotic evergreens, including a Chinese sequoia. The garden is part of the Thuya Lodge, which was originally a private estate and which contains a botanical library. Weddings by prearrangement. Wheelchair accessible. Open daily, 8–dusk. Fee: None. Located on Peabody Dr. about ¼ mile from central Northeast Harbor. Tel. (Thuya Lodge): 207-276-5130.

## PORTLAND: DEERING OAKS ROSE GARDEN

This circular garden is an accredited All-America Rose Selections Garden containing seven hundred bushes and fifty-seven varieties. Peak bloom is June through August. Located on Park Avenue in Deering Oaks Park, where there are also lawns, shade trees, and benches. Picnicking. Wheelchair accessible. Group tours by prearrangement. Garden available for weddings. Open sunrise to 10 P.M. Fee: None. For further information, write to the Dept. of Parks and Public Works, 55 Portland St., Portland, ME 04101. Tel.: 207-775-5451.

## SOUTH BERWICK: HAMILTON HOUSE

Built in 1785 on a bluff over the Piscataqua River, this restored mansion is now owned by the Society for the Preservation of New England Antiquities. The grounds are enhanced by flower-lined paths, terraced formal gardens enclosed by clipped hedges, and statuary. Open June to mid-Oct., Tues., Thurs., Sat., and Sun. only, 12–5. Fee: $2/adults, $1.50/seniors, $1/children. Location: South Berwick is located in the southern tip of Maine along the New Hampshire state line, 5 miles northeast of Dover, NH; Hamilton House can be found 2 miles south of downtown South Berwick; take State Rte. 236 to Brattle St. to Vaughan's Lane. Address: Vaughan's Lane, South Berwick, ME 03908. Tel.: 207-384-5269.

# *Maryland*

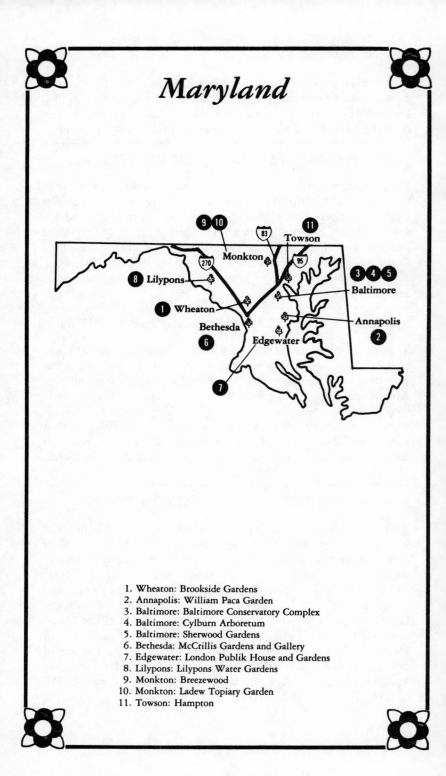

1. Wheaton: Brookside Gardens
2. Annapolis: William Paca Garden
3. Baltimore: Baltimore Conservatory Complex
4. Baltimore: Cylburn Arboretum
5. Baltimore: Sherwood Gardens
6. Bethesda: McCrillis Gardens and Gallery
7. Edgewater: London Publik House and Gardens
8. Lilypons: Lilypons Water Gardens
9. Monkton: Breezewood
10. Monkton: Ladew Topiary Garden
11. Towson: Hampton

# *Maryland*

## "DON'T MISS" GARDENS

### WHEATON: BROOKSIDE GARDENS

*A publicly supported garden with excellent azalea and rhodo-dendron collections, conservatory floral displays, and colorful permanent and seasonal plant exhibits.*

Opened in 1969 and operated by the Maryland-National Capital Park and Planning Commission, this 50-acre public display is designed for the enjoyment of its visitors. Supported entirely by county tax dollars and free to the public, Brookside's displays are of wide variety and high quality. Most popular are its conservatory floral displays, which include the Winter (mid-January to March), Easter (April), Summer (May to October), Fall Chrysanthemum (November) and Christmas Poinsettia (mid-December to mid-January) displays.

Brookside Gardens offers a fine array of outdoor gardens: Its Azalea Garden contains over four hundred varieties of azaleas and rhododendrons in bloom April to June, as well as thirty varieties of viburnum with their bright, colorful fruit; the Formal Gardens provide a progression of flowers from spring to fall; the Fragrance Garden stimulates the senses; the Trial Garden offers new ideas and new plants in imaginative patterns and designs; the Rose Garden contains recent All-America award winners; and the Gude Garden is an area of grassy hills and ponds planted with flowering cherry and crab apple trees—awarded top honors in 1977 at the Landscape Awards Program of the American Association of Nurserymen.

LOCATION: 15 miles north of downtown Washington, DC. Take Georgia Ave. (State Rte. 97) to Randolph Rd., go east to Glenallan Ave.

ADDRESS: 1500 Glenallan Ave., Wheaton, MD 20902.

TELEPHONE: 301-949-8230.

HOURS: Open daily; grounds 9–sunset, conservatories 9–5; closed Christmas Day.

FEE: None.

TOURS: Recorded Tour on hand-held cassette player is available. Guided tours provided for groups or schools by prearrangement.

RESTAURANT: None on grounds.

SHOPS: None on grounds.

WHEELCHAIR ACCESS: Partially accessible.

SPECIAL ACTIVITIES: Year-round schedule of free lectures, demonstrations, guided walks, special workshops and trips. 2,000 volume horticultural library. Free videotape and slide shows about Brookside Gardens are available for group viewing by prearrangement.

TIPS: 1. Outstanding spring bulb displays in April; the Azalea Garden peaks in mid-May.

2. Have a question? The garden staff will answer horticulture questions by phone, Tues.–Thurs., 9:30–noon. Call 301-949-8227.

3. The Formal Gardens make an unforgettable location for a wedding (weekends only, by prearrangement).

4. The Computer Vegetable Program provides a personalized computer printout for your vegetable garden; fee is $7.00.

# EXCELLENT GARDENS

## ANNAPOLIS: WILLIAM PACA GARDEN

This garden, representing an eighteenth-century urban garden, was rescued and restored by Historic Annapolis, Inc., and the state of Maryland. William Paca, governor of Maryland and a signer of the Declaration of Independence, developed his 2-acre garden according to the English style popular in the late 1700s. Broad stairways and clipped hedges lead from the house toward a wilderness area of fruit trees and wildflowers. Closer to the house are a series of terraces containing an herb garden and a physick (medicinal) garden, plus four parterre gardens (flora planted in intricate patterns) of holly and boxwood, and a rose garden. In late May there is an annual day celebrating roses and May flowers, with flower displays and special exhibits. Group tours by prearrangement. Gift shop. Wheelchair access to parts of garden. Horticultural library. Open daily, Mon.–Sat., 10–4; Sun., May–Oct., 12–5, and Nov.–Apr., 12–4; closed Christmas and Thanksgiving. Fee: mid-Mar. to Nov., $1.50/adults, $1.25/seniors, $.75/ages 6–18; Dec. to mid-Mar., $.75/adults and seniors, $.50/ages 6–18. Located at Martin and King George Sts. Address: 1 Martin St., Annapolis, MD 21401. Tel.: 301-267-6656.

## BALTIMORE: BALTIMORE CONSERVATORY COMPLEX

This historic conservatory (built in 1888), with its three green-houses, offers about ¼ acre of permanent displays (tropicals, aroids, orchids), plus three annual shows. The Spring Flower Display is held in the weeks before and after Easter; the Chrysanthemum Display is in November, and the Poinsettia Show December to January. East of the conservatory is a 1-acre display garden containing bulbs in spring, and colorful annuals and perennials in summer. Tours by prearrangement. Wheelchair accessible. Gardens available for weddings. Open daily, 10–4. Fee: None. Address: Druid Hill Park, Gwynns Falls Pkwy. and McCulloh St., Baltimore, MD 21217. Tel.: 301-396-0180.

## BALTIMORE: CYLBURN ARBORETUM

This 176-acre complex serves as a display garden, wildflower preserve, bird sanctuary, and garden center. Collections include daylilies and tree peonies, an All-America Selections Display Garden of annuals, a perennial garden, a shade garden, an herb garden, and the Garden of the Senses for the visually impaired. Trails through natural woodlands offer many varieties of wildflowers. An arboretum contains fine collections of magnolias and Japanese maples. Originally a private estate, the city of Baltimore bought the property in 1942 and turned the mansion with its inlaid floors, mosaics, and tapestries into a horticulture center. Educational services include tours for schools, garden clubs, and other groups. Lectures, symposia, and workshops held regularly. Other attractions include a horticultural library, the Children's Nature Museum, and the Bird Museum. Grounds open daily, 6 A.M.–9 P.M.; mansion open weekdays, 8–4. Fee: None. Located northwest of downtown Baltimore, on Greenspring Ave. between Coldspring La. and Northern Pkwy. Address: 4915 Greenspring Ave., Baltimore, MD 21209. Tel.: 301-396-0180.

## BALTIMORE: SHERWOOD GARDENS

Begun in 1927, this 6½-acre garden boasts one of North America's most dazzling tulip displays, with over seventy thousand bulbs (thirty-five varieties) blooming in spring. Other collections of interest include azaleas, flowering trees (dogwoods and magnolias), boxwoods (some dating back to the eighteenth century), and rare trees from other countries. Peak bloom is late April to early May when masses of tulips, daffodils, pansies, and lilacs create a handsome spectacle. Annual Bulb Sale on the Saturday prior to Memorial Day. Open daily, all day. Fee: None. Located on Stratford Rd. between Greenway and Underwood Rds., approximately 2 miles north of downtown Baltimore; take Charles St. north to Stratford Rd. east. For further information, write to Stratford Green, Inc., P.O. Box 4679, Baltimore, MD 21212. Tel.: 301-366-2672.

## BETHESDA: McCRILLIS GARDENS AND GALLERY

This garden began in 1941 as the private shade garden of Mr. McCrillis, an Assistant to the Secretary of the Interior under Presidents Roosevelt, Truman and Eisenhower. Originally collecting impressive arrays of azaleas and rhododendrons, McCrillis later added a variety of unusual woody plants including a Dawn Redwood, Japanese Snowbell, Stewartia, and a Japanese Umbrella Tree. Donated to the Maryland-National Capital Park and Planning Commission in 1978 and now managed by Brookside Gardens, the 5-acre McCrillis Gardens today feature over 750 varieties of azaleas representing native species and all major hybrid groups, including three hundred late-blooming Satsuki varieties imported in 1981. Further embellishing the garden are bulbs and perennials, ornamental trees and shrubs. Bloom season extends from late March into June, with peak bloom in early May. In addition, the McCrillis Gallery houses selections from the Montgomery County Contemporary Art Collection. There is an annual spring sculpture show. Garden available for weddings and receptions by prearrangement (call 301-949-8231). Garden open daily, 10–sunset; gallery open 12–4, weekends only in late Apr. and May, and for scheduled shows throughout the year. Fee: None. Location: Bethesda is located directly north of Washington, DC; from I-495, take Exit 36 onto Old

Georgetown Rd. south (Rte. 187), turn right on Greentree Rd. Address: 6910 Greentree Rd., Bethesda, MD 20034. Tel.: 301-469-8438 or 301-365-1657.

## EDGEWATER: LONDON PUBLIK HOUSE AND GARDENS

A National Historic Landmark, the Publik House is the sole remaining structure of a colonial town that lodged travelers between Philadelphia and Williamsburg, the colonies' two major capitals. Today the restored house is surrounded by 22 acres of handsome gardens, bordered by woodlands, streams, and the South River. Spring is heralded by thousands of daffodils, magnolias, and flowering cherries. In May azaleas and rhododendrons, and in summer daylilies, iris, and tree peonies abound. Other displays include collections of viburnums, camellias, and Japanese irises, the Waterfall Garden with ferns and wildflowers, and the Winter Garden of winter plants, flowers, and fruits. There is an annual Daffodil Show and a Horticulture Day, as well as other special activities relating to the Publik House itself (check for dates). Group or school tours by prearrangement; gardens available for weddings and receptions. Gift shop. Open Mar.–Dec., Tues.–Sat., 10–4, and Sun., 12–4. Fee: $2/adults, $1/ages 6–18. Located on State Rte. 253, 7 miles south of Annapolis. Address: 839 Londontown Rd., Edgewater, MD 21037. Tel.: 301-956-4900.

## LILYPONS: LILYPONS WATER GARDENS

Lilypons is an aquatic farm that sells everything from plants to pond frames by direct purchase or mail order. Pools of unusual and beautiful displays of waterlilies in shades of white, yellow, pink, red, blue, and magenta cover 20 landscaped acres and are complemented by water iris, lotus, and ornamental fish. Special festivities include the Lotus Blossom Festival in July and the Koi Festival (for the imperial Japanese carp) the weekend after Labor Day, when artisans, singers, and dancers provide entertainment and crafts in the gardens. The lilies themselves bloom June to mid-September. Open Mar.–Oct., Mon.–Sat., 10–5, and Sun., 12–5; Nov.–Feb., Mon.–Fri. only, 10–3. Fee: None. Located 9 miles south of Frederick on the Monocacy River. Address: 6800 Lilypons Rd., P.O. Box 10, Lilypons, MD 21717. Tel.: 301-874-5133.

## MONKTON: BREEZEWOOD

Breezewood is made up of several gardens surrounding the main house and museum. Foremost is the Oriental Garden with waterfalls, pagodas, and ponds. There is also an English-style formal garden enclosed by a stone wall. The museum contains a collection of Southeast Asian art, particularly Buddhist art from Thailand. Group tours by prearrangement. The garden and museum are open 2:00–5:30 on the first Sunday of each month from May through October. Fee: $2. Address: 3722 Hess Rd., Monkton, MD 21111. Tel.: 301-472-9438.

## MONKTON: LADEW TOPIARY GARDENS

Opened to the public approximately 10 years ago, Ladew Topiary Gardens has become famous quickly. A delight to both adults and children, this topiary garden is one of the two finest in North America (also see Green Animals). Displays include a third of a mile of uniquely trimmed hedges in the form of cones and chained walls, a floral horseman with his hounds chasing a fox across a lawn, and animals of diverse shapes and forms set atop geometric rings and spheres. The grand allee offers a unicorn, a sea horse, a heart pierced by Cupid's arrow, and a facsimile of a top-hatted Winston Churchill with his hand in a V-for-victory sign. The grounds consist of 22 acres and contain over a dozen gardens, including an herb garden, a Japanese garden, a pink garden, a rose garden, a wild garden, a Victorian garden, a terrace garden, an iris garden, and a waterlily garden. The large white clapboard Ladew house, part of which dates from the late 1700s, is filled with English antiques, paintings, and memorabilia. A collection of carriages is on display in the barn. Lectures are held in spring and fall, and concerts on Sunday afternoons in summer. Gift shop. Cafe open for lunch. Group tours by prearrangement. Garden open Tues.–Sat., 10–4, and Sun., 12–5; house open on Wed., Sat., and Sun. only. Fee: Garden only, $2.50/adults, $2/students and seniors, $.50/children under 12; house and garden, $4/adults, $3/students and seniors, $1/children under 12. Located on Rte. 146, north of Baltimore and Towson; look for exit 27 from the Beltway (I-695), go north on Rte. 146 about 15 miles. Address: 3535 Jarrettsville Pike, Monkton, MD 21111. Tel.: 301-557-9466.

# TOWSON: HAMPTON

A National Historic Site, Hampton consists of an elegant Georgian-style mansion and twenty-two other historic structures, plus 60 acres of lovely landscaped grounds possessing several rare specimen tress. The grounds include a series of terraces with formal beds and parterres and a landscaped park all faithfully designed in the nineteenth-century English style, and also a sweeping evergreen terrace. Grounds open daily, 9–5; mansion viewed by guided tour every half hour, Mon.–Sat., 11:00–4:30, and Sun, 1:00–4:30; closed Christmas and New Year's Day. Fee: None. Located just off the Beltway (I-695); take exit 27 onto State Rte. 146 north, turn right onto Hampton La. Address: Hampton National Historic Site, 535 Hampton La., Towson, MD 21204. Tel.: 301-823-7054.

# *Massachusetts*

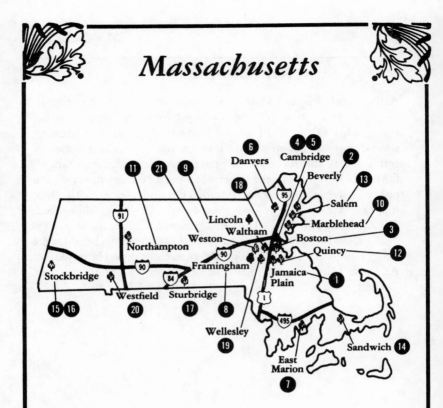

1. Jamaica Plain: Arnold Arboretum
2. Beverly: Sedgwick Gardens at Long Hill
3. Boston: Isabella Stewart Gardner Museum
4. Cambridge: Longfellow National Historic Site
5. Cambridge: Mount Auburn Cemetery
6. Danvers: Glen Magna
7. East Marion: Great Hill Farm
8. Framingham: Garden in the Woods
9. Lincoln: Codman House
10. Marblehead: Jeremiah Lee Mansion
11. Northampton: Botanic Garden of Smith College
12. Quincy: Adams National Historic Site
13. Salem: Ropes Mansion and Garden
14. Sandwich: Heritage Plantation
15. Stockbridge: Berkshire Garden Center
16. Stockbridge: Naumkeag
17. Sturbridge: Old Sturbridge Village
18. Waltham: Lyman Estate and Greenhouses
19. Wellesley: Wellesley College
20. Westfield: Stanley Park
21. Weston: Case Estates

# *Massachusetts*

## "DON'T MISS" GARDENS

### JAMAICA PLAIN: ARNOLD ARBORETUM

*Founded in 1872, the Arnold Arboretum is North America's oldest arboretum and front-runner in the introduction of exotic plant species. Today, boasting approximately seven thousand types of trees and shrubs, this garden will be of greater interest to the student of horticulture, though the general traveler may find the extensive lilac and bonsai collections, or the fall foliage, well worth a visit.*

Founded (but not funded) by Harvard University, Arnold Arboretum was incorporated into the Boston Park System in 1882. The 265-acre arboretum was planned and designed by Charles Sprague Sargent, its director from 1872–1927, and Frederick Law Olmsted, the father of American landscape architecture (among his many works: city parks of Boston and New York, the Biltmore Estate, as well as innumerable private gardens). Sargent's goal was a farsighted one—to assemble every variety of tree and shrub that could survive the harsh New England winter. During its first century, Arnold Arboretum has introduced more than two thousand new plants, many of them via Ernest "Chinese" Wilson, whose Far Eastern expeditions at the turn of the century have become part of horticultural legend.

LOCATION: On State Rte. 203, about 4 miles southwest of downtown Boston.

ADDRESS: Arnold Arboretum, The Arborway, Jamaica Plain, MA 02130.

TELEPHONE: 617-524-1718.

HOURS: Daily, sunrise to sunset. Propagating greenhouses open Wed., 1:30–4:00.

FEE: None.

TOURS: Guided tours by van on a regular basis—check for times. Group tours by prearrangement.

RESTAURANTS: None on grounds.

SHOPS: Gift shop in Hunnewell Building.

WHEELCHAIR ACCESS: Handicapped individuals can obtain permits to view the grounds from their own vehicles.

SPECIAL ACTIVITIES: The Arnold Arboretum offers an impressive array of lectures, workshops, exhibits, walks, trips, exhibitions, and an annual Plant Giveaway Sale. The arboretum maintains an active program of research and specimen collection, and it publishes a quarterly journal, a newsletter, and a magazine. In addition, the Visitor's Center can be reserved for weddings, receptions, or meetings.

TIPS: 1. Don't miss:
   a. Bonsai collection with specimens over two hundred years old, the oldest and third largest collection in the United States.
   b. Lilacs, over 550 types, magnificent in bloom.
   c. Trees in spring—magnolias, cherries, crab apples, and hawthorns.
   d. Azaleas in bloom April through June.
   e. Autumn foliage.
   f. A calendar of peak blooming periods is available upon request.
2. Arnold Arboretum is a must for the horticulture enthusiast interested in particular plant species.

# EXCELLENT GARDENS

## BEVERLY: SEDGWICK GARDENS AT LONG HILL

The gardens of this 114-acre estate were originally laid out around 1916 by Mabel Cabot Sedgwick, an accomplished horticulturist and garden writer. Her work was carried on by other family members until 1979 when the property was given to the Trustees of Reservations, a nonprofit organization that has preserved sixty-eight Massachusetts properties since 1891. Today Sedgwick Gardens at Long Hill features tree peonies, azaleas, and rhododendrons. The carefully maintained grounds also offer a series of gardens such as the Hosta Garden, the South Lotus Pool, the Grey Garden, croquet lawns, terraces, the Horseshoe Garden, the Tree Peony Garden, and the Cut-Flower Garden. There is an excellent array of flowering trees (Japanese cherries, magnolias, Stewartias, crab apples), many of them rarely seen this far north, and the estate is further embellished by such ornaments as a circular ironwork pavilion from France, a Chinese gate from Beijing, a Chinese pagoda, and statuary. Peak bloom is May through June. The house, built in 1921, is a reproduction of the 1802 Isaac Ball House of Charleston, South Carolina. The house serves as the headquarters of the Trustees of Reservations and contains interesting architectural features, such as handsome woodwork and eighteenth-century Chinese wallpaper. Long Hill promotes a lecture series and an annual plant sale. Tours by prearrangement. The house and gardens are available for rental by garden clubs, historical societies, and community groups. Gardens open daily, 8–sunset. Garden fee: $1/ages 15 and over; house tour: $2 per person (house seen by prearrangement only). Located on State Rte. 22, approximately 30 miles northeast of downtown Boston. Address: 572 Essex St., Beverly, MA 01915. Tel.: 617-922-1536.

## BOSTON: ISABELLA STEWART GARDNER MUSEUM

This small but charming courtyard garden with its fountain, evergreens, and ancient Greek, Roman, and Egyptian statuary, reflects the Venetian character of the museum itself. A continual array of potted flowers (hydrangeas, chrysanthemums, orchids) add grace and color. The four seasonal displays are especially attractive (Easter: lilies, cineraria, and hanging nasturtiums; Spring: azaleas and jasmines; Fall: chrysanthemums and begonias; Christmas: poinsettias and cyclamen). Outside the museum building are gardens that are quite colorful in spring. Open Tues., 1:00–9:30; Wed.–Sun., 1:00–5:30. Fee: None ($2 donation requested). Address: 280 Fenway, Boston, MA 02115. Tel.: 617-566-1401.

## CAMBRIDGE: LONGFELLOW NATIONAL HISTORIC SITE

The house, where Henry Wadsworth Longfellow lived from 1837 to 1882, is an outstanding example of eighteenth-century Georgian-style architecture. The 1½-acres of grounds are maintained as the poet himself kept them—with open lawns, stately trees, beds of lilacs, and a formal garden. Concerts are held in the gardens on alternate Sundays in summer. The house is seen by guided tour; group tours of grounds by prearrangement. Wheelchair access to grounds and first floor of house by prearrangement. Open daily, 9–5. Fee: Garden, none; house, $.50. Address: 105 Brattle St., Cambridge, MA 02138. Tel.: 617-876-4491.

## CAMBRIDGE: MOUNT AUBURN CEMETERY

Consecrated in 1831, Mount Auburn is the United States' oldest garden cemetery. The 170-acre grounds possess over 380 varieties of rare trees and flowering shrubs. There are over twenty-five hundred trees in all, hundreds of them flowering types, as well as drifts of blossoms, several ponds and lakes, a greenhouse, and a 62-foot tower offering an outstanding view of downtown Boston. Wheelchair accessible. Public tours sponsored year round; group tours by prearrangement. Chapels and gardens available for weddings and other functions. Open daily May–Sept., 8–7, and Oct.–Apr., 7–5. Fee: None. Address: 580 Mount Auburn St., Cambridge, MA 02138. Tel.: 617-547-7105.

## DANVERS: GLEN MAGNA

Glen Magna mansion was the home of the Peabody-Endicott families for more than a hundred years starting in 1814, when Captain Joseph Peabody bought the land to use as a place to hide valuable cargoes from British ships blockading the eastern seaboard during the War of 1812. The gardens, which consist of formal and informal areas surrounded by acres of fields and woods, are said to have been laid out by British statesman Joseph Chamberlain (Neville's father). Also present is the unique McIntyre Teahouse, a National Historic Landmark. Glen Magna can be reserved for weddings, receptions, or meetings. Mansion seen by tour, June–Sept. only, Tues. and Thurs., 10–4; garden open 9–dusk. Fee: Mansion tour, $1/adult, $.50/ages 12–18; garden, no fee. Located at 57 Forest St., approximately 30 miles north of downtown Boston. For further information, write to the Danvers Historical Society, P.O. Box 381, Danvers, MA 01923. Tel.: 617-774-9165.

## EAST MARION: GREAT HILL FARM

Best known for its large orchid collection and its acacias in spring, this large estate also offers azaleas, rhododendrons, perennials, mountain laurel, an arboretum, and a salt marsh. Group tours by prearrangement. Open Mon.–Fri., 8–4; also open weekends in Dec.; closed holidays. Fee: None. Location: East Marion is located just east of I-195 and U.S. 6 in southeast Massachusetts, about 20 miles east of New Bedford. Address: 1 Great Hill Drive, East Marion, MA 02738. Tel: 617-748-1052.

# FRAMINGHAM: GARDEN IN THE WOODS

Owned by the New England Wild Flower Society since 1965, this garden was originally created in the 1930s by the persistent efforts of two men, Will C. Curtis and Dick Stiles, who, by hand, cleared paths through this native woodland. Curtis's dream was to develop a garden of wildflowers and exotic plants within the natural, glacier-molded meadows and forests. His determination to collect and propagate rare and diverse species for the garden led to its attaining the status of a botanical garden in the 1940s, and today it is considered one of the best wildflower gardens in North America. Garden in the Woods consists of 30 acres of natural sanctuary and 15 acres of landscaped gardens, which include the Lily Pond, the Sunny Bog, the Rhododendron Grove, the Brookside, the Meadow, and the Lady-Slipper paths. Over 3 miles of trails course the gardens, which contain over fifteen hundred varieties of native wildflowers and shrubs. Bloom period extends from April through October. The trails and gardens are meticulously maintained, and most rare specimens are labeled. Tours available by prearrangement. Full schedule of plant sales, lectures, and workshops for all ages. Open mid-Apr.–Oct., Tues.–Sun., 9–4. Fee: $4/adult, $3/ages 3–15 and seniors. Location: Framingham is located approximately 25 miles west of central Boston. Address: Hemenway Rd., Framingham, MA 01701. Tel.: 617-877-6574.

# LINCOLN: CODMAN HOUSE

Built around 1740, the house and grounds are maintained by the Society for the Preservation of New England Antiquities. The parklike terrain offers unusual trees and other plantings and the restored Italian Garden consisting of terraces of flowers, reflecting pool and fountains, and classic statuary. Garden open all day, June–Oct.; house open Wed.–Sun., 12–5. Garden fee: None; house fee: $2/adults, $1.50/seniors, $1/children. Location: Approximately 3 miles west of Lincoln and 19 miles west of Boston, off of State Rte. 126 (Concord Rd.), just north of the junction with State Rte. 117 (South Great Rd.) Address: Codman Rd., P.O. Box 429, Lincoln, MA 01773. Tel.: 617-259-8843.

## MARBLEHEAD: JEREMIAH LEE MANSION

Maintained by the Marblehead Garden Club, this well-tended period garden adjacent to the 1768 home is primarily composed of plants of the colonial period. It contains an herb garden, a sunken garden, and a variety of flower beds. The 1768 mansion, with its elegant woodworking and antique furnishings, is maintained by the Marblehead Historical Society. Group tours by prearrangement. Garden available for weddings and parties. Open daily, spring–fall; closed, winter months. Fee: None. Located approximately 20 miles north of downtown Boston; take State Rte. 1A to Rte. 129 to Marblehead. Address: 16 Beacon St., Marblehead, MA 01945. Tel.: 617-631-1069.

## NORTHAMPTON: BOTANIC GARDEN OF SMITH COLLEGE

The grounds of Smith College's 125-acre campus were designed to serve as a botanical garden and arboretum. Planned in the 1890s by the Olmsted brothers, the present garden possesses well over three thousand species and varieties. The Lyman Plant House, dating back to 1895, contains collections of palms, ferns, orchids, begonias, bromeliads, and more. The grounds are utilized for educational purposes for the students and interested visitors. For pure enjoyment, two excellent shows are held annually: the Bulb Show in early March and the Chrysanthemum Show in early November. These week-long shows attract as many as fifteen thousand visitors. Hours: Outdoor garden open daily, all day; greenhouse open daily, 8:00–4:15. Fee: None. Wheelchair accessible. Tours available for groups by prearrangement. Located on College La., just off State Rte. 9 (Elm St.), 1 mile west of central Northampton in western Massachusetts. Address: Smith College, Northampton, MA 01063. Tel.: 413-584-2700.

## QUINCY: ADAMS NATIONAL HISTORIC SITE

Maintained by the National Park Service, the Old House was built in 1730 and in 1787 became the home of John Adams, then John Quincy Adams, and subsequent generations. The garden includes a 1731 boxwood hedge, a nineteenth-century flower garden, and the York Rose carried from England by Abigail Adams. Hours: House and garden open daily, Apr.

19–Nov. 10, 9–5. Fee: None (guided tours, $.50 per adult). Located on the corner of Adams St. and Newport Ave. in central Quincy, 8 miles south of Boston. Address: 135 Adams St., P.O. Box 351, Quincy, MA 02269. Tel.: 617-773-1177.

## SALEM: ROPES MANSION AND GARDEN

Built before 1750, the Ropes mansion contains collections of eighteenth and nineteenth-century glass, ceramics, and porcelain. The 1-acre formal garden was landscaped in 1912 with a variety of flower beds in geometric design. Botanical lecture series in March. Garden available for weddings. Hours: Garden open spring–fall, Mon.–Sat., 8–4; mansion open June–Oct., Tues.–Sat., 10–4 (tours every ½ hour). Fee: Garden, none; mansion, $1.50/adults, $1/seniors, $.75/children; group rates. Located in central Salem, about 18 miles northeast of Boston. Address: 318 Essex St., Salem, MA 01970. Tel.: 617-744-0718.

## SANDWICH: HERITAGE PLANTATION

Heritage Plantation includes a number of museums of Americana located on 76 beautifully landscaped acres. From 1921 to 1943 Charles Dexter lived here, developing and disseminating hybrid rhododendrons, which have become famous for their large flowers and clarity of color. Today the nearly thirty-five thousand Dexter rhododendrons, as well as azaleas and other flowering shrubbery, create a magnificent spectacle in May and June. By summer thousands of daylilies (550 varieties) are in bloom. The terrain is primarily natural woodland with trails winding along Upper Shawnee Lake. The museums, housing antique cars (Rolls-Royce, Pierce-Arrow, Dusenberg, Cord, Packard—thirty-four in all), antique firearms, military miniatures, Currier and Ives lithographs, ancient and unusual hand tools, and an operational 1912 hand-carved carousel, add an interesting dimension. There are regularly scheduled concerts, entertainment, and special exhibitions. One of New England's best family attractions. Open mid-May to mid-Oct., daily, 10–5. Fee: $5/over age 12, $2/ages 5–12; group rates available. Located on the northwest end of Cape Cod, 1 mile from downtown Sandwich. Reachable by historic train from Hyannis, Buzzards Bay, and Falmouth. Address: Heritage Plantation of Sandwich, Inc., Grove and Pine Sts., Sandwich, MA 02563. Tel.: 617-888-3300.

## STOCKBRIDGE: BERKSHIRE GARDEN CENTER

This 15-acre botanic garden presents a wide variety of displays and also serves as a gardening information center for the Berkshire area. Displays include the Old-Fashioned Rose Garden, the Herb Garden, the Vegetable Garden, the Pond Area Garden, the Idea Garden, and several landscaped flower gardens and walks. Collections include primroses, daylilies (over two thousand varieties), perennials, shrubs, and conifers. Color from spring into fall. In addition, there are several greenhouses offering tropical and other exhibits, and the Sap House where maple sap is converted into syrup. The center sponsors several seasonal shows: Daffodil Show (May), Herb Symposium (June), Flower Show (August), and Harvest Festival (October). There are also regularly scheduled courses, lectures, and symposia. Gift shop, Herb shop, library; staff makes itself available for gardening questions. Tours every Tuesday and Saturday morning; groups tours by prearrangement. Wheelchair access to parts of garden. Hours: Outdoor gardens open daily, mid-May to mid-Oct., 10–5; greenhouses open daily, year-round, 10–5. Fee (May–Oct.): $3/adults, $2/seniors, $.50/ages 6–12. Located in western Massachusetts on State Rte. 102, 2 miles west of central Stockbridge, about 12 miles south of Pittsfield. Address: Stockbridge, MA 01262. Tel.: 413-298-3926.

## STOCKBRIDGE: NAUMKEAG

Completed in 1886, this 26-room Norman-style mansion of former ambassador Joseph Choate is today owned and maintained by the Trustees of Reservations. The house is surrounded by 50 acres, 7 of which constitute the elegantly landscaped gardens originally designed by Nathaniel Barrett and later improved by Fletcher Steele, working with Choate's daugter, Mabel. *Naumkeag* is an Indian word meaning "Haven of Peace," and the gardens were patterned to provide serene walks amid grass terraces and sequestered gardens, which include the Flower Garden, the Rose Garden, the Afternoon Garden (offering pools and welcome shade in summer), the Rock Garden, the Cutting Garden (to provide blossoms for the house), and the splendid Chinese Garden. The house (viewed by guided tour) contains an array of turn-of-the century furnishings, antiques, and artwork. Wheelchair access to parts of garden and first floor of home. House available for weddings, but not receptions or meetings. Open late June to Labor Day, Tues.–Sun., 10–5; open weekends and holidays in late May, early June, Sept. and early Oct., 10–5. Fee: $4/adults for house and garden, $3 for house only, $2 for garden only; $1/children ages 6–16 for house and garden. Location: Stockbridge is located in western Massachusetts, 12 miles south of Pittsfield; Naumkeag can be found in Stockbridge on Prospect St. For further information, write to The Trustees of Reservations, P.O. Box 792, Stockbridge, MA 01262. Tel.: 413-298-3239.

## STURBRIDGE: OLD STURBRIDGE VILLAGE

Six authentic gardens (two flower, three vegetable, one herb) have been created to complement the forty historical homes, meeting houses, museums, craft shops, mills, and farm of this living museum of 200 acres. The flower gardens serve as the centerpiece of the Summer Garden Weekend. The Herb Garden is extensive with over four hundred varieties. In August, Garden Days is held with slide talks, workshops, tours, and other activities. A full schedule of workshops, concerts, craft displays, magic shows, contests, exhibits, and other family events and entertainment attracts over half a million visitors annually. Open Apr.–Oct., daily, 9–5; Nov., daily, 10–4; Dec.–Mar., Tues.–Sun., 10–4; closed Christmas and New Year's Day. Fee: $8.50/adults, $4/ages 6–15. Located on U.S. 20, just off I-86 and I-90, in southcentral Massachusetts. Address: Sturbridge, MA 01566. Tel.: 617-347-3362.

## WALTHAM: LYMAN ESTATE AND GREENHOUSES

Another estate owned by the Society for the Preservation of New England Antiquities, this mansion was built around 1795. Theodore Lyman was an enthusiastic horticulturist who filled the estate's 30 acres with broad lawns, garden beds, ornamental trees and shrubs, and a collection of rhododendrons. He also built five greenhouses, four of which are still utilized (the fifth, though no longer in use, is thought to be the oldest standing greenhouse in the United States). Hours: Garden open Thurs.–Sun., 10–4; mansion open only for group tours by appointment. Fee: $2/adults, $1.50/seniors, $1/children. Located in central Waltham, 10 miles northwest of Boston; take U.S. 20 (N. Beacon St., Main St.) to Lyman St. Address: 185 Lyman St., Waltham, MA 02154. Tel.: 617-891-7095 (greenhouse) or 617-893-7431 (house).

## WELLESLEY: WELLESLEY COLLEGE

The Wellesley College campus offers two horticultural attractions. The Margaret C. Ferguson Greenhouses offer over one thousand kinds of plants including collections of orchids, ferns, desert plants, aquatic plants, tropical and subtropical plants. Special shows include bulbs, azaleas and spring flowers (March through May), and a chrysanthemum exhibit (late October through November). The 22-acre Alexandra Botanic Garden and Hunnewell Arboretum possesses over five hundred species of woody plants, including specimens of hickory and walnut, Chinese golden larch, Chinese cork, and tulip trees. Collections of lilacs, azaleas, rhododendrons, and flowering trees (dogwoods, crab apples, cherries) provide blossoms in spring; oaks and lindens provide autumn color. Other collections include hydrangeas, waterlilies, the Jennings Biblical Garden, plus native forest and wildflowers. Group tours by prearrangement. Picnicking in designated areas. Wheelchair accessible. Weddings by prearrangement. Advice on plants can be obtained by phone or in person at the greenhouses. Open daily, 8:00–4:30. Fee: None. Location: Wellesley is located just off State Rte. 135, 10 miles west of Boston and 3 miles west of I-95. For further information, write to Wellesley College, Dept. of Biological Sciences, Wellesley, MA 02181. Tel.: 617-235-0320.

## WESTFIELD: STANLEY PARK

Conceived by Frank Stanley Beveridge, founder of Stanley Home Products, and opened to the public in 1949, Stanley Park offers 180 acres of gardens, playgrounds, historical displays, and picnic areas to its two hundred thousand annual visitors. Among the gardens, the best known is the Rose Garden, which serves as a test garden for All-America Rose Selections. This garden possesses twenty-five hundred bushes (fifty varieties) and in 1983 received the Outstanding Garden Award. Other horticultural displays include the Japanese Garden, the Rhododendron Display Garden, the Flowering Gardens of the World, a 5-acre arboretum, as well as an 85-acre wildlife sanctuary with hiking trails. Stanley Park's other attractions include a covered bridge, the Old Mill Wheel, the Blacksmith's Shop (with genuine forge, bellows, tools, and anvil), ball fields, tennis and basketball courts, a jogging track, a children's playground, picnic groves, and a pavilion. There is a 98-foot carillon tower, which provides bell concerts, and various bands and singing groups provide summer Sunday evening entertainment on the Acre Lawn. Weddings are permitted, and the pavilion can be reserved. Open daily, mid-May–mid-Oct., 8–dusk. Fee: None. Location: Westfield is located on U.S. 20, 10 miles west of Springfield; Stanley Park can be found southwest of downtown Westfield, along Western and Kensington Aves. For further information, write to The Stanley Park of Westfield, Inc., 400 Western Ave., Westfield, MA 01085. Tel.: 413-568-9312.

## WESTON: CASE ESTATES

The nursery for Arnold Arboretum, Case Estates offers fine displays of its own. The perennial garden and herbaceous beds provide color spring to fall, including collections of peonies, narcissus, iris, and daylilies. The Rhododendron Display Garden, still in the early stages of development, is nonetheless spectacular. Planned and maintained in conjunction with the Massachusetts Chapter of the American Rhododendron Society, one acre of these sensational plants is already planted, putting on quite a show in May and June. There is also a Hosta Display Garden, created in conjunction with the New England Hosta Society. The ground cover and mulch display contains over 150 beds providing ideas for the home gardener. In addition to all this, there are natural woodlands and wildflower trails. Courses, workshops, tours, and lectures are offered throughout the year. Facilities are available for meetings, weddings, and receptions. On the third Sunday in September, the popular Rare Plant Sale and Auction is held. Open daily, 9–sunset. Fee: None. Located on Wellesley St., just south of U.S. 20, approximately 10 miles west of downtown Boston. Address: 135 Wellesley St., Weston, MA 02193. Tel.: 617-524-1718.

# *Michigan*

Mackinac Island **7**

**75**

**75**

**27**

Midland **8**

Bloomfield Hills **3**

**69**

**6** Holland **5**

**96**

East Lansing **4**

Grosse Pointe Farms

**94**

Detroit

Tipton Ann Arbor

Niles **4**

Belle Isle

**9** **10** **2** **1**

1. Belle Isle, Detroit: Anna Scripps Whitcomb Conservatory
2. Ann Arbor: Matthai Botanical Garden
3. Bloomfield Hills: Cranbrook Hills
4. East Lansing: Michigan State University Horticulture Gardens
5. Grosse Pointe Farms: Grosse Pointe Garden Center
6. Holland: Veldheer Tulip Gardens, Inc.
7. Mackinac Island: Grand Hotel
8. Midland: Dow Gardens
9. Niles: Fernwood
10. Tipton: Hidden Lake Gardens

# *Michigan*

## "DON'T MISS" GARDENS

### BELLE ISLE DETROIT: ANNA SCRIPPS WHITCOMB CONSERVATORY

*An elegant conservatory offering superb floral shows and collections, as well as colorful outdoor gardens.*

The 15-acre Anna Scripps Whitcomb Conservatory and grounds are located on Belle Isle in the midst of the Detroit River. The 1,000-acre island is a city park, designed in 1883 by Frederick Law Olmsted. It presents a myriad of activities for individuals and families, including a zoo, an aquarium (five thousand fish), a casino (dances, parties, senior center), a museum, a nature center, playing fields and courts, fishing areas, bicycle paths, a canoe lake, horse trails, and a 238-acre natural woodland where deer and other wildlife can be spotted.

The conservatory dates back to 1904, but several renovations have opened and enlarged it. More than a quarter million plants are displayed each year. Permanent collections include palms, ferns, cacti, tropical plants, and America's largest municipally owned orchid collection (over fifty-five hundred plants). Whitcomb's most popular displays—attracting over a million visitors annually—are its flower shows. Six of them keep nearly continuous color in the conservatory throughout the year (Winter Show, mid-January to Easter; Easter Show, Easter to early May; Mother's Day Show, early May to June 1; Summer Show, June to October; Chrysanthemum Show, early November to early December; Christmas Show, mid-December to mid-January). The outdoor grounds include broad lawns bordered by clipped hedges, a sunken garden and lily pool; large, colorful dahlia and perennial gardens provide blossoms spring to fall.

---

LOCATION: On Belle Isle, 2 miles from downtown Detroit. Take Jefferson Ave. or E. Grand Blvd. to the MacArthur Bridge.

ADDRESS: Belle Isle, Detroit, MI. For information, write to the Recreation Dept./City of Detroit, Water Board Bldg., 735 Randolph St., Detroit, MI 48226.

TELEPHONE: 313-267-7133 (Conservatory Office) or 313-224-1100 (Recreation Dept.).

HOURS: Conservatory, daily, 9–6; Belle Isle Park, daily, sunrise to sunset.

FEE: None.

TOURS: Group tours by prearrangement.

RESTAURANT: None in conservatory. Several snack bars in park.

SHOPS: None in conservatory.

WHEELCHAIR ACCESS: Access throughout.

---

TIPS: 1. Don't miss any of the six flower shows. The Chrysanthemum Show is the most popular.
2. The outdoor gardens are impressive, especially the excellent dahlia garden, which peaks in late summer/early fall.
3. When entering Belle Isle, notice the 30-foot floral clock made from twenty-two thousand plants and flowers.
4. Even in winter Belle Isle offers something for everyone. In addition to the indoor activities at the conservatory, aquarium, and museum, there is outdoor ice skating, sledding, sleigh and pony-cart rides, and feeding the deer that venture out of the woods.

---

# EXCELLENT GARDENS

---

## ANN ARBOR: MATTHAI BOTANICAL GARDEN

Associated with the University of Michigan, the Matthai Botanical Garden is dedicated to research and education. The garden comprises 250 acres, most of it natural woodland, prairie, and bog. Approximately 5 acres are landscaped and include a rose garden, an herb knot garden, a rock garden, and a perennial garden. There are lawns, trails, and a pond. The 1-acre conservatory is mainly reserved for research, but part of it houses permanent collections of tropicals and cacti and is open to the public. Here it holds Easter and Christmas floral shows. Wheelchair access to most areas. Guided tours and group tours available. Adult education classes are presented on a variety of topics. Weddings and meetings can be held by prearrangement. Open: Outdoor gardens, daily, 8–sunset; conservatory, daily, 10–4; closed Thanksgiving, Christmas, and New Year's Day. Fee: $1/adult, $.75/senior, $.50/children ages 6–12. Address: 1800 N. Dixboro Rd., Ann Arbor, MI 48105. Tel.: 313-763-7060.

## BLOOMFIELD HILLS: CRANBROOK HILLS

Cranbrook Hills offers 40 acres of magnificently terraced gardens, colorful flower beds, tranquil pools, statuary, and fountains, with a diversity of flowering plants that insures beautiful blooms from May to October. The gardens were designed to augment the Cranbrook House, an elegant English manor built at the turn of the century for publisher George Booth. Today Cranbrook is a well-known educational community, consisting of several schools, an academy of art, an institute of science, and more. Gardens open May and Sept., daily, 1–5; June–Aug., daily, 10–5; Oct., weekends only, 1–5; house tours on Sun., July and Aug., 2–4, plus the last Sun. of the month in Apr., May, June, Sept., Oct.; group tours of house, Sept.–June by prearrangement. Fee: $2/adults, $1.50/students and seniors. Located approximately 15 miles northwest of downtown Detroit; take Woodward Ave. (State Rte. 1) or Telegraph Rd. (U.S. 24) to Lone Pine Rd. Address: 380 Lone Pine Rd., P.O. Box 801, Bloomfield Hills, MI 48013. Tel.: 313-645-3149.

## EAST LANSING: MICHIGAN STATE UNIVERSITY HORTICULTURE GARDENS

Dedicated to research, testing, and display, the 2½-acre Horticulture Gardens contain an All-America Rose Selections trial garden (four hundred bushes), plus gardens of annuals, perennials, bulbs, and water plants. There are propagation greenhouses that can also be viewed. Bloom period extends from April into October. Guided tours by prearrangement. Picnicking. Gardens available for weddings. Gardens open daily, sunrise to sunset; greenhouses open Mon–Fri., 8:00–4:30. Fee: None. Located on the north side of the MSU campus, near Grand River Rd. (Note: In 1988 the gardens will be moved to another location on campus; please check for details.) For further information, write to MSU Horticulture Gardens, East Lansing, MI 48823. Tel.: 517-355-0348.

## GROSSE POINTE FARMS: GROSSE POINTE GARDEN CENTER

Originally the Italian Renaissance home of the Alger family, this colorful, award-winning garden of circular beds and brick pathways overlooks Lake St. Clair. The Garden Center is dedicated to horticultural and gardening education, and the annual and perennial beds and other plantings are cared for by Garden Center members. The Center also sponsors lectures, workshops, and horticultural and bonsai exhibitions. Library and meeting rooms are available to members. Open Tues., Wed., and Thurs., 10–4; closed in Aug. and Dec. Fee: $5 (annual membership fee). Location: Grosse Pointe Farms is located on Lake St. Clair, approximately 10 miles northeast of downtown Detroit; take Jefferson Ave. north, which becomes Lake Shore Dr. Address: 32 Lake Shore Rd., Grosse Pointe Farms, MI 48236. Tel.: 313-881-4594.

## HOLLAND: VELDHEER TULIP GARDENS, INC.

A mail-order and retail flower farm offering one of the largest selections of tulips in the world. From April to May, over 2 million tulips can be seen here, complete with windmills, canals, and Dutch drawbridges. During this time the garden also participates in Holland's Tulip Time Festival. In summer the garden produces fields of dahlias, gladiolus, begonias, and bedding plants. There is a gift shop and a garden shop. On the grounds are the Deklomp Wooden Shoe Factory and the Delftware Factory. Open Mon.–Sat., 8:00–5:30; open Sun. in season; in May, open daily, 8–dusk. Fee: $2 per person in May only. Location: Holland is located in southwestern Michigan, 30 miles south of Muskegon and 20 miles west of Grand Rapids; take U.S. 31 north past I-196 to Quincy St. Address: 12755 Quincy St. and U.S. 31, Holland, MI 49423. Tel.: 616-399-1900 or 616-399-1803.

## MACKINAC ISLAND: GRAND HOTEL

The beautifully landscaped grounds of this Victorian hotel consist of sixteen planting areas, gardens, and a greenhouse. A vast array of bedding plants are employed including tulips (24,000), daffodils (3,000), begonias (5,000), marigolds (1,500), and geraniums (5,000)—over 100,000 in all. The gardens include the Lilac Collection, the Gazebo Garden, the English Nice Garden, the Begonia Bend, the Daylily Collection, and the English Tea Garden. An annual Lilac Festival is held in mid-June, and a Flower and Garden Weekend just after Labor Day. Located in the Straits between Lakes Michigan and Huron, Mackinac (MACK-IN-awe) Island is majestic yet serene, especially since bicycle or horse and carriage are the only forms of transportation allowed (the island is accessible by ferry, airplane, or private boat). The hotel, opened in 1887, is one of the most famous and distinguished on the American continent. Walking Tour brochure (recommended) available in gift shop for $.25. Gardens (and hotel) available for weddings and meetings. Hotel open May–Nov. Day fee (hotel and gardens): $3. Location: Mackinac Island is located in the far northwestern corner of Lake Huron, in the straits separating upper and lower Michigan. Address: Mackinac Island, MI 49757. Tel.: 906-847-3331.

## MIDLAND: DOW GARDENS

This former estate garden consists of 35 acres of lawns, gardens, ponds, waterfalls, shrubs, and trees. There is a small but well-groomed rose garden in bloom July to September. Color is provided by tulips in spring and a flower garden of annuals in summer. Wheelchair accessible. Wedding portraits can be taken here by prearrangement. Group tours by prearrangement. Open daily, 10–9; closed major holidays. Fee: None. Location: Midland is located in central Michigan, northeast of Saginaw (15 miles), Flint (50 miles), and Detroit (72 miles). Address: 1018 West Main St., Midland, MI 48640. Tel.: 517-631-2677.

## NILES: FERNWOOD

Conceived as an educational center for gardening, nature study, and arts and crafts, this 105-acre botanic garden and nature center contains 6 acres of landscaped gardens, a 45-acre arboretum, an 18-acre wilderness area, and 30 acres of natural woodland along the Saint Joseph River. Landscaped areas include a lilac collection, an herb garden, shrub roses, the Japanese Garden, the iris and daylily collections, the hosta and fern collections, a ground cover collection, a rock garden, a vine collection, an azalea ravine, a prairie garden, a vegetable garden, a boxwood garden, numerous beds of flowering annuals and perennials, and a greenhouse with collections of cacti, orchids, bromeliads, and other tropicals. The gardens are designed to provide ideas to home gardeners, as well as to offer color from spring to fall. Peak bloom is in April and May; good color also in July and August and in autumn. There is an annual Mothers' Day Herb and Garden Festival with a choral concert. Art exhibits in main Meeting House. Group tours by prearrangement. Wheelchair accessible. Over 140 classes and events are held each year covering a wide variety of topics. Library. Gift shop. Open Mar. 15 to Dec. 15, Mon.–Fri., 9–5; Sat., 10–5; Sun., 12–5; open year-round, dawn to dusk, to members. Fee: $2/people ages 13 and up; no fee to members or children 12 and under. Location: Niles is located in the far southwest of Michigan, at the intersection of U.S. 33 and State Rtes. 51 and 140; Fernwood can be found west of Niles, just north of Buchanan. Address: 1720 Range Line Rd., Niles, MI 49120. Tel.: 616-695-6491 or 616-683-8653.

---

## TIPTON: HIDDEN LAKE GARDENS

Donated to Michigan State University in 1946, these 670 acres of rolling hills and forest encompass many choice collections. The arboretum possesses over twenty-five hundred species of woody plants, a fine assortment of flowering trees (magnolias, cherries, crab apples, hawthorns), the Harper Collection of Dwarf and Rare Conifers, an array of rhododendrons and azaleas, and more. There is also a large All-America Trial Garden for bedding annuals, and a conservatory with tropical, arid, and temperate plant collections. The grounds offer over 6 miles of picturesque drives and 5 miles of hiking trails. The Garden Center Building contains exhibits, a library, a gift shop, a meeting room, and an auditorium where classes are held. Picnic area. Wheelchair accessible. Guided tours by prearrangement. Garden open Apr.–Oct., Mon.–Fri., 8–sundown, and Sat.–Sun., 9–sundown; Nov.–Mar., Mon.–Fri., 8:00–4:30, and Sat.–Sun., 9:00–4:30; Garden Center Building and conservatory hours vary slightly—check for times. Fee: $1. Location: Tipton is located in southeastern Michigan on State Rte. 50, southwest of Ann Arbor (30 miles) and Detroit (60 miles); the gardens can be found on Rte. 50, just west of Tipton. Address: Tipton, MI 49287. Tel.: 517-431-2060.

# *Mississippi*

## EXCELLENT GARDENS

### BELZONI: WISTER GARDENS

This beautifully landscaped, award-winning 14-acre garden embodies broad lawns, graceful gazebos, and paths meandering beneath towering trees. Peak season is spring when four thousand tulips and thousands of other bulbs burst into bloom, quickly followed by over eight thousand azaleas and a variety of flowering fruit trees. In summer, a broad array of bedding plants are in blossom; in autumn, chrysanthemums, and in winter, camellias and hollies provide color, plus the plants in the Garden House. A 4-acre lake serves as home to swans, flamingos, and ducks. The sixteen-room Colonial House contains antiques and Oriental rugs. Garden available for weddings. Open daily, 8–5. Fee: None. Location: Belzoni is located in west-central Mississippi, at the junction of U.S. 49W and State Rtes. 12 and 7; the garden is on Rte. 12, just east of the junction. For further information, write to Wister Gardens, P.O. Box 237, Belzoni, MS 39038. Tel.: 601-247-3025.

### BILOXI: BEAUVOIR

Beauvoir is the restored plantation house of Jefferson Davis, president of the Confederacy during the Civil War. The grounds consist of 66 acres, about a quarter of which contain azaleas and camellias in a naturalized setting. Peak bloom is in spring. Beauvoir is one of the featured houses of the Biloxi Spring Pilgrimage. Group tours by prearrangement. Open daily, 8:30–5:00; closed Christmas. Fee: $3.75/adults, $3/seniors, $1.75/children ages 13–17, $1.25/children ages 7–11; group rates available. Location: Biloxi is located on the Gulf Coast; Beauvoir can be found 5 miles west of downtown Biloxi. Addess: 200 W. Beach Blvd. (U.S. 90), Biloxi, MS 39531. Tel.: 601-388-1313.

### JACKSON: MYNELLE GARDENS

This 6-acre garden displays beautiful flower beds along with lagoons, gazebos, statuary, and fountains, and it includes a wild bird sanctuary. Collections include azaleas, irises, daylilies, bulbs,

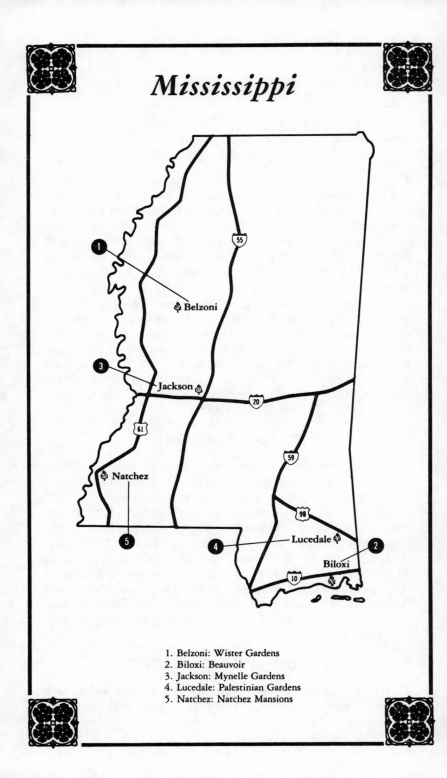

# Mississippi

1. Belzoni: Wister Gardens
2. Biloxi: Beauvoir
3. Jackson: Mynelle Gardens
4. Lucedale: Palestinian Gardens
5. Natchez: Natchez Mansions

annuals and perennials by the thousands, plus amaryllis, dianthus, camellias, magnolias, and other flowering trees—nearly a thousand varieties in all. Garden areas include the Rustic Garden and Summerhouse, the Formal Garden, the Old-fashioned Garden, the Medical and Herb Garden, the English Bog Garden, the Japanese Garden Island, and the Wedding Lawn. Among the many rare plants, its old-fashioned rose collection contains specimens whose lines date back to the seventeenth century. Group tours by prearrangement. Garden available for weddings, receptions, meetings, and classes. Open daily, dawn to dusk. Fee: $2/people ages 12 and over. Located approximately 4 miles west of downtown Jackson; take Capitol St. to Clinton Blvd.—the garden is just west of I-220. Address: 4738 Clinton Blvd., Jackson, MS 39209. Tel.: 601-922-4011.

## LUCEDALE: PALESTINIAN GARDENS

This 20-acre garden is actually a scale model of the Holy Land complete with miniaturized replicas of the ancient cities of Jerusalem, Jericho, Bethlehem, Tiberias, and Capernaum. Also featured are shrubs and plants mentioned in the Bible. The garden is nondenominational, and individuals and groups of all faiths are welcome. Guided tours, picnic area, gift shop. Open daily, Mar.–Nov., 8–4. Fee: $1.50/adult, $.50/child; group rates available. Location: Lucedale is located in southeastern Mississippi at the junction of U.S. 98 and State Rtes. 63 and 26, 45 miles northwest of Mobile, Alabama; take U.S. 98 north from Lucedale, go 12 miles and look for signs, turn right, and proceed 6.5 miles to garden. For further information, write to Palestinian Gardens, Rte. 9, Box 792, Lucedale, MS 39452. Tel.: 601-947-8422.

## NATCHEZ: NATCHEZ MANSIONS

Natchez is well known for its many grand old mansions and its famous Spring Pilgrimage. Four mansions in particular are noted for their gardens. Foremost among these is Cherokee (217 High St.), built around 1800, with its azalea gardens, bulb and pansy beds, white garden, mauve garden, hollies, and flowering dogwoods. D'Evereux (D'Evereux Dr.), a classic columned mansion built around 1840, possesses gardens with large terraces amid shrubs and stately trees, plus reflecting pools and fountains. Hope Farms (147 Homochitto St.), built in the late 1700s and filled with family heirlooms and rare antiques, has a garden with spring bulbs and flower beds. Stanton Hall (401 High St.), a palatial antebellum mansion built in 1857 and filled with period antiques and furnishings, has a beautifully landscaped courtyard, plus lawns surrounded by azaleas, dogwoods, and live oaks. Cherokee is open only for limited periods in spring and autumn; other mansions open daily. Tours and visits organized year-round by Natchez Pilgrimage Tours; D'Evereux and Hope Farms offer bed and breakfast accommodations. Hours and fees: Vary with types of tours. For further information, write to Natchez Pilgrimage Tours, P.O. Box 347, Natchez, MS 39120. Tel.: 601-446-6631.

# New Hampshire

## EXCELLENT GARDENS

### CORNISH: SAINT-GAUDENS NATIONAL HISTORIC SITE

This historic site includes the home, studio, and landscaped grounds of the sculptor, Augustus Saint-Gaudens. Flowing vines, shaped hedges, and terraces of flowers characterize this monument to the famous artist. Concerts and exhibitions are offered during summer months. Open late May through Oct.; gardens, open 8–dark; house, open 8:30–4:30. Fee: $.50/adult. Located in west-central New Hampshire, just off State Rte. 12A, 12 miles north of Claremont. For further information, write to Saint-Gaudens National Historic Site, RR #2, Cornish NH 03745. Tel.: 603-675-2175.

### FITZWILLIAM: RHODODENDRON STATE PARK

A National Natural Landmark, 15 acres of this state park are filled with five native wild rhododendron species. There are also wildflower trails through natural woodland. Peak bloom is in early July. Open daily, dawn to dusk. Fee: $1 during season (late May–Sept. 1). Location: The park is located on State. Rte. 119, about 3 miles west of Fitzwilliam and 22 miles east of Brattleboro. For further information, write to Division of Parks and Recreation, State of New Hampshire, P.O. Box 856, Concord, NH 03301. Tel.: 603-271-3254.

### NORTH HAMPTON: FULLER GARDENS

Each year twenty thousand visitors frequent the colorful grounds once the home of the former governor Alvan Fuller. Beautifully designed with sculptured hedges and flower walks, this 2-acre garden possesses an All-America Rose Display Garden (fifteen hundred bushes), a Japanese garden, and a conservatory with collections of tropical and desert plants. In spring hundreds of tulips and wildflowers burst into bloom, followed by azaleas and rhododendrons. In summer there are beds of annuals and perennials, plus roses, and in fall a display of chrysanthemums. Open daily, mid-May through Oct., 10–6. Fee: $2/adult; $1.50/seniors; children admitted free if accompanied by an

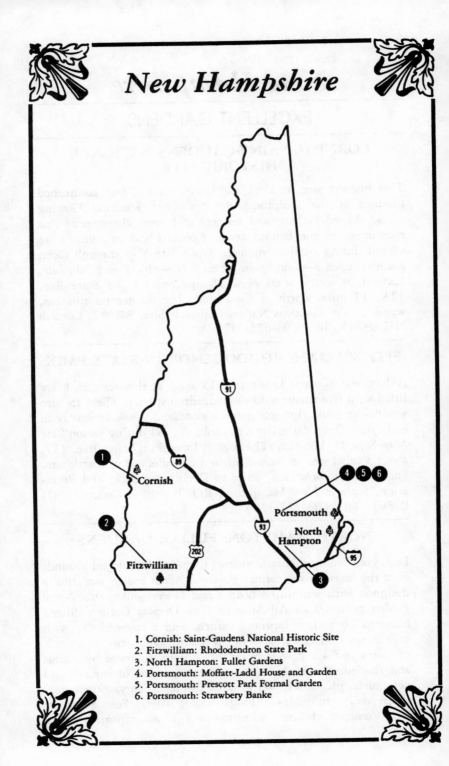

# New Hampshire

adult; group rates. Location: North Hampton is located approximately 12 miles south of Portsmouth; take State Rte. 1A to Willow Ave. Address: 10 Willow Ave., North Hampton, NH 03862. Tel.: 603-964-5414.

## PORTSMOUTH: MOFFATT-LADD HOUSE AND GARDEN

Built in 1763, this National Historic Landmark has been restored by the National Society of Colonial Dames of America in the state of New Hampshire. The 1½-acre old-fashioned garden consists of four terraces, brick walks, grass steps, rose arbors, fruit trees, an herb garden, beds of flowers in bloom May to October, tall lilac hedges, and 100-year-old wisteria. The towering chestnut tree, a Big Tree Champion, was planted in 1776 by William Whipple, a signer of the Declaration of Independence. The house is a classic of eighteenth-century architecture and furnishings. Group tours, weddings, meetings, receptions by prearrangement. Open Jun. 15–Oct. 15, Mon.– Sat., 10–4, and Sun., 2–5. Fee: $2/adult, $.75/child; group rates available. Address: 154 Market St., Portsmouth, NH 03801. Tel.: 603-436-8221.

## PORTSMOUTH: PRESCOTT PARK FORMAL GARDEN

A magnificent flower garden is the centerpiece of this public park along the historic Portsmouth waterfront. Visited by over two hundred thousand people last year, the award-winning Prescott Park Formal Garden punctuates its beautifully designed displays (thousands of flowering plants in six hundred varieties) with walkways and fountains. Designated an All-America Selection Demonstration Garden and maintained in conjunction with the University of New Hampshire Cooperative Extension Service, it also includes trial gardens, the Josie F. Prescott Memorial Garden, a floral wall, weeping Japanese crab apples, and in winter, 2 miles of Christmas lights. In addition to the formal garden, Prescott Park offers picnic areas, a fishing pier, boat moorings, outdoor concerts, and arts and crafts exhibits. Garden available for weddings. Open daily, sunrise to sunset. Fee: None. Located in the historic waterfront district, across from Strawbery Banke Restoration. For further information, write to the Cooperative Extension Service, University of New Hampshire, Nesmith Hall, Durham, NH 03824. Tel.: 603-862-1520.

## PORTSMOUTH: STRAWBERY BANKE

This family attraction consists of thirty-seven authentically restored original buildings and gardens of old Portsmouth. There is a flower walk, an herb garden, and a flower garden, as well as eight period gardens in various stages of restoration. A New England Gardening Day is held in June and offers garden tours, displays, and workshops. Open May–Oct., 10–5. Fee (grounds and museums): $5.50/adults, $4.50/seniors, $3/children ages 6–16, or $15/families. Located on Marcy St. in the Portsmouth waterfront district, across from Prescott Park. For further information, write to Strawbery Banke, P.O. Box 300, Portsmouth, NH 03801. Tel.: 603-436-8010.

# New Jersey

## "DON'T MISS" GARDENS

### SOMERVILLE: DUKE GARDENS

*A 1-acre pearl of a garden with eleven indoor displays showing garden designs from around the world.*

"Perfection Under Glass" is the motto of Duke Gardens, and it lives up to the claim. Although originally erected by James Duke as working greenhouses for his estate, it was his daughter, Doris, who planned and carried out the conversion of the structure into a showcase. The author remembers her visiting Longwood in the 1950s when she was developing her ideas. Very talented in garden design, Doris Duke had an eye for detail and a knack for having everything in the right place; scale, color—all the factors involved in producing a superior visual display. Carefully selecting the plants and flowers she would use, Miss Duke wisely chose not to rival the larger gardens in terms of collections or species, but instead concentrated on the theme that characterizes her gardens—visual harmony and beauty.

Doris Duke also came up with a novel display concept. She conceived the idea of creating, in her various greenhouse rooms, eleven distinct gardens, each representing a different era or culture. This serves to produce a compelling experience for the visitor. Not only is one swept away by the sheer diversity and beauty of garden styles, but one also gets an intimate glimpse into the diverse cultures as represented by their garden traditions. For example, one quickly appreciates the preciousness of water when viewing the Islamic Symmetry garden. Water is the central thread of this garden, where the brickwork is patterned after the Shalamar Gardens of Lahore, Pakistan. Filled with plants in geometric designs and surrounded by a high wall, the Persian name for this type of garden is *pairidaeza,* the root of our own word "paradise."

LOCATION: In central New Jersey, just south of Somerville on State Rte. 206, 40 miles west of New York City, 17 miles north of Princeton.
ADDRESS: State Rte. 206 South, Somerville, NJ 08876.
TELEPHONE: 201-722-3700.

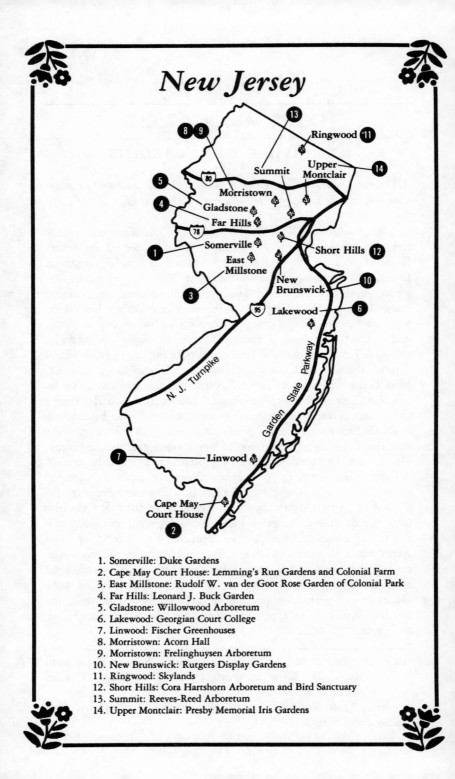

# New Jersey

1. Somerville: Duke Gardens
2. Cape May Court House: Lemming's Run Gardens and Colonial Farm
3. East Millstone: Rudolf W. van der Goot Rose Garden of Colonial Park
4. Far Hills: Leonard J. Buck Garden
5. Gladstone: Willowwood Arboretum
6. Lakewood: Georgian Court College
7. Linwood: Fischer Greenhouses
8. Morristown: Acorn Hall
9. Morristown: Frelinghuysen Arboretum
10. New Brunswick: Rutgers Display Gardens
11. Ringwood: Skylands
12. Short Hills: Cora Hartshorn Arboretum and Bird Sanctuary
13. Summit: Reeves-Reed Arboretum
14. Upper Montclair: Presby Memorial Iris Gardens

HOURS: Daily, 12–4; advance reservations required. Closed holidays and summer months.

FEES: $5.00/people ages 12 and up, $2.50/children ages 6–12. Cameras and high-heeled shoes not permitted.

TOURS: All visitors are guided through the gardens in small groups. Larger group tours by prearrangement. School-sponsored group tours admitted free on Mon. and Fri. by prearrangement.

RESTAURANTS: None on grounds.

SHOPS: Only slides and postcards are sold.

WHEELCHAIR ACCESS: No.

---

TIPS: Duke Gardens is a remarkable sight from fall to spring (it is closed in summer because of uncomfortably high temperatures and humidity within). However, winter is a particularly good time to visit, when the bare northern countryside makes these meticulous gardens all the more refreshing and impressive.

## EXCELLENT GARDENS

### CAPE MAY COURT HOUSE: LEMMING'S RUN GARDENS AND COLONIAL FARM

This is one of the few gardens in North America landscaped entirely with annuals. Established in 1977, the twenty-seven individual gardens unfold along a winding sandy path including a yellow garden, a blue and white garden, an English cottage garden, a houseplant garden, an orange garden, a fern garden, a begonia garden, and a rose garden. The seventeenth-century colonial farm contains a log cabin and an herb garden. Peak bloom is late May into October. Special summer programs and tours are scheduled weekly. Gift shop. Wheelchair accessible. Open daily, 9:30–5:00. Fee: $3/adult, $1/ages 6–12. Located just off U.S. 9 near Swainton in New Jersey's southern tip, about 30 miles south of Altantic City and 18 miles north of Cape May. Address: 1845 Rte. 9 North, Cape May Court House, NJ 08210. Tel.: 609-465-5871.

## EAST MILLSTONE: RUDOLF W. van der GOOT ROSE GARDEN OF COLONIAL PARK

Owned and operated by the Somerset County Park Commission, this 1-acre garden has been an accredited All-America Rose Selection display garden since 1973. The van der Goot collection totals over four thousand bushes (275 varieties), including the newest All-America Award winners. All plants are clearly labeled. Blooming period is June into October. In addition, Colonial Park contains an arboretum emphasizing trees and shrubs of the central New Jersey area, as well as lilacs and flowering cherries. Group tours by prearrangement for garden clubs, schools, and other interested groups. Hours: Rose garden open daily, June–Aug., 10–dusk, and Sept.–Oct., 10:00–4:30; arboretum open year-round, daily, during daylight hours. Fee: None. Located on Mettler's Rd.; take State Rte. 533 (River Rd.) to Amwell Rd., then to Mettler's Rd. For further information, write to the Horticulture Dept., Somerset County Park Commission, P.O. Box 5327, North Branch, NJ 08876. Tel.: 201-873-2459.

## FAR HILLS: LEONARD J. BUCK GARDEN

Leonard J. Buck was a mining engineer who became fascinated by the rock outcroppings on his land, and the relationship of the soil's mineral composition to the plants that grew there. After building a dam and laying out pathways, Buck filled his valley with a profusion of native and exotic plant life. In 1950 Buck received the Gold Medal of the National Association of Gardeners for his transformation of this naturally rocky terrain into a first-rate alpine garden. Now owned and operated by the Somerset County Park Commission, this public garden contains eleven diverse rock gardens in a natural setting that includes masses of rhododendrons, ferns, and wildflowers. Group tours by prearrangement. Meeting rooms available to garden clubs and civic organizations. Open: Mon.–Sat., 10–4 and Sun., 10–6. Fee: None. Located in central New Jersey, approximately 40 miles west of New York City, at the junction of I-287 and State Rte. 512. Address: Layton Rd., Far Hills, NJ 07931. Tel.: 201-234-2677.

## GLADSTONE: WILLOWWOOD ARBORETUM

This 130-acre arboretum possesses more than 3,500 kinds of flora including oaks (35 kinds), maples (50 kinds), willows (100 kinds), masses of ferns and wildflowers, and a hillside of pink lady's-slippers. Also featured are collections of lilacs, magnolias, cherries, hollies, and conifers. This is perhaps the best collection of temperate-zone plants in New Jersey. The residence dates back to 1792. There are educational programs for all ages and a children's garden. Summer Music Festival outdoor concerts are held here and at the adjacent Bamboo Brook Outdoor Education Center. Tours by prearrangement. Open Mon.–Fri., 9:00–4:30, and open some weekends (check for times). Fee: None. Location: Gladstone is located in central New Jersey, 40 miles west of New York City, near the junction of U.S. 206 and State Rte. 512; take 512 (Pottersville Rd.) west from Gladstone, turn right onto Union Grove Rd., left onto Longview. For further information, write to the Morris County Park Commission, P.O. Box 1295R, Morristown, NJ 07960. Tel.: 201-829-0474.

## LAKEWOOD: GEORGIAN COURT COLLEGE

Formerly the Gould estate, Georgian Court College's 200-acre campus possesses an Italian garden, a sunken garden, and a formal garden. There is also an authentic, 1-acre Japanese garden designed and created around 1915 by Takeo Shiota (who also designed the Japanese garden at the Brooklyn Botanic Garden). Tours of estate and grounds by appointment. Fee: $2. Location: Lakewood is located in east-central New Jersey on U.S. 9. Address: Lakewood Ave., Lakewood, NJ 08701. Tel.: 201-364-2200.

## LINWOOD: FISCHER GREENHOUSES

This retail and mail-order nursery of 50 acres specializes in African violets and related plants. Individual and group visits are encouraged, with Mr. Charles Fischer himself often serving as guide. Additional formal gardens and nature walks are planned in the near future. Open daily, 9–5. Fee: None. Location: Linwood is located on State Rte. 585, 10 miles west of Altantic City; take Central Ave. west from Linwood, turn right on Oak. Address: Oak Ave., Linwood, NJ 08221. Tel.: 609-927-3399.

## MORRISTOWN: ACORN HALL

Restored in 1971 by the Home Garden Club of Morristown, Acorn Hall's 2 acres of cultivated grounds consist almost entirely of flora representative of the period 1853 to 1888, when the garden was originally created. Plantings include wildflowers, ferns, laurels, rhododendrons, azaleas, peonies, bulbs, old-fashioned roses, herbs, hydrangeas, dogwoods, and weeping cherries. Several specimens date from the original garden. Good color from April into October. There are also wooded areas with a path connecting the lawn and barn areas. The house, an excellent example of Victorian Italianate architecture, was completed in 1853 and now serves as home for the Morris County Historical Society. Wheelchair access to garden and first floor of house. Gardens open daily, daylight hours; house open on Thurs., 11–3, and Sun., 1:30–4:00. Fee: None for garden; house, $1/adult, $.50/seniors. Location: Acorn Hall is in central Morristown, which is located 30 miles west of New York City at the junction of State Rte. 24 with I-187 and U.S. 202. Address: 68 Morris Ave., Morristown, NJ 07960. Tel.: 201-267-3465.

## MORRISTOWN: FRELINGHUYSEN ARBORETUM

Formerly the Frelinghuysen estate, these 127 undulating acres offer 4 miles of trails through collections of flowering trees (crab apple, cherry, magnolia, dogwood), azaleas and rhododendrons, peonies, ferns, a vast array of wildflowers, and spring and fall bulbs. There is also a rose garden and a lilac garden. Plantings are designed to provide diverse color from early spring into fall. Library. Classes and programs for all ages and interests, including garden excursions. Meeting rooms available for weddings, receptions, or affairs. Wheelchair accessible. Group tours by prearrangement. Summer Music Festival offering outdoor concerts June to August. Garden open daily, 9–dusk; house hours limited—check for times. Fee: None. Location: Morristown is located 30 miles west of New York City at the junction of State Rte. 24 with U.S. 202 and I-287; take Morris Rd. east from Morristown to Whippany Rd., turn left onto E. Hanover Ave. Address: 53 E. Hanover Ave., P.O. Box 1295R, Morristown, NJ 07960. Tel.: 201-829-0474.

## NEW BRUNSWICK: RUTGERS DISPLAY GARDENS

Best known for its excellent azalea and rhododendron display (over five hundred varieties) from late April to mid-June, the 50-acre gardens also offer an evergreen garden, a hedge and vine display, a shrub garden, a large collection of American and Japanese hollies, and a garden of annuals in bloom July and August. North of the gardens is the Frank G. Heylar Woods, offering paths through virgin forest. Open house programs are scheduled throughout the year. Open daily, 8:30–dusk, May–Sept.; 8:30–4:30, Oct.–April; closed Saturdays during hunting season. Fee: None. Located just east of U.S. 1 on Ryders Lane. For further information write to Rutgers Display Gardens, College of Agriculture and Environmental Science, Rutgers University, New Brunswick, NJ 08903. Tel.: 201-932-9639.

## RINGWOOD: SKYLANDS

Located in Ringwood State Park, this impressive 115-acre garden was designated the official New Jersey Botanical Garden in 1974. Originally part of an estate, the grounds were designed with formal and informal areas, bright with color from January to October. The formal plantings near the manor house contain a succession of gardens (azalea, lilac, winter, octagonal, perennial, annual, summer, and peony gardens), broad lawns, a magnolia walk, a honeysuckle lane, and in spring, thousands of tulips and other spring bulbs. Beyond the Crabapple Vista (formed by 162 flowering trees) lie the naturalized areas with wildflower, heather, bog, and rhododendron gardens, beyond which lie miles of paths through the estate's 1,000 acres of woodlands. Group tours by prearrangement. Gardens available for weddings and receptions. Full schedule of lectures, slide shows, garden walks, excursions to other gardens, and an Annual Floral Fair and Plant Sale. The Visitor Center is located in the original Carriage House. The forty-five-room Tudor Revival mansion, designed by John Russell Pope (who designed the National Gallery and National Archives), contains impressive interiors shipped intact fom Europe. The mansion is temporarily closed as it undergoes restoration—check for reopening date. Gardens open daily, dawn to dusk; mansion open May–Oct., 10–4. Fee:

No fee for gardens; mansion fee is $1/weekdays, $2/weekends. Location: Ringwood is located in northern New Jersey on State Rte. 511, 3 miles below the state line and 40 miles northwest of New York City; Skylands is 1 mile north of Ringwood. Address: Ringwood State Park, Box 1304, Ringwood, NJ 07456. For further information, write to Skylands Association, P.O. Box 302, Ringwood, NJ 07456. Tel.: 201-962-7031.

## SHORT HILLS: CORA HARTSHORN ARBORETUM AND BIRD SANCTUARY

This arboretum has 3 miles of trails through 17 acres of natural forest enhanced by eighty varieties of wildflowers, azaleas, and rhododendrons, a great diversity of ferns, flowering trees, mountain laurels, and lady's-slippers. Committed to public recreation and education, the arboretum hosts a full schedule of workshops, lectures, and programs for small children, juveniles, and families. Peak bloom is in spring, foliage color in fall. Group tours by prearrangement. Arboretum open daily; Stone House (reception center) open May and Oct. only, Tues.–Thurs., 2:30–4:30; Sat., 9:30–11:30; Sun., 3–5. Location: about 20 miles west of New York City; take I-78 to the Morris-Essex Turnpike, turn north onto Forest Dr. Fee: None. Address: 324 Forest Drive South, Short Hills, NJ 07078. Tel.: 201-376-3587.

## SUMMIT: REEVES-REED ARBORETUM

A 12½-acre garden, consisting of rolling lawns, formal gardens, native woodland, and a house. Collections include wildflowers, ferns, bulbs, daffodils, roses, azaleas, herbs, conifers, and flowering trees (dogwood, magnolia, cherry, crab apple). Plantings are arranged to provide excellent color from spring through fall foliage season (a guide to seasonal bloom is available upon request). Dedicated to conservation and education, the arboretum holds a full schedule of classes and programs for adults (gardening and gardens, art, birds, geology, plant clinics, travelogues, concerts, cooking, plus field trips and group tours) and children (over fifteen hundred children are enrolled in programs held in the Discovery Center). A Rose Day is held in June. Free concerts in summer. Wheelchair accessible. Group tours by prearrangement. House and gardens available for weddings and meetings. Open daily, daylight hours; office open Mon., Tues., and Thurs. 9–3. Fee: None. Location: Summit is located on State Rte. 512, 20 miles west of New York City; take I-78 west to the Morris-Essex Turnpike, turn left onto Hobart Ave. Address: 165 Hobart Ave., Summit, NJ 07901. Tel.: 201-273-8787.

---

## UPPER MONTCLAIR: PRESBY MEMORIAL IRIS GARDENS

Named after the founder of the American Iris Society and located in Mountainside Park, Presby Gardens contains over six thousand varieties of iris, some whose origins date back to the sixteenth century. The iris was named after the Greek goddess of the rainbow, and she would not be disappointed by the spectrum of color seen here during the peak blooming period in late May and early June. Good color also viewable the remainder of May and June, and again in September and early October. Guided tours for schools, garden clubs, or senior groups by prearrangement. Wheelchair accessible. Open daily, sunrise to sunset. Fee: None. Location: Upper Montclair is located approximately 12 miles northwest of New York City; take State Rte. 3 to junction with U.S. 46, turn left onto Valley Rd., turn right onto Normal Ave., turn left onto Upper Mtn. Ave. Address: 474 Upper Mountain Ave., Upper Montclair, NJ 07043. Tel.: 201-783-5974.

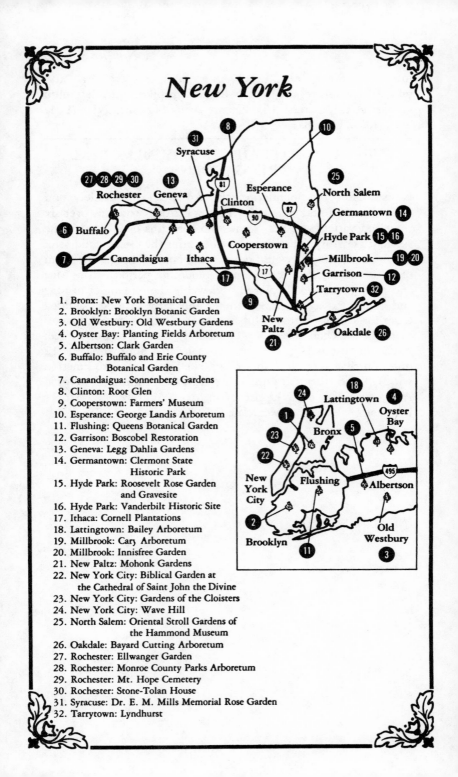

# New York

1. Bronx: New York Botanical Garden
2. Brooklyn: Brooklyn Botanic Garden
3. Old Westbury: Old Westbury Gardens
4. Oyster Bay: Planting Fields Arboretum
5. Albertson: Clark Garden
6. Buffalo: Buffalo and Erie County
       Botanical Garden
7. Canandaigua: Sonnenberg Gardens
8. Clinton: Root Glen
9. Cooperstown: Farmers' Museum
10. Esperance: George Landis Arboretum
11. Flushing: Queens Botanical Garden
12. Garrison: Boscobel Restoration
13. Geneva: Legg Dahlia Gardens
14. Germantown: Clermont State
       Historic Park
15. Hyde Park: Roosevelt Rose Garden
       and Gravesite
16. Hyde Park: Vanderbilt Historic Site
17. Ithaca: Cornell Plantations
18. Lattingtown: Bailey Arboretum
19. Millbrook: Cary Arboretum
20. Millbrook: Innisfree Garden
21. New Paltz: Mohonk Gardens
22. New York City: Biblical Garden at
       the Cathedral of Saint John the Divine
23. New York City: Gardens of the Cloisters
24. New York City: Wave Hill
25. North Salem: Oriental Stroll Gardens of
       the Hammond Museum
26. Oakdale: Bayard Cutting Arboretum
27. Rochester: Ellwanger Garden
28. Rochester: Monroe County Parks Arboretum
29. Rochester: Mt. Hope Cemetery
30. Rochester: Stone-Tolan House
31. Syracuse: Dr. E. M. Mills Memorial Rose Garden
32. Tarrytown: Lyndhurst

# New York

## "DON'T MISS" GARDENS

### BRONX: NEW YORK BOTANICAL GARDEN

*One of America's oldest botanical gardens, with a wide spectrum of specialized displays, a fine collection of stately trees, and most important, the classic Enid A. Haupt Conservatory.*

Founded in 1891 with the purpose of giving the United States a garden rivaling the Royal Botanical Garden at Kew, the New York Botanical lists among its founding fathers Cornelius Vanderbilt and Andrew Carnegie. New York Botanical's original conservatory was designed after the internationally famous Crystal Palace built for the London Exhibition of 1851. The Crystal Palace represented a revolutionary concept in conservatory architecture, wherein splendidly delicate glass-and-iron structures replaced the traditional brick buildings of the past (as seen at Dumbarton Oaks). It is said that the source of inspiration for this architectural innovation by Sir Joseph Paxton was the symmetrical vein patterning of a giant waterlily leaf.

Today, New York Botanical's restored Enid A. Haupt Conservatory contains some outstanding displays under an acre of glass. The dome of this magnificent structure rises 90 feet over the collection in the Palm Court. Other displays include plants of economic importance together with a display box or can of the ultimate product engendered, ferns and orchids overflowing a volcanic crater, a tree covered with an array of bromeliads (nonparasitic plants that use tree limbs for support), and a collection of insect-eating plants. Beyond all this are the colorful seasonal shows featuring fall chrysanthemums, Christmas poinsettias, Easter lilies, and seasonal summer displays.

New York Botanical's most unusual outdoor garden is the Rock Garden. Planted among rocks deposited on the grounds by receding glaciers, the species represented in this dramatic garden are those that surmount the forbidding conditions of the Alps, Rockies, and Himalayas. Strong winds and severe temperatures keep these plants compact, which serves to make their brief but profuse flowering in early spring only the more dramatic. The popularity of this particular garden has prompted a Rock Garden Festival in mid-April.

LOCATION: On Southern Blvd., across from the famous Bronx Zoo and Fordham University.

ADDRESS: Bronx, NY 10458.

TELEPHONE: 212-220-8700.

HOURS: Grounds open daily, 8–dusk; conservatory, Tues.–Sun., 10–5.

FEE: Grounds, free. Enid A. Haupt Conservatory, $2.50/adults, $1.25/seniors and children. Parking costs $3.00.

TOURS: Group tours by prearrangement.

RESTAURANT: In the Old Snuff Mill, a National Historic Place built in 1840 and used as a tobacco mill until 1870.

SHOPS: Garden shop.

WHEELCHAIR ACCESS: Most areas accessible.

SPECIAL ACTIVITIES: Seasonal shows in the conservatory. Rock Garden Festival in mid-April. Educational classes for adults and children year-round.

---

TIPS: 1. In addition to the Haupt Conservatory and Rock Garden, don't miss:
   a. Jane Watson Irwin Perennial Garden with its massed blossoms (peak June–Aug.).
   b. Rhododendron Valley, further embellished with mountain laurel and narcissus (peak May–June).
   c. Azalea Way, beautiful in April.
   d. Trees, many rare, as well as flowering cherries, dogwoods, witch hazels, and tulip trees (peak April).
2. It's helpful to get a Visitors Map and Guide ($.25) before setting out on foot.
3. The renowned Bronx Zoo lies just across Fordham Rd.

---

## BROOKLYN: BROOKLYN BOTANIC GARDEN

*A world-famous garden offering the finest Japanese garden in the eastern United States (if not the entire Western Hemisphere), one of America's best bonsai collections, an excellent collection of flowering cherry trees (thirty varieties, some over seventy-three years old), and the third largest public rose collection in the United States.*

A true oasis in the midst of a city of concrete and brick, Brooklyn Botanic Garden was established in 1910 on a rock-strewn piece of city wasteland, within view of a dump where rubbish was incinerated around the clock. Not content merely to collect plant specimens and research materials, the Brooklyn Botanic pioneered an approach unique at the time. Emphasizing education to anybody wanting to learn, in 1914 this garden became the world's first botanic garden to initiate a children's garden and to offer in-service training for school teachers. Courses for adults were later added, and the garden's quarterly Record evolved into its *Plants & Gardens* series of internationally known handbooks. It is probably not coincidental that one of the authors grew up near this garden, spent a great deal of time walking its paths and learning its flora, and eventually became director of two of America's great gardens (see "About the Authors").

Brooklyn Botanic's best-known garden is its Japanese Hill-and-Pond Garden. Designed in 1915 by landscape architect Takeo Shiota, this garden presents a series of four Japanese garden styles: palace garden, Shinto, Buddhist temple garden, and tea garden. Each of these reflects the Japanese concept of the garden as a place for contemplation, a "mirror of nature." Carefully placed rocks and painstakingly pruned trees and shrubs are all blended to create natural scenes in miniature. Unlike most Western gardens, flowering plants are used sparingly in order not to disrupt the unchanging, eternal essence of this type of garden. For this reason Japanese gardens are essentially evergreen gardens in which trees are often trained to have a windswept appearance, and plant life is balanced by rocks and water. Water, in particular, is a vital element. Its smooth surface reflects a calm serenity, while the music of a waterfall represents the ceaseless rhythm of change. In designing the waterfall here, Mr. Shioto is said to have reset the rockbed repeatedly until the sound of the waterfall was just right.

The Brooklyn Botanic Garden is an immaculately designed and carefully tended garden, even more remarkable considering its location in the heart of urban Brooklyn. A 52-acre oasis, the Brooklyn Botanic represents the ultimate in inner-city gardens. It's no surprise that its visitors number more than three quarters of a million per year.

---

LOCATION: In the heart of Brooklyn, next to the Brooklyn Museum and Prospect Park.

ADDRESS: 1000 Washington Ave., Brooklyn, NY 11225.

TELEPHONE: 718-622-4433.

HOURS: Apr. 1–Sept. 30: Tues.–Fri., 8–6; Sat., Sun., and holidays, 10–6. Oct. 1–Mar. 30: Tues.–Fri., 8:00–4:30; Sat.,

Sun., and holidays, 10:00–4:30. Closed Mon. except on legal holidays. The Hill-and-Pond Garden is closed Nov.–Feb.

FEE: Garden, free (donations appreciated). Nominal fees on weekends for the Japanese Hill-and-Pond Garden.

TOURS: On Sun. at 1 P.M., mid-March to mid-Nov. Tours for groups or schools via prearrangement.

RESTAURANT: Snacks available at the Terrace Cafe. No picnicking.

SHOPS: Shop offering books, gifts, plants, and materials.

WHEELCHAIR ACCESS: Most of garden is accessible.

SPECIAL ACTIVITIES: Annual benefit plant sales in May and Nov. A broad range of ongoing educational activities, classes, lectures, concerts. The children's garden program, in which more than fifteen thousand children have over the years cultivated the same patch of city soil, has been in existence for more than 70 years.

---

TIPS: 1. Don't miss:
   a. Award-winning rose garden with five thousand bushes.
   b. Flowering trees include cherries, crab apples, and magnolias—dazzling in spring.
   c. A new three-pavilion (Desert, Tropical, Temperate) conservatory, along with greenhouses holding the excellent bonsai, orchid, and water gardens, is due to open in late 1987.
2. Peak times: Apr.–May for the cherry blossoms and other flowering trees; May– June for the luxuriant stands of azaleas and rhododendrons; June to early Oct. for roses.
3. The adjacent Brooklyn Museum and Prospect Park offer attractions of merit and family recreational facilities.

---

# OLD WESTBURY: OLD WESTBURY GARDENS

*A lovely estate in which both house and grounds were designed to augment each other's beauty. Perhaps the most colorful estate garden in New York.*

Listed in the National Register of Historic Places, Old Westbury was built at the turn of the century by John Shaffer Phipps, the son of steel magnate Henry Phipps (who endowed Phipps Conservatory). John Phipps's dream was to build an English-style country estate. The mansion house was to be fashioned in the architectural style of Charles II, and the gardens in the nineteenth-century English tradition of an expanse of lawns, reflecting pools, and distant vistas. To this blueprint George Crawley, the architect for both the house and gardens, added broad walkways and formal gardens imbued with color, creating a combination so attractive that Old Westbury is unfailingly ranked among America's top gardens.

The garden tour should actually begin with Westbury House, a handsome, nineteen-room brick structure containing carved oaken paneling, marble mantlepieces, antique gilded mirrors, and crystal chandeliers, furnishings by Chippendale and Hepplewhite, and paintings by Gainsborough, Constable, Reynolds, and John Singer Sargent. The house appears today just as it did 80 years ago, and as its originators intended, its windows offer some of the finest views of the 100-acre garden.

Upon leaving the Westbury Manor, notice the broad avenue of European beeches, the largest collection in the state. Moving down a staircase past an embankment of rhododendrons, one now enters the gardens. Just as the gardens can be viewed from the house, Old Westbury was designed so that the house would appear to advantage from the gardens. Notice the view of it from the Boxwood Garden as it is reflected across the pond.

Farther on, beyond the lilac walk (which in May offers a feast of its own) is the Walled Garden, Old Westbury's most colorful garden. The view from the entrance, through lovely wrought-iron gates, is simply magical. Two acres of flowers, nurtured and rotated by a staff of three, provide an unbroken succession of intense color from May through October. Planted along brick walls and bluestone paths are processions of tulips, poppies, peonies, irises, fuschias, primroses, pansies, Sweet Williams, foxgloves, daisies, and chrysanthemums, as well as a wide variety of other perennials.

---

LOCATION: On Long Island, about 30 miles from New York City. Take exit 39S from the Long Island Expressway, follow the service road east for 1.2 miles, then turn right onto Old Westbury Rd. Also reachable by taxi from Westbury Station on the Long Island Railroad.

ADDRESS: P.O. Box 430, Old Westbury, NY 11568.

TELEPHONE: 516-333-0048.

HOURS: Open late Apr. through early Nov., Wed.–Sun. and holidays, 10–5.

FEE: For garden, $3/adults, $1/children ages 6–12 years, $2/seniors. For mansion, $2/adult, $1/child. Group rates available.

TOURS: At regular intervals daily.

RESTAURANTS: Snack bar. Picnicking in designated areas.

SHOPS: Garden shop open Wed.–Sun., 11:00–4:30.

WHEELCHAIR ACCESS: Majority of garden and house is accessible via special tour map.

SPECIAL ACTIVITIES: A full schedule of shows and exhibits including art exhibits, plant sales, antique car shows, lectures, and concerts; Christmas Open House in Dec.

---

TIPS: 1. In addition to the mansion and the Walled Garden, don't miss:

   a. Cottage Garden: charming playhouse and miniature garden.

   b. Rose Garden: designed in the tradition of a seventeenth century parterre.

   c. Answer Gardens: Four small gardens (includes vegetable, evergreen, and Japanese) offering ideas for the home gardener. Behind this is the Demonstration Perennial Garden and All-America Rose Test Garden.

   d. Autumn Walk and Lake Trail provide spring daffodils and fine fall color.

2. As far as concentrated color is concerned, Old Westbury ranks second to none in the northeastern United States.

3. While May through June are undoubtedly the best months to visit, every month from spring into fall provides something sensational. In October, for example, the Walled Garden is teeming with asters and chrysanthemums, and the Autumn Walk is ablaze with fall color.

4. Don't miss the other nearby English estate garden, Planting Fields, to see how two gardens of similar style have been developed so differently.

---

# OYSTER BAY: PLANTING FIELDS ARBORETUM

*A 409-acre horticultural garden possessing one of the finest collection of azaleas and rhododendrons in the Northeast, an excellent indoor collection of camellias, an orchid collection with over four thousand specimens, and an impressive collection of stately trees, especially beeches and lindens.*

The name "Planting Fields" dates back to the Matinecock Indians who cultivated this fertile soil (known as Haven Loam) for a millennium before the colonists arrived. In 1913 the land was purchased for an estate by W. R. Coe. The original house burned down in 1918, and it took from then through 1921 for the seventy-five-room Coe House to be built. This dwelling was styled after English Tudor mansions of the sixteenth and seventeenth centuries, and it is considered one of the finest examples of Elizabethan architecture in America.

Born in Worcestershire, England, Mr. Coe came to the United States at the age of 14, bringing with him his love of British architecture and landscaping. Consequently the garden, like the house, reflects the style of an English country estate. Designed in part by the Olmsted brothers, the English estate style is exemplified by the sweeping lawns with their huge specimen trees, the wooded paths lined with rhododendrons and azaleas, and the customary conservatory. Despite damage caused by the 1985 hurricane, the trees at Planting Fields, which include linden, beech, elm, dogwood, cedar, holly, and a separate Dwarf Conifer Garden, represent some of the finest of their kind. One of these, a purple beech, was carted full grown from Mrs. Coe's childhood home in Fairhaven, Massachusetts. The tree was shipped across Long Island Sound to Oyster Bay where a dock was built to receive it. Electrical and telephone wires were taken down along the way as a team of seventy-two horses carried it to its present home. Another tree, a weeping hemlock, is perhaps the largest of its kind you will ever see. Only 15 feet high, it offers an exceedingly dense canopy over 40 feet in diameter. Indeed, the late Henry Hicks, the nurseryman who originally sold the tree to the Coes, told the author some 30 years ago that when Hicks first saw the tree, it was so thick that a goat had been able to climb upon it and was placidly resting on the tree's apex.

Planting Fields also boasts the finest collection of rhododendrons and azaleas north of the Mason-Dixon Line. Consisting of over eight hundred species, thousands upon thousands of these magnificent plants explode into bloom April to June, covering hillsides and lining tree-shaded paths. And when this occurs in concert with the flowering magnolias, dogwoods, cherries, and crab apples, the total effect is wondrous.

---

LOCATION: Oyster Bay is located along the North Shore of Long Island off State Rte. 106 and Rte. 25A, about 25 miles from New York City.

ADDRESS: Planting Fields Road, Oyster Bay, NY 11771.

TELEPHONE: 516-922-9200.

HOURS: Garden open daily, 9–5. Coe Hall open Apr.–Sept., Tues.–Thurs. only, 1:00–3:30.

FEE: Garden, $1.50/people ages 12 and over; no garden fee from Labor Day through Apr., Mon.–Fri.; Coe Hall $1/adults, $.50/seniors and children.

TOURS: For groups by appointment (call 516-922-9201).

RESTAURANT: None on grounds.

SHOPS: Gift shop at Arboretum Center near main greenhouses.

WHEELCHAIR ACCESS: Access to most areas.

SPECIAL ACTIVITIES: Educational programs held year-round.

---

TIPS: 1. In addition to the specimen trees and azaleas, don't miss:
   a. Greenhouses, over 1½ acres, with superb orchid and camellia displays.
   b. Italian Garden with its graceful lilac and wisteria.
   c. Carshalton Gates, fashioned in 1712 in England but never used. Mr. Coe spent more than $1 million (in 1930!) in their transport and installation here.
2. The best time to visit is April through early June, for the azaleas and rhododendrons, dogwoods and cherries. Other peak times: summer for begonias, geraniums, and annuals; autumn for outdoor foliage and the indoor Chrysanthemum Show; Dec. for the Christmas Show (poinsettias and cyclamen); Feb. for indoor camellias and orchids. Truly any time of year is a good one at Planting Fields.
3. If you are visiting Apr.–Sept., Tues.–Thurs., the Coe House, with its crafted limestone, leaded glass windows, stained glass, and statuary, is worth viewing.
4. While in the area, be sure to visit the other nearby English estate garden, Old Westbury, to see how gardens of similar schools have been so differently developed.

---

# EXCELLENT GARDENS

---

## ALBERTSON: CLARK GARDEN

A branch of the Brooklyn Botanic Garden, this 12-acre garden emphasizes commercially available species usable under Long

Island's climatic conditions. Displays include the Hunnewell Rose Garden (125 varieties), the Braisted Wildflower Garden (250 species of native shrubs, ferns, and flowering shade plants), Long Island Daylily Society Display Garden (250 cultivars), selections of rhododendrons, azaleas, roses, spring bulbs, perennials, daylilies, dwarf conifers, bog plants, vegetables, and herbs. There is also a good collection of flowering trees (cherries, dogwoods, crape myrtles, witch hazels), as well as the Children's Garden and the Seniors' Garden. Special activities include a Sunday Afternoon Fireside Lecture Series (on outstanding horticultural attractions from around the world), Summer Evening Garden Programs (garden topics, photography, astronomy, square dancing), Thursday Evening Concerts, Spring Plant Fair, Fall Plant Sale, and Holiday Traditions (Christmas and winter programs). Group tours by prearrangement. Picnicking. Gift shop. Most of garden is wheelchair accessible. Lecture hall and classrooms available for garden groups. Garden available for wedding pictures by prearrangement. Open weekdays, 8:00–4:30, and weekends and holidays, 10:00–4:30. Fee: $1.50/adults, $.75/seniors and children under 12. Located in Nassau County, Long Island, 20 miles east of New York City; take the Long Island Expressway (Rte. 495) to exit 37 (Roslyn Rd.), turn right and go to I.U. Willets Rd., turn right; by train, take Long Island Railroad (Oyster Bay Line) to Albertson—garden is immediately east of station. Address: 193 I.U. Willets Rd., Albertson, NY 11507. Tel.: 516-621-7568.

## BUFFALO: BUFFALO AND ERIE COUNTY BOTANICAL GARDEN

This garden consists of twelve greenhouses offering more than 2 acres of indoor gardens, as well as outdoor gardens in season. The indoor displays include a 30-foot waterfall and collections of cacti, orchids, ferns, and economic plants (coffee, cocoa, palms). A separate "market place" is being developed for children where there will be selected flora with the finished market product (e.g., rice plants and packaged rice, cereal plants and packaged cereals). The garden also produces two attractive floral shows (Spring Show at Easter time, Chrysanthemum Show in early Nov.), and a smaller Christmas display. Open daily, 9–4. Fee: None. Address: South Park Ave. and McKinley Pkwy., Buffalo, NY 14220. Tel.: 716-828-1040.

## CANANDAIGUA: SONNENBERG GARDENS

Listed by the Smithsonian as "one of the most magnificent late Victorian gardens ever created in America," this superb 50-acre estate possesses nine formal gardens, a conservatory, arboretum, smooth lawns, giant trees, and a graceful 100-year-old mansion. Among the formal gardens is a rose garden containing over four thousand bushes, an authentic Japanese garden with tea house, a sunken Italian garden in which thousands of blossoms are blended into a giant fleur-de-lis, and a rock and water garden. Statues, gazebos, fountains, and ponds further embellish the grounds. There is a café near the conservatory, or you can have lunch on the mansion's second floor overlooking the Italian garden. The mansion also contains a gift shop selling Victorian reproductions, sachets, collectibles, and potpourris. A garden shop offering plants and related items is located in the greenhouse. Special events include performances, lectures, and exhibits. Guided tours of gardens and mansion at 10, 1, and 3. Open daily, May–mid-Oct., 9:30–4:30 (to 5:30 during summer months). Fee: $4.25/adults, $3.75/seniors, $1.25/children ages 6–18. Location: Canandaigua is located 25 miles southeast of Rochester; Sonnenberg is located on Gibson St. (State Rte. 21), east of Main St. For further information, write to Sonnenberg Gardens, Box 663, Canandaigua, NY 14424. Tel.: 716-394-4922.

## CLINTON: ROOT GLEN

Originated by Oren and Nancy Root in 1850, this 7½-acre wooded garden is now owned and maintained by Hamilton College. The rolling slopes of the garden contain some fifty-five tree species (including many original plantings such as a Norway pine 13 feet in circumference) and many varieties of shrubs and flowers including peonies, irises, lilies, daffodils, heathers, primroses, and other annuals and perennials. The garden is dedicated to public enjoyment and education and to the conservation of plants and birds (seventy-five species). Guided tours available by prearrangement by calling Bristol Campus Center (315-859-7193). Open daily, dawn to dusk. Fee: None. Location: Clinton is located in central New York on State Rte. 12B, 9 miles southwest of Utica. Address: 107 College Hill Rd., Clinton, NY 13323.

## COOPERSTOWN: FARMERS' MUSEUM

An extensive herb garden, containing 130 medicinal plants, is located next to the apothecary shop. Farmers' Museum, an educational family attraction, consists of a collection of authentically restored buildings filled with Americana. Open daily, May–Oct., 9–6; call for winter hours; closed Thanksgiving, Christmas, and New Year's Day. Fee: $4/adults, $1.50/children ages 7–15; combined rates available, which include Fenimore House and Baseball Hall of Fame, also located in Cooperstown. Location: Cooperstown is located in central New York at the junction of State Rtes. 80 and 28, 70 miles west of Albany. For further information, write to Farmers' Museum, P.O. Box 800, Cooperstown, NY 13326. Tel.: 607-547-2533.

## ESPERANCE: GEORGE LANDIS ARBORETUM

Over twenty-five hundred kinds of plants can be found at the 100-acre George Landis Arboretum. Collections include spring bulbs, lilacs, rhododendrons, peonies, ferns, roses, perennials, annuals, conifers, and southern Appalachian plants. Peak bloom is April to June. Group tours by prearrangement. Scheduled programs and tours on Saturday mornings in summer. Weddings by prearrangement. Open daily, sunrise to sunset. Fee: None. Location: Esperance is located 21 miles west of Schenectady on U.S. 20. Address: Esperance, NY 12066. Tel: 518-875-6935.

## FLUSHING: QUEENS BOTANICAL GARDEN

This lovely 26-acre garden is a fit companion for New York City's other botanical gardens. It offers a feast of gardens including the largest rose garden on the East Coast, the Formal Display Garden containing beautiful floral designs (utilizing fifty thousand tulips in spring, for example), and the Wedding Garden complete with white gazebo, willow trees, waterfall, and festive blossoms everywhere. There is also a bird garden, and a bee garden where hundreds of pounds of pollen are gathered yearly. In addition, Queens Botanical promotes lectures, classes, special exhibitions, educational programs, and children's activities attracting over thirty thousand participants per year. Plant and gift shops. Wheelchair accessible. Open daily, 8–sunset. Fee: None. Address: 43-50 Main St., Flushing, NY 11355. Tel.: 718-886-3800.

## GARRISON: BOSCOBEL RESTORATION

Originally built in 1805, Boscobel is another of New York's meticulously restored estates. The 36 landscaped acres include a rose garden, an herb garden, and many large trees on the broad terraces overlooking the Hudson. A greenhouse contains a good collection of orchids as well as orange trees—quite unusual for this area. Sound and Light program on Wed. and Sat. evenings. Open Apr.–Oct., daily, 9:30–5:00; Nov., Dec., and Mar., daily, 9:30–4:00; closed Jan. and Feb. Fee: $4/adults, $2/children ages 6–14. Location: Garrison is located on State Rte. 9D just across the Hudson from West Point, 70 miles north of New York City. Address: Rte. 9D, Garrison, NY 10524. Tel.: 914-265-3638.

## GENEVA: LEGG DAHLIA GARDENS

The dahlia is a magnificent star-burst of a flower, and Legg Gardens, a commercial nursery, presents 3 acres teeming with them. With sizes varying from Ping-Pong balls to larger than a dinner plate, the dahlia is displayed in nearly every color of the rainbow including deep red, bright yellow, lavender, snow white, orange, tan, as well as blends and bicolors. Here are five hundred varieties from all over the globe. Peak bloom July to October. Tours available August through October; groups and bus tours welcome at no charge. Open daily, 8–sunset. Fee: None. Location: Geneva is located on the northern shore of Lake Seneca, 53 miles west of Syracuse and 45 miles southeast of Rochester; the gardens are located west of downtown Genevea— take U.S. 20 west to State Rte. 14A south to Hastings Rd. Address: Hastings Rd., R.D. 4, Box 168, Geneva, NY 14456.

## GERMANTOWN: CLERMONT STATE HISTORIC PARK

Perched on 450 wooded acres overlooking the Hudson, Clermont is a well-maintained park with a picnic area, hiking trails, a stand of fine old black locust trees, and formal gardens around the historic home, which dates back to the Revolution. The park is open daily; the mansion can be toured June through October. Fee: None. Location: Germantown is located on State Rte. 9G on the east bank of the Hudson, 40 miles south of Albany and 115 miles north of New York City; take Rte. 9G south from Germantown, turn west on State Rte. 6. Address: R.D. 1, Germantown, NY 12526. Tel.: 518-537-4240.

# HYDE PARK: ROOSEVELT ROSE GARDEN AND GRAVESITE

Located at the Home of Franklin D. Roosevelt National Historic Site, this rose garden was designed and developed in 1912. Surrounded by a 14-foot hemlock hedge dating back before 1867, the rose garden contains approximately 560 bushes representing twenty-eight varieties. The gravesite marks the burial spot of President Roosevelt as well as his wife Eleanor. Their well-known pets, Fala and Chief, are also buried in the garden. The home, part of which was built in the early 1800s, was FDR's birthplace and contains original furnishings and art. Nearby is the Franklin D. Roosevelt Library, which also contains a museum filled with models, gifts, and other mementos from the careers of this accomplished couple. Open daily, 9–5. Fee: $1.50. Location: Hyde Park is located on the east bank of the Hudson River, on U.S. 9 at the junction with State Rte. 82, approximately 80 miles north of New York City; the garden and grave site can be found on U.S. 9. Address: Home of Franklin D. Roosevelt National Historic Site, 249 Albany Post Rd., Hyde Park, NY 12538. Tel.: 914-229-8114.

# HYDE PARK: VANDERBILT HISTORIC SITE

This fifty-four-room mansion with its Italian garden is an impressive reminder of the elegant way of life of the Hudson River valley landowners at the turn of the century. Bequeathed to the National Park Service in 1940, the gardens fell into disrepair during World War II and only recently have undergone restoration. Frederick W. Vanderbilt is said to have held a deep interest in horticulture, and his design included a central cherry walk, terraced flower gardens, a rose garden, pools and statuary, and propagation greenhouses. Interpreters available in summer for questions and tours. Grounds available for small weddings (no tents, chairs). Open daily, 9–5. Fee: $1.50. Location: Hyde Park is located on the east bank of the Hudson on U.S. 9 at the intersection of State Rte. 82, approximately 80 miles north of New York City; Vanderbilt Historic Site can be found on U.S. 9. Address: Dutchess County, Hyde Park, NY 12538. For further information, contact the National Park Service at 914-229-9115, or the Frederick W. Vanderbilt Garden Association, P.O. Box 239, Hyde Park, NY 12538. Tel.: 914-229-7770.

## ITHACA: CORNELL PLANTATIONS

Adjacent to and part of the Cornell University campus, this 2,800-acre area contains a botanical garden, arboretum, lake, ponds, waterfalls, and woodland trails. The gardens, which are as attractive as they are diverse, include an excellent herb garden, a rhododendron and azalea garden, an alpine garden, and a lavishly colorful garden of annuals and perennials in the American Peony Society Garden. Several well-marked trails course alongside the steep and beautiful Cascadilla and Fall Creek gorges, leading to waterfalls or views of Lake Cayuga. There is also a wildflower area that is very beautiful in spring. Group guided tours available by prearrangement. Open daily, sunrise to sunset. Fee: None. Tour books and pamphlets available in gift shop (open weekdays, 8–4, and weekends in summer, 12–4). Located on the Cornell University campus; take Dryden Rd. or Tower Rd. east to Judd Falls Rd. and turn left, go to Plantations Rd. and turn left, look for entrance to headquarters and parking area. Address: The Plantations, Cornell University, One Plantations Rd., Ithaca NY 14850. Tel.: 607-256-3020.

## LATTINGTOWN: BAILEY ARBORETUM

Bailey Arboretum is a tranquil 42-acre tract, providing nature trails amid specialized collections of rare trees. Frank Bailey, who bequeathed the estate to Nassau County in 1968, collected trees from all over the world, including a towering black walnut, dwarf Nikko fir, dawn redwood, Oriental spruce, Chinese witch hazel, and oak, maple, and tulip trees. Bedded gardens of tulips, daffodils, irises, chrysanthemums, and roses add color from spring through fall. Another focal point is a hand-chiseled miniature castle of granite and marble, fashioned in Germany in the 1930s. Grounds available for group meetings or wedding portraits by appointment. Open mid-Apr.–mid-Nov., daily, 9–4. Fee: $1. Location: The village of Lattingtown is located on the North Shore of Long Island, 3 miles from Glen Cove and approximately 20 miles from Manhattan; the arboretum is found just beyond Lattingtown on the road to Bayville. Address: Bayville Rd. and Feeks La., Lattingtown, Nassau County, Long Island, NY 11560. Tel.: 516-676-4497.

## MILLBROOK: CARY ARBORETUM

Originally a branch of the New York Botanical Garden, Cary
Arboretum now allows public access to 600 of its 2,000 acres.
Among its many varieties of trees is a rare collection of hardy
trees from Russia. The most popular display is its Fern Glen—
two lushly landscaped acres containing about 125 varieties of
ferns and related flora, many rare. There is also a greenhouse
with a tropical collection. Gift shop. Open Mon.–Sat., 9–4;
Sun., 1–4; closed holidays and in hunting season (late Nov.–
early Dec.). Fee: None. Location: Millbrook is located on U.S.
44 approximately 80 miles north of New York City, 4 miles
east of the Taconic State Pkwy. Address: Institute of Ecosystem
Study, Box AB, Millbrook, NY 12545. Tel.: 914-677-5343.

## MILLBROOK: INNISFREE GARDEN

This 1,000-acre estate includes a series of gardens surrounding
the mansion. Designed and built at the turn of the century by
Walter Beck, the gardens reflect his deep interest in the principles of Far Eastern art. By diverting streams, creating waterfalls, and plotting terraces and rock walls, he sought to blend
his creation with the natural beauty of the surrounding area of
rolling hills and forest. Open Wed.–Fri., 10–4, and Sat.–Sun.,
11–5. Fee: None. Location: Millbrook is located on U.S. 44, 80
miles north of New York City and 5 miles east of the Taconic
State Pkwy.; garden can be found on Tyrrell Rd., 1 mile south
of U.S. 44. Address: Millbrook, NY 12545. Tel.: 914-677-8000.

## NEW PALTZ: MOHONK GARDENS

Adjacent to the Mohonk Mountain House Hotel, these gardens
were started in 1888. Today they boast a spectacular show
garden whose seventy-five formal beds are filled with as diverse
a group of flowering plants as is found at most botanical
gardens. Packed with blossoms April to October, the Show
Garden also features carpet bedding—the use of colorful plants
to create patterns or designs. Mohonk Gardens also offers an
herb garden, a wildflower-fern trail through native woodlands,
elegant gazebos, and lovely vistas including one from which six

states can be seen on a clear day (New York, New Jersey, Pennsylvania, Massachusetts, Connecticut, and Rhode Island). Peak garden bloom is from July to August. Beyond all this is the hotel itself, a magnificent antique of a place atop sheer cliffs overlooking Lake Mohonk. The resort offers tennis, golf, swimming, fishing, horse trails, ski trails, or if rest is your aim, total tranquillity. The hotel also holds numerous special programs throughout the year such as its Winter Carnival, Music Week, Hikers Holiday, Mystery Weekend, and Chocolate Binge. Gardens are open daily, 7–dusk. Fee: Free for hotel guests; for visitors, fee for adults is $3/weekdays or $5/weekends, fee for children is $2 at all times; there is a family fee of $8/weekdays or $10/weekends. Garden visitors are not permitted to tour the hotel, but hotel facilities can be utilized for a fee. Location: New Paltz is located on U.S. 87, about 75 miles north of New York City; Mohonk Mountain House is 6 miles west of New Paltz—follow Main St. (State Rte. 299) to Mountain Rest Rd. Address: Mohonk Mountain House, Lake Mohonk, New Paltz, NY 12561. Tel.: 914-255-1000 or 212-233-2244.

## NEW YORK CITY: BIBLICAL GARDEN AT THE CATHEDRAL OF ST. JOHN THE DIVINE

On the grounds of the world's largest Gothic cathedral, this ¼-acre garden contains more than a hundred kinds of plants mentioned in the Bible, including flowers, herbs and bitter herbs (chicory, dandelion), grains, and vegetables. Trees include papyrus, fig, quince, plum, and apricot. Cedars, pines, walnuts, willows, and cypresses provide shade for the benches along the paths. Nonhardy trees such as olives are potted and moved to greenhouses in winter. All plants are labeled with pertinent biblical verses: mustard, a seed of which "a man took, and cast into his garden; and it grew and waxed a great tree" (Luke 13:19). The cathedral itself, with its tapestries, sculptures, and stained glass, is worth a visit, as is the museum. Music, dance, and drama performances are scheduled throughout the year. The garden is wheelchair accessible. Groups can obtain guided tours, workshops, or a slide show by prearrangement. Gift shop. Garden open daily, 9–sunset; cathedral open daily, 7–5; gift shop open daily, 9–5. Fee: None. Location: Take Westside Hwy. to 96th St. exit. Address: 1047 Amsterdam Ave. and 112th St., New York, NY 10025. Tel.: 212-678-6886 or 212-864-3760.

# NEW YORK CITY: GARDENS OF THE CLOISTERS

A must for medieval history buffs and plant historians, the Cloisters, a branch of the Metropolitan Museum of Art, overlooks the Hudson River from Fort Tryon Park at the northern tip of Manhattan. Enhancing its medieval architecture and art are three small gardens, composed almost entirely of plants from the Middle Ages. Among these is an authentically reproduced herb garden possessing 250 species, while another garden contains all the plants depicted in the seven exquisite Hunt of the Unicorn Tapestries that belong to the museum. The museum itself is derived from elements of fine French monasteries, and it houses the Metropolitan's medieval art. There are frequent exhibits, lectures, and concerts. Open Mar.–Oct., Tues.–Sun., 9:30–5:15; Nov.–Feb., Tues.–Sun., 9:30–4:45. Fee: Donation of $4.50/adults, $2.25/students and seniors is requested; some donation is required. Located in Fort Tryon Park at the northern tip of Manhattan, about a mile north of the George Washington Bridge. Address: Fort Tryon Park, NY, 10040. Tel.: 212-923-3700.

# NEW YORK CITY: WAVE HILL

Built in 1848, this house and its 28 acres graced by fine trees and views represent the only Hudson River estate within the city limits to have been preserved for the public. Once enjoyed by Mark Twain, Teddy Roosevelt, and Toscanini, this garden enjoys a spendid balance between formal plantings and natural woodland. Wave Hill serves as an educational center through its work with city schools and frequent public programs. It also offers art and sculpture exhibitions, theater, and concerts. Open daily, 10:00–4:30. Fee: Weekdays, none; weekends and holidays, $2/adults, $1/seniors. Located in the northwest area of the Bronx, at 252nd St. and Independence Ave. Address: 675 West 252 St., Bronx, NY 10471. Tel.: 212-549-2055.

# NORTH SALEM: ORIENTAL STROLL GARDENS OF THE HAMMOND MUSEUM

The Hammond Museum's 3½-acre garden is actually a collection of fifteen different gardens and landscapes (such as the waterfall garden, the azalea garden, the fruit garden, the Zen garden), all blended together in the style of a seventeenth-century Japanese stroll garden. This is a quiet, contemplative place, richly adorned with shrubbery, willows, rhododendrons, and reflecting pools. Hammond Museum is also open to the public and offers fine art displays and live performances. Tip: The fare in the terrace restaurant, which is adorned by trees, flowers, and a bubbling fountain, has been awarded four stars by one restaurant reviewer. Open May–Oct., Wed.–Sun., 11–5. Fee: $2/adults, $1/children ages under 12. Location: North Salem is located on State Rtes. 121 and 116, just west of the New York-Connecticut state line, about 50 miles north of New York City. Address: Deveau Rd., North Salem, NY 10560. Tel.: 914-669-5033.

## OAKDALE: BAYARD CUTTING ARBORETUM

Located on Long Island's South Shore, 50 miles from New York City, this arboretum was begun in 1887 as part of a private estate. One hundred thirty of the property's 690 acres are now open to the public, and they offer exceptionally fine collections of evergreen and deciduous trees. Massed plantings of azaleas, rhododendrons, and mountain laurel provide color March through June. Indigenous beauty is afforded by wildflowers and vistas of the Connetquot River. The Cutting residence, which can be toured, contains fourteenth-century fireplaces, intricately carved woodwork, and Tiffany-style leaded windows. Wheelchair accessible. Concerts, art exhibits, and educational programs held regularly. Open Apr. 15–Oct. 30, Wed.–Sun., 10–5. Fee: $1.50/adult. Location: Oakdale is located in central Long Island near the South Shore, off exit 45 of the Montauk Hwy. For further information, write to Bayard Cutting Arboretum, P.O. Box 466, Oakdale, NY 11769. Tel.: 516-581-1002.

## ROCHESTER: ELLWANGER GARDEN

This ½-acre Victorian garden was first opened to the public in 1985. Originally started as a pear orchard in 1867, it has been kept as a private garden within the same family until acquired in 1983 by the Landmark Society of Western New York. Today the garden is in the process of being renovated. Displays include over twenty-five beds of perennials including peonies and irises, as well as specimen trees and new and old-fashioned roses. Peak bloom May to June. Wheelchair accessible. Open mid-May–

July, Tues., 10–4, and Sun., 2–4; group tours Mon.–Fri., 10–4, by appointment. Fee: $1.50/adults, $.75/seniors. Located 1 mile south of downtown Rochester, next to the Rose Mansion Bed and Breakfast; parking is on McLean St. Address: 625 Mt. Hope Ave. For further information, write to the Landmark Society of Western New York, 130 Spring St., Rochester, NY 14608. Tel.: 716-546-7028.

## ROCHESTER: MONROE COUNTY PARKS ARBORETUM

Monroe County Parks Arboretum is the collective name for three distinct parks, each within the city of Rochester. Highland Park consists of 150 acres and possesses many rare specimens from Europe and Asia. It also boasts one of the world's largest collections of lilacs, with over twelve hundred bushes covering 22 acres, and promotes a 10-day Lilac Festival in May. Highland Park also offers collections of magnolias, crab apples, maples, and rhododendrons, as well as a woodland garden, a rock garden, a sunken garden, and Lamberton Conservatory. Another Monroe County Park Arboretum garden is the Maplewood Rose Garden, an All-America Rose Selections test garden of 12 acres featuring forty-five hundred roses. Located on the bank of the Genesee River gorge, this garden is surrounded by stands of crab apples, oaks, maples, and evergreens. The third Monroe County Parks Arboretum garden is the Durant-Eastman Park, 942 acres of wildflowers amid tall trees on steep slopes. Peak wildflower bloom occurs in late April and early May. All parks of the Monroe County Parks Arboretum are open dawn to dusk. Fee: None. For further information, write to the County of Monroe, Dept. of Parks, County Office Bldg., 39 W. Main St., Rochester, NY 14614. Tel.: 716-428-5301.

## ROCHESTER: MT. HOPE CEMETERY

Dedicated in 1838, this Victorian cemetery was designed to provide an imaginative and attractive landscape. Perched on 54 glacier-etched acres, which once formed the westward expansion of the Pinnacle mountain range, the grounds are marked by sharp rises and cliffs. Today Mt. Hope, with its great lawns and many flower beds, features flowering dogwoods, Japanese maples, several exotics, and 300-year-old red and black oaks. Also noteworthy are the many historic monuments, chapels, and buildings. Self-guided tour brochure available on request. Open daily, sunrise to sunset. Fee: None. Located at 791 Mt. Hope Ave. For further information, write to the Mt. Hope Cemetery, Bureau of Parks, Cemetery Division—Dept. of Recreation and Community Services, 1133 Mt. Hope Ave., Rochester, NY 14620. Tel.: 716-473-2755.

## ROCHESTER: STONE-TOLAN HOUSE

Owned and maintained by the Landmark Society of Western New York, the Stone-Tolan House is a faithful restoration of a 1790s farmstead. The original house was built by Orringh Stone in 1792, then expanded in 1805. The grounds have been revitalized with descendants of plants known to have been imported by the colonists, or trees, shrubs, and wildflowers native to New York. The garden has been restored in the style of an early frontier farm, including a kitchen garden (herbs) and an orchard. Flowering annuals and perennials have been planted to add color. The house gives us some insight into rural colonial daily life. Guided tours available to schools and groups by prearrangement. Lectures and exhibitions are held on a wide range of topics. The renovated Stone-Tolan barn, which serves as a craft center, is available to community groups for meetings or special events. Open Wed.–Sat., 10–4, and Sun., 1–4. Fee: $1.50/adults, $.75/seniors, $.50/students, $.10/children ages 13 and under (fees subject to change in near future). Located on State Rte. 96, approximately 2 miles east of downtown Rochester. Address: 2370 East Ave., Rochester, NY. For further information, write to the Landmark Society of Western New York, 130 Spring St., Rochester, NY 14608. Tel.: 716-546-7029.

## SYRACUSE: DR. E. M. MILLS MEMORIAL ROSE GARDEN

Maintained through the cooperation of the city of Syracuse's Department of Parks and the Syracuse chapter of the American Rose Society, this impressive rose garden is made up of a hundred beds of roses, fifty beds representing All-America Rose Selection varieties. Overall, this garden contains 2,350 bushes with forty arbors. The Mills Memorial Rose Garden is located in Thornden Park, a recreational park with playing fields, picnicking, and a pool. The park also possesses several stands of lilacs and a greenhouse, which is open to the public. Wheelchair accessible. Garden available for weddings by prearrangement. Open daily, 9–9; in summer, 9–10. Fee: None. Location: The park is located off Ostrom Ave., S. Beech St. and Madison St. For further information, write to the Dept. of Parks, City of Syracuse, 412 Spencer St., Syracuse, NY 13204. Tel.: 315-473-4333.

## TARRYTOWN: LYNDHURST

This Gothic mansion, set on 67 parklike acres above the Hudson, was built in 1838 and later on became the residence of Jay Gould. The Lyndhurst greenhouse was the largest in the United States at the time Gould built it in 1881, and the first in America to use metal framing, predating its more famous cousin at the New York Botanical Garden by 10 years. Once holding a magnificent orchid collection, the greenhouse fell on lean years after World War II, but it is now being restored. Lyndhurst's grounds possess many fine trees, including magnolias, dogwoods, sassafras, Japanese maples, and Oriental spruce. A lovely rose garden contains over five hundred bushes of a hundred different varieties. A wrought-iron gazebo adorns the grounds, as do several other buildings, including the mansion, a Greek Revival indoor swimming-pool building, and a bowling alley. Lyndhurst is owned and maintained by the National Trust for Historic Preservation, the only national private, nonprofit organization chartered by Congress to encourage the public preservation of historic buildings, objects, and sites. Open Apr.–Oct., daily, 10:00–4:15, and Nov.–Dec., weekends. Fee: $4/adults, $3/senior citizens, $2/children. Location: Tarrytown is located on U.S. 9 about 1 mile north of the Tappan Zee Bridge and 20 miles north of Manhattan. Address: 635 S. Broadway, Tarrytown, NY 10591. Tel.: 914-631-0046.

# North Carolina

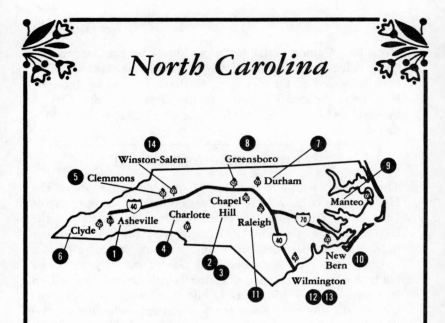

1. Asheville: Biltmore Estate
2. Chapel Hill: Coker Arboretum
3. Chapel Hill: North Carolina Botanical Garden
4. Charlotte: University of North Carolina at Charlotte
   Botanical Gardens
5. Clemmons: Tanglewood Park
6. Clyde: Campus Arboretum of Haywood Technical College
7. Durham: Sarah P. Duke Gardens
8. Greensboro: Bicentennial Garden
9. Manteo: Elizabethan Gardens
10. New Bern: Tryon Palace
11. Raleigh: North Carolina State University Arboretum
12. Wilmington: Greenfield Gardens
13. Wilmington: Orton Plantation
14. Winston-Salem: Reynolda Gardens

# North Carolina

## EXCELLENT GARDENS

### ASHEVILLE: BILTMORE ESTATE

It took a thousand workers five years to build this 250-room French chateau, and several more years to develop the garden, which was designed by Frederick Law Olmsted, America's foremost name in landscape design. Today over half a million people visit the Biltmore House and Garden annually. The garden contains both formal and naturalized areas. The formal gardens cover 25 acres and include a 4-acre walled English garden packed with blossoms (fifty thousand tulips in spring), an Italian garden with pools and statuary, a rose garden (eighty varieties), and large plantings of native laurel, azaleas, rhododendrons, and hollies. The remainder of the 11,000-acre estate is dedicated to forestry. America's first attempt at large-scale forest management, as well as its first school of forestry, took place here at the turn of the century. Garden bloom period extends from April through September. A Festival of Flowers is held in the latter half of April, and Christmas at Biltmore, with madrigal singers, candlelight tours, and hundreds of poinsettias decorating the house, is held in December. Also recommended is the tour of the house, which contains works by Renoir, Sargent, Whistler, and Dürer, and Flemish tapestries and much more. There is also a winery that can be toured. Group tours by prearrangement. Deerpark restaurant is open for lunch and available to groups for dinner by prearrangement. Wheelchair access to parts of house and garden. Open May–Oct., daily, 8:30–5:00; Nov.–Apr., daily, 9–5; closed Thanksgiving, Christmas, and New Year's Day. Fee: $15/adults, $12/children ages 12–17, free for children ages 11 and under with an adult; group rates available. Location: Asheville is located in western North Carolina; Biltmore Estate can be found just off U.S. 25, three blocks from I-40—look for signs. Address: One Biltmore Plaza, Asheville, NC 28803. Tel.: 704-274-1776.

### CHAPEL HILL: COKER ARBORETUM

Located on the campus of the University of North Carolina, this 5-acre arboretum offers collections of native and exotic trees and shrubs, plus colorful displays of daffodils, tulips, daylilies, and other seasonal blossoms. Open daily, sunrise to sunset. Fee: None. Located at Cameron St. and Raleigh Rd., adjacent to the Morehead Planetarium. Address: Chapel Hill, NC 27514. Tel.: 919-962-8100.

## CHAPEL HILL: NORTH CAROLINA BOTANICAL GARDEN

A center for research, conservation, and interpretation of regional native plants, this 168-acre garden possesses a variety of display gardens and more than 2 miles of trails through natural Piedmont woodland. There is an excellent herb garden made up of culinary, evergreen, and medicinal plants (some quite beautiful, such as the foxglove from which digitalis is derived). There is a shade garden, an economic plant garden, a carnivorous plant collection (one of America's most comprehensive), as well as displays of aquatic plants, ferns, mountain plants, and wildflower propagation beds. The garden offers lectures, workshops, classes, field trips, and special plant sales. A regularly scheduled introductory tour is given on weekends, spring through fall (Sat., 10:30; Sun., 3:00). The garden is open daily, sunrise to sunset; visitor center open daily—check for times. Fee: None. Located on Laurel Hill Rd., just south of U.S. 15 and 50 and the U.S. 54 Bypass. Address: North Carolina Botanical Garden, University of North Carolina at Chapel Hill, Totten Center 457a, Chapel Hill, NC 27514. Tel.: 919-967-2246.

## CHARLOTTE: UNIVERSITY OF NORTH CAROLINA AT CHARLOTTE BOTANICAL GARDENS

The University of North Carolina at Charlotte has two kinds of gardens and a greenhouse. The Van Landingham Glen is a 7½-acre forested area possessing native plants from every part of the Carolinas, including over fifty species of ferns and a broad array of wildflowers. Also of great interest is an excellent collection of several thousand rhododendrons—one of the Southeast's finest rhododendron gardens. The Susie Harwood Garden consists of 2½ acres landscaped in an Oriental motif with gazebo, moon gate, and arched bridges. This garden includes exotic and ornamental plants from around the world, plus colorful spring bulbs and crape myrtles. The McMillan Greenhouse features displays of American and African desert plants, tropical plants, and orchids. Hours: Outdoor gardens open daily, dawn to dusk; greenhouse open by appointment (call 704-597-4055). Fee: None. Located on the UNCC campus, which is on State Rte. 49, about 6 miles east of downtown Charlotte. Address: University of North Carolina at Charlotte, Dept. of Biology, Charlotte, NC 28223.

## CLEMMONS: TANGLEWOOD PARK

This 1,150-acre family resort in central North Carolina is colorfully landscaped with flower beds and flowering trees (dogwood, magnolia, cherry, crab apple, burning bush, purple plum leaf). Its foremost display, located in front of the 1859 manor house, is a ¼-acre All-America Rose Selections rose garden with eight hundred bushes. Open daily. Fee: Admission to park grounds, $1/car. Location: Tanglewood is located on U.S. 158 about 4 miles west of Winston-Salem and 1 mile past Clemmons. For further information, write to Tanglewood Park, P.O. Box 1040, Highway 158 West, Clemmons, NC 27012. Tel.: 919-766-0591.

## CLYDE: CAMPUS ARBORETUM OF HAYWOOD TECHNICAL COLLEGE

Established in 1970, the arboretum is spread throughout the 80-acre college campus. Collections include a 1-acre rhododendron garden, a dahlia garden, a rose garden, a terrace garden, a perennial garden, a fruit orchard, a pond area with a mill house and waterwheel, a small conservatory, drifts of spring bulbs and summer flowers, and a large collection of trees. The woodland areas contain nature paths. Individual or group tours by prearrangement. Open daily, 9:00–4:00. Fee: None. Located in western North Carolina, about 25 miles west of Asheville; from I-40 take Exit 27 onto U.S. 19 and 23, follow signs to campus. Address: Freelander Dr., Clyde, NC 28721. Tel.: 704-627-2821, ext. 269.

## DURHAM: SARAH P. DUKE GARDENS

This 55-acre garden was opened to the public in 1934. Today it ranks as one of North Carolina's finest, attracting over two hundred thousand visitors yearly. The 15 acres of formal gardens include the Terrace Garden, a visual delight and a testimony to the art of garden architecture. Comprised of stone terraces, languid pools, and two fountains, this area is accented by a procession of flowering plants—twenty-five thousand in number, March through November. Other highlights of the formal area include the Hanes Iris Garden, the Bloomquist Fern Glen, and the Grass and Sky Garden. The remaining 40 acres are natural pine forest embellished with plantings of narcissus, ground myrtle, and other flora. Peak bloom is in May. Open daily, 8–dusk. Fee: None. Location: Duke University is located off Duke University Rd. and Academy Rd., about 1 mile west of downtown Durham; the gardens are on the western side of the campus. Address: Duke University, Durham, NC 27706. Tel.: 919-684-5579.

## GREENSBORO: BICENTENNIAL GARDEN

Spring bulbs (over thirty thousand), flowering trees, camellias, and azaleas fill this 7½-acre garden with color during its peak bloom in spring. There is also a rock garden, a wildflower garden, a daylily garden (105 varieties), a sun-dial garden, bird areas, a small rose garden, and a fragrance garden for the blind. Thousands of annuals and perennials provide color in summer. Group guided tours by prearrangement. Weddings by prearrangement. Open daily, dawn to dusk. Fee: None. Located between Holden and Hobbs Rds., one block north of Friendly Ave. For further information write to Greensboro Beautiful Inc., Drawer W-2, Greensboro, NC 27402. Tel. 919-373-2558.

## MANTEO: ELIZABETHAN GARDENS

Conceived and maintained by the Garden Club of North Carolina, these gardens are located on Roanoke Island next to the Lost Colony Waterside Theater and historic Fort Raleigh. Dedicated to America's first English colony, they were designed to represent an Elizabethan pleasure garden, with year-round color from winter camellias, spring bulbs, azaleas, and flowering trees, to summer gardenias, roses, crape myrtle, and geraniums. Wildflower trails wind through native forest along Roanoke Sound. Guided tours by prearrangement. Wheelchair accessible. Plant and gift shops. Garden available for weddings. Open daily, 9–5; in summer, 9–8. Fee: $1.50/people ages 12 and over, $1.35/seniors; group and school rates available. Location: Manteo is located on Roanoke Island in eastern North Carolina, just north of the Cape Hatteras National Seashore and west of Nags Head. For further information, write to Elizabethan Gardens, P.O. Box 1150, Manteo, NC 27954. Tel.: 919-473-3234.

---

## NEW BERN: TRYON PALACE

Tryon Palace was built in 1767 for (and named after) the royal governor of the colony. By 1777 the British rule was gone, and from then till 1794 Tryon Palace served as governor's house for the newly founded state of North Carolina. Most of the building burned in 1798, but in 1952 a reconstruction was begun, using the original architectural plans. Today, Tryon Palace stands as a historical monument filled with antiques and artifacts representative of the colonial era. During the restoration, no blueprint of the original gardens was available, so the gardens have been patterned after the English schools of the eighteenth and nineteenth centuries. This means that most of the garden consists of closely tended, precisely clipped flora trained to form interesting designs and pleasing patterns (eighteenth-century design). Farther out, the garden becomes more naturalized (nineteenth-century design) and uses native plants in their untrained state along with open spaces and sweeping vistas. These two approaches create an interesting combination, so well orchestrated that the Tryon Palace gardens are uniformly considered one of North America's finest replicas of a colonial English garden. Among its displays are the Maude M. Latham Garden (an elaborate swirl of pruned shrubbery, highlighting beds of tulips, chrysanthemums, and other seasonal flowers), the Green Garden (an intricate display of clipped shrubs best viewed from the palace), and a wilderness area (a naturalized garden with fine views of the palace and Trent River). Peak bloom April to May; good color from spring bulbs to fall foliage. Gift and garden shop. Wheelchair access to most of house and gardens; wheelchairs available. Open Tues.–Sat., 9:30–4:00, and Sun., 1:30–4:00; closed most holidays. Fee: $6/adult. Location: New Bern is located in eastern North Carolina, on U.S. 70. For further information, write to Tryon Palace, P.O. Box 1007, New Bern, NC 28560. Tel.: 919-638-5109.

## RALEIGH: NORTH CAROLINA STATE UNIVERSITY ARBORETUM

Dedicated in 1980, this arboretum has accomplished much in just a few years. Possessing only 8 acres, there are nevertheless over five thousand species of rare and unusual plants. Exhibits include an All-America Selections display of annual plants, also collections of rare dwarf pine and juniper cultivars, and a lath house containing fifteen hundred species of shade-loving plants. There is a White Garden in which weddings can be held, a Japanese garden, and a 300-foot perennial border containing common and unusual blossoms of every color of the rainbow. Wheelchair accessible. Group tours by prearrangement. Open daily, 8–5. Fee: None. Located about 2 miles west of downtown Raleigh; take Hillsborough St. toward the state fairground, make first left at the railroad tracks, then left onto Beryl Rd. Address: Beryl Rd., Raleigh, NC 27606. Tel.: 919-737-3133.

## WILMINGTON: GREENFIELD GARDENS

This municipal park contains azaleas by the thousands, which can be viewed by car, boat, bicycle, or foot. Within the garden is the 180-acre Greenfield Lake, which provides a sight-seeing boat as well as summer rentals of canoes and paddleboats. Lake Shore Drive encircles the lake and offers a 5-mile road and bicycle path through the gardens. In addition, Greenfield includes a fragrance garden, a nature trail, dogwoods, bald cypresses covered with Spanish moss, and massive plantings of spring and summer blossoms. An azalea festival is held in early April when the azaleas are at their peak. Picnicking. Concession stands and boat rentals open on weekends in spring and fall, daily in summer. Area available for weddings by prearrangement. Waterskiing and motorboat races in summer. Open daily 8 A.M.–11 P.M. Fee: None. Location: In central Wilmington. For further information, write to the City of Wilmington, Dept. of Parks, P.O. Box 1810, Wilmington, NC 28402. Tel.: 919-763-9871.

## WILMINGTON: ORTON PLANTATION

One of North Carolina's finest gardens, the antebellum Orton Plantation house and gardens are situated amid lagoons, lakes, and a riverbank, as well as ubiquitous moss-draped live oaks.

Winding paths lead through a variety of small gardens filled with azaleas, camellias, rhododendrons, gardenias, irises, hydrangeas, wisteria, roses, magnolias, and crape myrtles—providing blossoms from March to September. Wheelchair access to most of garden. Gardens available for weddings and receptions. Open Mar.–Aug., 8–6; Sept.–Nov., 8–5. Fee: $4.50/adult, $2.00/children 6–12. Located about 12 miles south of Wilmington in southeast North Carolina, just off State Rte. 133. Address: Winnabow, NC 28479. Tel.: 919-371-6851.

## WINSTON-SALEM: REYNOLDA GARDENS

Created in 1916 and donated to Wake Forest University in 1958, Reynolda Gardens consists of 130 acres, most of it woodlands. Four acres of the gardens, however, are beautifully landscaped and offer a variety of flowering trees (cherries, magnolias), an All-America Rose Garden, herb and vegetable displays, and a colorful flower garden, along with broad lawns, arbors, statuary, and fountains. There are also greenhouses and a conservatory (built in 1912 and recently restored) in which tropical plants are displayed and an annual Christmas open house is held. Paths meander along ponds and streams and through the woodland area and are lined with wildflowers and dogwoods in spring. Peak bloom in spring and fall. Grounds open daily; conservatory, Mon.–Fri., 9–3. Fee: None. Located on Reynolda Rd. (State Rte. 67), about 3 miles west of downtown Winston-Salem. Address: 100 Reynolda Village, Winston-Salem, NC 27106. Tel.: 919-761-5593.

# Ohio

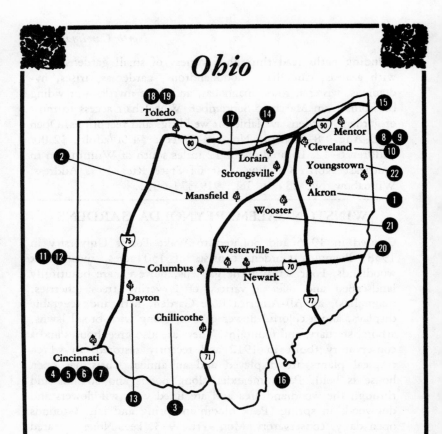

1. Akron: Stan Hywet Hall and Gardens
2. Mansfield: Kingwood Center
3. Chillicothe: Adena
4. Cincinnati: Ault Park
5. Cincinnati: Krohn Conservatory
6. Cincinnati: Mt. Airy Arboretum
7. Cincinnati: Spring Grove Cemetery
8. Cleveland: Cleveland Cultural Gardens and Rockefeller Park
   Greenhouses
9. Cleveland: Garden Center of Greater Cleveland
10. Cleveland: Lake View Cemetery
11. Columbus: Franklin Park Conservatory and Garden Center
12. Columbus: Park of Roses
13. Dayton: Cox Arboretum
14. Lorain: Lakeview Park Rose Garden
15. Mentor: Holden Arboretum
16. Newark: Dawes Arboretum
17. Strongsville: Gardenview Horticultural Park
18. Toledo: George P. Crosby Gardens
19. Toledo: Toledo Zoo
20. Westerville: Inniswood Botanical Garden and Nature Preserve
21. Wooster: Secrest Arboretum
22. Youngstown: Fellows Riverside Gardens

# *Ohio*

## "DON'T MISS" GARDENS

### AKRON: STAN HYWET HALL AND GARDENS

*Thirty-two lovely gardens and displays on 70 acres, plus a sixty-five-room house representing one of America's finest examples of Tudor architecture.*

A National Historic Landmark visited by 175,000 people in 1985, Stan Hywet (pronounced STAN HEE-wit, meaning "stone quarry" in Old English) was built in 1915 by F. A. Seiberling, the founder of Goodyear Rubber. Fascinated by English history, the Seiberlings studied the manors and gardens of England before concluding plans for Stan Hywet. Warren Manning, one of the founders of the American Society of Landscape Architects, designed the 3,000-acre grounds in which a variety of English influences were blended, using the natural terrain and flora. After Seiberling's death in 1955, the gardens fell into neglect. About 2,000 acres returned to natural woodland and were absorbed into the Akron parks system. In 1971, restoration of the 70 acres nearest the hall was begun. Thirty-two gardens were revitalized using original photographs and plans. Today these include the Rose Garden, the Plum Tree Garden, the Alpine Garden, the Japanese Garden, the English Walled Garden, the Birch Allee (path), the Rhododendron Allee, the Conservatory and Greenhouse, as well as the newly restored Breakfast Room Garden. Lavish plantings of daffodils (over 50,000), tulips (20,000), wildflowers, azaleas, peonies (300 kinds), and chrysanthemums (over 8,000), and other annuals and perennials add color spring to fall.

LOCATION: About 4 miles northwest of downtown Akron; take W. Market St. (State Rte. 18) west, turn right onto Portage Path.

ADDRESS: 714 North Portage Path, Akron, OH 44303.

TELEPHONE: 216-836-5533.

HOURS: Gardens open till 5; closed Mon. and holidays. House tours Tues.-Sat., 10–4, and Sun., 1–5.

FEE: $5/adults, $2/children ages 6–12. Group rates.

TOURS: House viewed by guided tour. Self-guided tour map available for garden.

RESTAURANT: None on grounds. Picnicking in designated area.

SHOPS: Plant sales at greenhouse. Gift shop sells souvenirs, crystal, pottery, toys, jewelry, porcelains.

WHEELCHAIR ACCESS: Special tours for wheelchairs and mothers with strollers (admission free).

SPECIAL ACTIVITIES: A full schedule of shows and exhibits (art, doll show, Ohio Mart, stitchery, antique cars, decorated eggs), book reviews, travelogues, concerts, Christmas Open House, Madrigal Dinner, Midsummer Dance— something nearly every week of the year. Auditorium available for meetings and events.

---

TIPS: 1. Don't miss the tulips, daffodils, and flowering trees in early spring, the annuals and perennials starting in July, and the chrysanthemums in October.

2. The hall offers masterful examples of skilled woodcarving, masonry, and stonework. The furnishings consist of sixteenth- and seventeenth-century Tudor and Stuart pieces, plus antique silver, pewter, tapestries, and portraits. Four presidents visited Stan Hywet, and Leopold Stokowski, Will Rogers, and other famous artists performed here.

3. The diversity of events held at Stan Hywet offers something for every age and taste.

---

## MANSFIELD: KINGWOOD CENTER

*Twenty-seven acres of exceptional floral displays, including major collections of tulips, daffodils, dahlias, irises, hostas, daylilies, peonies, roses, and chrysanthemums.*

Originally the estate of Charles Kelley King, Kingwood is now a private, nonprofit institution emphasizing education as well as visual beauty. Kingwood consists of 47 acres: 20 acres of natural woodland and 27 acres landscaped into seventeen individual gardens. Each of these gardens contains plants numbering in the thousands: forty-five thousand tulips in spring; in summer the Iris Garden is filled with more than a hundred cultivars. Other collections include daylilies (400 kinds), dahlias (50 varieties), lilies (50 cultivars), peonies (400 kinds), plus daffodils, gladiolus, chrysanthemums, and wildflowers in great abundance. Suffice it to say, from spring to fall the sweeping grounds and lawns are awash with color. In addition, there is an excellent herb garden. Special flower shows are held frequently throughout the growing season, highlighted by state and national exhibitions. Mr. King was also a bird enthusiast, so there is a duck pond area where waterfowl and other birds are plentiful. There is also a chain of seven greenhouses and an orangery containing year-round indoor displays.

---

LOCATION: About 3 miles west of downtown Mansfield on Park Ave. West (State Rte. 430), 1 mile south of U.S. 30.

ADDRESS: 900 Park Ave. West, Mansfield, OH 44906.

TELEPHONE: 419-522-0211.

HOURS: Grounds open daily, 8–sunset. Hall open Tues.–Sat., 9–5; also open Sun., 1:30–4:30, Easter through Oct. only.

FEE: None.

TOURS: For groups by prearrangement.

RESTAURANT: None on grounds.

SHOPS: Gift and plant shops.

WHEELCHAIR ACCESS: Buildings and grounds accessible.

SPECIAL ACTIVITIES: A regular schedule of lectures and classes. Staff members will answer questions regarding plant identification and care. Plant sales and auctions are held during the growing season. The library is available for public use, as is the meeting hall.

---

TIPS: 1. Don't miss:
   a. Tulip display in May. A regular May event is the Mother's Day weekend plant sale.
   b. Irises in bloom: late May to early June.
   c. Annuals: June to Oct.
   d. Chrysanthemums in bloom: Sept. to Nov.
   e. Truly any time from Apr. to Nov. offers luxuriant color.
2. Kingwood hosts a number of excellent shows—Ohio State African Violet Society Show, Ohio Hemerocallis Society, Fall Harvest Show, and more—check for updated schedule.
3. Also worth a visit is Kingwood Hall, a Normandy-style mansion built in 1926 (at a cost of $400,000), filled with art and furniture collected by Mr. King.

# EXCELLENT GARDENS

## CHILLICOTHE: ADENA

An early nineteenth-century mansion and outbuildings, restored by the Ohio Historical Society with a small yet colorful period garden of roses, and annual and perennial blossoms. Lovely vistas. Wheelchair accessible. Fee for mansion and garden: $2/people ages 13 and up, $1/children under 13. Hours: Memorial Day– Labor Day, Wed.–Sat., 9:30–5:00, and Sun., 12–5; Labor Day–Oct. 31, open weekends only; closed Nov.–late May. Located about 2 miles west of downtown Chillicothe; take U.S. 35 west, exit onto State Rte. 104 north, turn left onto Adena Rd. Address: Adena State Memorial, Adena Rd., P.O. Box 831-A, Chillicothe, OH 45601. Tel.: 614-772-1500.

## CINCINNATI: AULT PARK

The gardens of this public park are maintained in part by volunteers through a successful Adopt-a-Plot Program. Plots include a rock garden, a Japanese garden, a kitchen herb garden, a dwarf and miniature plot, plus collections of annuals and perennials, roses, ferns, hardy succulents, exotic plants, and other ornamentals. Ault Park also possesses a nice stand of flowering cherry and crab apple trees. Open daily, dawn to dusk. Fee: None. Located near U.S. 50 just off Heeking Rd., approximately 10 miles east of downtown Cincinnati. For further information, write to the Cincinnati Park Board, 950 Eden Park Dr., Cincinnati, OH 45202. Tel.: 513-352-4080.

## CINCINNATI: KROHN CONSERVATORY

This 20,000 square-foot conservatory consists of four permanent display houses (tropical, palm, orchid, desert), plus a floral display house in which, since 1933, six excellent seasonal shows are presented (Pre-Spring, Easter, Mother's Day, Summer, Chrysanthemum, Christmas). Group tours by reservation (call 513-352-4091). Special Birthday Party Safari tours for children, ages 5–12. Gift shop. Open daily, 10–5 (later hours for Easter and Christmas shows). Fee: None. Located in Eden Park in central Cincinnati; take the Columbia Pkwy. (U.S. 50) to Martin Dr. exit, turn right onto Eden Park Dr. Address: 950 Eden Park Dr., Cincinnati, OH 45202. Tel.: 513-352-4090.

# CINCINNATI: MT. AIRY ARBORETUM

Mt. Airy Arboretum contains an excellent collection of evergreens (Meyer Lake Garden), a wildflower trail, collections of
rhododendrons and azaleas, a green garden (shrubs, ground
covers, vines, and herbs), a lovely perennial garden sponsored by
Cincinnati garden clubs, and trails through dense woodland.
Adjacent to the 120-acre arboretum is the 1,466-acre Mt. Airy
Forest (sixteen hundrend species of trees and shrubs), the first
municipal reforestation project in the United States. Guided
tours by prearrangement. Open daily, dawn to dusk. Fee: None.
Located about 4 miles northwest of downtown Cincinnati; take
I-75 to U.S. 27 (Colerain Pike). Address: 5083 Colerain Ave.,
Cincinnati, OH. Tel.: 513-541-8176.

# CINCINNATI: SPRING GROVE CEMETERY

The largest nonprofit cemetery in the United States, Spring
Grove was chartered in 1845 with a commitment to landscape
architectural design. Today the grounds cover 733 acres of
lawns, rolling hills, woodlands, fourteen lakes, streams, and
waterfalls. Plantings produce masses of color in spring with
more than 100,000 daffodils, 30,000 tulips, 10,000 pansies,
and thousands of crocuses, hyacinths, rhododendrons, and flowering trees (cherries, dogwoods, crab apples, and magnolias). In
summer there are more than 40,000 annuals, and in autumn
several thousand chrysanthemums. Spring Grove contains an
important collection of more than 800 indigenous and exotic
tree varieties, including sixteen state champions and two national champions. Of architectural interest are the gatehouses and
chapels, plus many monuments from the Civil War. Guided
group tours by prearrangement; walking tour-guide brochure
available on request. For the physically impaired, much of the
grounds can be viewed via 37 miles of paved road. Chapel and
grounds available for weddings and recitals. Open daily, 7:30–5:30.
Fee: None. Address: 4521 Spring Grove Ave., Cincinnati, OH
45232. Tel.: 513-681-6680.

# CLEVELAND: CLEVELAND CULTURAL GARDENS
# & ROCKEFELLER PARK GREENHOUSES

Located in Rockefeller Park are the Cultural Gardens consisting
of a string of nineteen distinct displays, each offering sculpture

and landscaping typical of one of the nationalities that have made the Cleveland area their home. Included among these are British, German, Greek, Hebrew, Irish, Italian, Russian, Ukranian, Afro-American, American Indian. Interesting garden designs, colorful blossoms, marble sculptures and fountains can be seen in abundance. The Rockefeller Park greenhouses contain collections of tropical plants, economic plants, cacti and succulents, palms, ferns, and orchids. Seasonal flower shows are scheduled regularly. Adjacent to the greenhouses is a Japanese style garden. The Cultural Gardens are open daily, dawn to dusk. Fee: None. Located about 4 miles west of downtown Cleveland along East and Liberty Blvds., between St. Clair and Superior Aves. For further information, write to Cleveland Cultural Garden Foundation, Westgate Legal Bldg., 20088 Center Ridge Rd., Rocky River, OH 44116. The Rockefeller Park Greenhouses are open Mon.–Fri., 9:30–4:00, and Sun., 8–6. Fee: None. Address: 750 E. 88th St., Cleveland, OH. Tel.: 216-664-3103.

## CLEVELAND: GARDEN CENTER OF GREATER CLEVELAND

Established as a resource center for garden enthusiasts, this garden contains a library of over twelve thousand volumes and offers a full schedule of courses, lectures, and workshops for all ages. Display gardens include a Japanese garden, a rose garden, an herb garden, and a colorful perennial garden. Indoor displays and seasonal shows are held in the Garden Center Building. Guided tours. Gift shop. Wheelchair accessible. Open: Mon.– Fri., 9–5, and Sun., 2–5; closed Sat. Fee: None. Located about 4 miles west of downtown Cleveland, just across Magnolia Dr. from Case-Western Reserve Law School; take Euclid Ave. to East Blvd. Address: University Circle, 11030 East Blvd., Cleveland, OH 44106. Tel.: 216-721-1600.

## CLEVELAND: LAKE VIEW CEMETERY

Established in 1869, Lake View Cemetery offers a surprising number of superior gardens on its 285-acre grounds. Collections include azaleas (2,000), daffodils (nearly 100,000), irises (1,300), mountain laurel (nearly 1,000), lilacs (600), rhododendrons (1,500—some nearly 20 feet high), and viburnums (800). There are hundreds of specimen trees, and the flowering trees (cherries, magnolias, dogwoods, and crab apples) number more than a thousand. The cemetery also contains some architecturally interesting monuments, particularly the Victorian Gothic-styled, 180-foot-tall James A. Garfield Monument. Almost half the grounds remain heavily wooded with numerous species of birds and wildlife. Blossoms can be found spring into fall, and tour routes are marked and altered as various plantings come into bloom. An Azalea Sunday is held each spring. The gardens can be toured by car or foot. Group tours by prearrangement. Open daily, 7:30–5:30. Fee: None. Located approximately 7 miles west of downtown Cleveland; entrance is near junction of Euclid Ave. (U.S. 6 and 20) and E. 123rd St. Address: 12316 Euclid Ave., Cleveland, OH 44106. Tel.: 216-421-2665.

## COLUMBUS: FRANKLIN PARK CONSERVATORY AND GARDEN CENTER

Modeled after the 1893 Columbian Exposition in Chicago's Glass Palace (which was itself modeled after London's famous Crystal Palace), the 90-year-old Franklin Park Conservatory is on the National Register of Historic Places. Today the renovated conservatory covers over 12,000 square feet and contains permanent collections of orchids (over six hundred), desert plants (hundreds of species of cacti and succulents), bonsai, and a tropical forest. Four major seasonal shows (Easter Lily, Summer Foliage, Chrysanthemum, Poinsettia) are held annually. During Halloween a Witches Walk is presented, and at Christmas a special Candlelight Tour. Seminars, workshops, and lectures are offered to children and adults. A reference library of over a thousand volumes is open to the public. Wheelchair accessible. Group guided tours by prearrangement; a self-guided tour brochure is available to visitors (recommended). Gift shop. The conservatory and garden center are available for weddings, meetings, and special events. Open daily, 10–4. Fee: None. Located in central Columbus just off I-70 and 270. Address: 1777 E. Broad St., Columbus, OH 43203. Tel.: 614-222-7447.

## COLUMBUS: PARK OF ROSES

Located in Whetstone Park, this superb 13-acre All-America Rose Selections Display Garden contains seven thousand rose bushes (190 varieties), plus a collection of miniature roses and the Heritage Garden of eighty-two antique rose plants. In addition, there is a large daffodil garden (five thousand bulbs), a perennial garden and an herb garden. Peak bloom is June through September. Summer activities include Saturday and Sunday evening concerts and the Thursday-Morning-in-the-Park program for children. Wheelchair accessible. Picnic facilities with reservable shelter house. Area available for weddings by prearrangement. Open daily, dawn to dusk. Fee: None. Location: Whetstone Park is located 4 miles north of downtown Columbus. Address: 3923 N. High St. For further information, write to the Dept. of Parks and Recreation, 420 W. Whittier St., Columbus, OH 43215. Tel.: 614-222-7520.

## DAYTON: COX ARBORETUM

Miles of trails wind by streams, and through meadows and natural woodlands in this 158-acre reserve. Gardens include an herb garden, a rock garden, and a shrub garden, and there is a greenhouse. Collections include conifers and crab apples. Spring Festival is the weekend after Mother's Day. Garden shop, library, and art gallery. Wheelchair accessible. Group tours by prearrangement. Garden open daily, 8–dusk, buildings, 8:00–4:30. Fee: None. Located about 6 miles south of downtown Dayton; take I-75 south to Springboro Pike exit. Address: 6733 Springboro Pike, Dayton, OH 45449. Tel.: 513-434-9005.

## LORAIN: LAKEVIEW PARK ROSE GARDEN

Established in 1935, this public rose garden, bordering Lake Erie, consists of a large circular display divided into forty-eight rose beds. All told, the garden contains some three thousand roses representing more than forty varieties. Peak bloom is June into fall. Permits can be obtained for weddings and other affairs in the garden. Open daily, sunrise–11 P.M.. Fee: None. Location: Lorain is located in north-central Ohio on Lake Erie, 30 miles west of Cleveland; the garden is just off W. Erie Ave. For further information, write to the Parks and Recreation Dept., City of Lorain, 329 Tenth St., Lorain, OH 44052. Tel.: 216-244-0705.

## MENTOR: HOLDEN ARBORETUM

One of North America's largest and finest arboretums, the 2,900-acre Holden Arboretum possesses more than four thousand different species and sixty-eight major plant collections. Among these are crab apples and rhododendrons, which together create exquisite color in spring. The extensive Maple Tree Collection produces maple syrup, which can be purchased in March at the Tree House Gift Shop. The Nut-Bearing Tree Collection is the only one of its kind in the United States. There are nature trails through natural woodlands and by streams and rare geological formations. Fall color is superb. In winter the trails provide excellent cross-country skiing. Holden maintains a year-round schedule of classes, workshops, lectures, and scheduled rare plant sales. Guided tours by prearrangement. Open Tues.–Sun., 10–5. Fee: $2.50/adults, $1.75/children ages 6–15 and seniors; group rates. Location: Mentor is located in northern Ohio about 20 miles west of Cleveland; the arboretum is 2 miles south of downtown Mentor; take State Rte. 306 south, go east on U.S. 6 to Sperry Rd. Address: 9500 Sperry Rd., Mentor, OH 44060. Tel.: 216-946-4400.

## NEWARK: DAWES ARBORETUM

The woodlands of oak, beech, maple, birch, and pine, and a vast collection of flowering crab apples and dogwoods in this 950-acre arboretum provide a perfect setting for its many trails. Dawes Arboretum possesses over two thousand kinds of trees and shrubs, including the world's longest hedge lettering. Display areas include azaleas, rhododendrons, a cypress swamp, a fern garden, an all-seasons garden, and a first-rate Japanese garden. The Visitors Center contains a bonsai collection. Picnicking. Grounds available for weddings, meetings. A full schedule of programs for all ages: from garden topics to apple-butter making to weaving. Youth programs. Cross-country skiing in winter. Plant sales. Floral shows. Gift shop. Group tours by prearrangement. Wheelchair accessible. Open daily, dawn to dusk; Visitors Center open weekdays, 9–5. Fee: None. Location: Newark is located in central Ohio, 33 miles west of Columbus; the arboretum can be found on State Rte. 13, 5 miles south of Newark and 1 mile north of U.S. 40. Address: 7770 Jacksontown Rd. SE, Newark, OH 43055. Tel.: 614-323-2355.

## STRONGSVILLE: GARDENVIEW
## HORTICULTURAL PARK

This surprising 16-acre garden possesses a multitude of fine displays and unusual touches. Designed as an informal park with winding paths, the 10-acre arboretum contains approximately two thousand flowering trees, including an excellent crab apple collection. Complemented in spring by wildflowers and over a hundred thousand daffodils, this display attracts thousands. The 6-acre garden area offers rich color spring through fall. Located here are groupings of azaleas and rhododendrons, a hosta collection, an unusually diverse display of perennials, and the Cottage Garden, containing foxglove, honeysuckle, iris, peony, chrysanthemum, and viburnum. There is a lily pond garden, and an English-style round garden consisting of silver and gold foliage plants. Open Sat.–Sun., 12–6. Fee: $2.50/adult, $1.50/child. Location: Strongsville is located 14 miles southwest of Cleveland; the garden can be found on U.S. 42, 1½ miles south of the junction with State Rte. 82. Address: 16711 Pearl Rd., U.S. 42, Strongsville, OH 44136. Tel.: 216-238-6653.

## TOLEDO: GEORGE P. CROSBY GARDENS

This 56-acre garden serves as both a cultural center and a botanical garden. Display gardens include an herb garden, a rose garden, a fern garden, a fragrance garden, a chrysanthemum garden, a miniature rose test garden, an All-America test garden for flowers and vegetables, flowering trees, plus a lovely 4-acre shade garden of azaleas, rhododendrons, hostas, perennials, and wildflowers. There is a pioneer cabin with pioneer garden using varieties dating back to 1850 and earlier. A planned expansion will add a bulb garden, a perennial garden, a series of ponds, and an aquatic garden. The cultural center hosts meetings, classes, and lectures for all ages, as well as garden society flower shows. The Artists' Village houses the studios of resident glassblowers, potters, sculptors, and painters; the public is invited to walk through and watch the crafts people at work. Annual festivals include a Main Street U.S.A. (early 1900s) fair in mid-May, Festival of the Arts (art exhibits) in late June, and a Fall Folk Festival (folk arts and crafts) in early October. Gift shop offers books, herbs, and spices, as well as original handcrafted artwork from the Artists' Village. Café open in summer. Picnicking area. Wheelchair access to parts of garden. Gardens available for weddings by prearrangement. Group guided tours by prearrangement; self-guide brochure upon request. Full schedule of classes, lectures, and demonstrations. Garden open 8–dark; cultural center, café, and gift shop hours vary—check for times. Fee: None (fee charged during festivals). Located on the west side of Toledo, 6 miles from downtown, just off I-475, U.S. 20 (Reynolds Rd.) and State Rte. 120 (Central Ave.); from downtown take Bancroft St. or Dorr St. (State Rte. 246) west to Elmer. Address: 5402 Elmer Dr., Toledo, OH 43615. Tel.: 419-536-8365.

## TOLEDO: TOLEDO ZOO

In addition to the profuse plant materials used for its wildlife exhibits, the Toledo Zoo also possesses several quality horticultural displays. Toward the left after entering the grounds, directly behind the aquarium, is the conservatory containing more than nine hundred species of tropical foliage plants and succulents. Major collections include orchids, cyclamens, amaryllis, palms, ferns, begonias, bromeliads, and ficus. The conservatory also offers an Easter display of lilies, hyacinths, cinerarias, and dahlias, and a Christmas display of poinsettias, kalanchoes, and Christmas cacti. Just beyond the conservatory is the formal garden with flowering perennials (hostas, irises, daylilies, delphiniums, foxgloves, peonies, asters, and wildflowers) and a rose garden with over four hundred plants surrounding a waterlily pool. Guided tours of conservatory and gardens by prearrangement. Wheelchair accessible. Snacks and picnicking. Gift shop. Needless to say, the zoo itself is an excellent attraction for all ages. Open daily, Apr.–Sept, 10–5, and Oct.–Mar., 10–4; closed Thanksgiving, Christmas, and New Year's Day. Fee: $2/adults, $.75/seniors and children ages 2–11; free on Mon., 10–12 (except holidays). Located just off U.S. 24 at Harvard Blvd., about 2 miles southwest of downtown Toledo. Address: 2700 Broadway, Toledo, OH 43609. Tel.: 419-385-4040.

## WESTERVILLE: INNISWOOD BOTANICAL GARDEN AND NATURE PRESERVE

This 92-acre park consists of formal and wooded areas. Collections include daylilies, daffodils, hostas, wildflowers, and roses (500 bushes), as well as extensive arrays of peonies (200 varieties) and irises (400 varieties) which offer fine color from late May to mid-June. The newly developed ¾-acre herb garden contains America's largest thyme collection. Group tours by prearrangement. Programs, workshops and lectures are held in the Innis House. Wheelchair accessible. Open Tue.–Sat., 8:00–4:30, and Sun., 12–5; open Tues. evenings in summer. Fee: None. Location: Westerville is located in central Ohio, about 12 miles north of downtown Columbus; from the I-270 loop, take Exit 29, proceed north on State Rte. 3. Address: 940 Hempstead Rd., Westerville, OH 43081. Tel.: 614-895-6216.

## WOOSTER: SECREST ARBORETUM

Part of the Ohio Agricultural Research and Development Center, Secrest Arboretum consists of 85 acres containing over 2,000 species, varieties, and cultivars of native and exotic plants. Collections include junipers (75 kinds), yews (100 types), shade trees (140 types), hollies (100 types), as well as the popular rose garden (1,500 plants representing 500 varieties) and flowering crab apple collection (over 150 kinds). The Secrest Arboretum's best-known collection is its 7-acre Rhododendron Display Garden, begun in 1917, now containing nearly 2,000 rhododendron and azalea plants (over 200 different kinds), in flower from mid-April to early July. Thousands of visitors come from all over Ohio and neighboring states to view these magnificent plants at their peak in late May. Open daily, dawn to dusk. Fee: None. Location: Wooster is located in central Ohio, about 60 miles south of Cleveland and 30 miles east of Mansfield; the Ohio Agricultural Research and Development Center can be found just off State Rte. 83, less than 1 mile south of the junction with U.S. 30. Address: Ohio Agricultural Research and Development Center, Wooster, OH 44691. Tel.: 216-263-3761.

## YOUNGSTOWN: FELLOWS RIVERSIDE GARDENS

Located in Mill Creek Park, this 6-acre garden contains many fine collections, including roses, azaleas, and rhododendrons. Color is also provided by tulips in spring, extensive plantings of annuals and perennials in summer, and chrysanthemums and fall foliage in September and October. The displays are further embellished by flagstone terraces, a reflecting pool and fountain, and a Victorian gazebo. Picturesque views of the city and of Lake Glacier can also be enjoyed from the garden. Adjacent to the garden is the Fred W. Green Memorial Garden Center in which lectures and workshops are held. Its auditorium is available for group meetings. Mill Creek Park is a 2,500-acre all-purpose public recreation area with picnic tables, hiking trails, a golf course, lakes for boating and fishing, tennis courts, playgrounds, sports fields, and in winter, ice skating and cross-country skiing. Weddings permitted in garden Mon.–Sat. by prearrangement; receptions held in park. Garden open 10–dark. Fee: None. Location: Fellows Riverside Garden is located along the northern aspect of the Mill Creek Park, on Mahonning Ave. (State Rte. 18), just off I-680. For further information, write to the Mill Creek Park Office, 816 Glenwood Ave., Youngstown, OH 44502. Tel.: 216-744-4171.

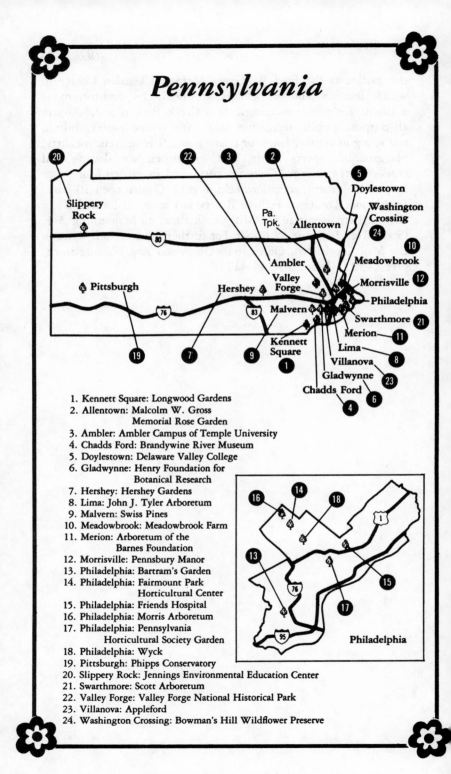

# *Pennsylvania*

1. Kennett Square: Longwood Gardens
2. Allentown: Malcolm W. Gross Memorial Rose Garden
3. Ambler: Ambler Campus of Temple University
4. Chadds Ford: Brandywine River Museum
5. Doylestown: Delaware Valley College
6. Gladwynne: Henry Foundation for Botanical Research
7. Hershey: Hershey Gardens
8. Lima: John J. Tyler Arboretum
9. Malvern: Swiss Pines
10. Meadowbrook: Meadowbrook Farm
11. Merion: Arboretum of the Barnes Foundation
12. Morrisville: Pennsbury Manor
13. Philadelphia: Bartram's Garden
14. Philadelphia: Fairmount Park Horticultural Center
15. Philadelphia: Friends Hospital
16. Philadelphia: Morris Arboretum
17. Philadelphia: Pennsylvania Horticultural Society Garden
18. Philadelphia: Wyck
19. Pittsburgh: Phipps Conservatory
20. Slippery Rock: Jennings Environmental Education Center
21. Swarthmore: Scott Arboretum
22. Valley Forge: Valley Forge National Historical Park
23. Villanova: Appleford
24. Washington Crossing: Bowman's Hill Wildflower Preserve

# Pennsylvania

## "DON'T MISS" GARDENS

### KENNETT SQUARE: LONGWOOD GARDENS

*One of America's greatest gardens according to garden experts, Longwood presents gardens, lakes, fountains, and conservatories in grand array. The ultimate indoor/outdoor pleasure garden and a first-rate horticultural center, Longwood produces the finest conservatory displays in the world, as well as fountains and fountain shows unparalleled by any other American garden.*

In the nineteenth century, a Quaker farm known as Peirce's Park possessed the finest collection of evergreen and deciduous trees in America. To avoid its destruction by lumbering interests, Pierre du Pont purchased the park in 1906 and began to construct what is generally considered the finest formal garden in the Western Hemisphere. Today, few gardens offer an array as diverse as Longwood's, and none do it better. From its formal European fountains to its whimsical topiary, from its broad, tree-lined paths to its creatively colorful indoor collections, Longwood is an ever-changing, ever-new experience. Longwood represents the epitome of pleasure gardens; a garden that is grand in every way—size, quality, and beauty. Witness the Main Fountain Garden, Longwood's most impressive outdoor garden. Located in the western section, this is an Italianate fountain garden in which stonework, statuary, urns, hedges, and trees all serve as punctuation to America's best garden fountains, from modest sprays to thunderous jets reaching 130 feet.

Longwood truly has too many gardens to list—350 acres of formal gardens, natural forest with lakes and vistas, and an excellent topiary display of diverse shapes and sizes up to 15 feet. Beyond all of these are Longwood's internationally famous conservatories. With nearly 4 acres under glass, Longwood presents breathtaking shows in its main conservatories and a seemingly endless succession of permanent collections, including orchids, roses, ferns, cacti and succulents, palms, economic and carnivorous plants, and many more.

LOCATION: On U.S. 1, 30 miles southwest of Philadelphia, 12 miles north of Wilmington.

ADDRESS: P.O. Box 501, Rte. 1, Kennett Square, PA 19348-0501.

TELEPHONE: 215-388-6741.

HOURS: Daily, 9-6, April–Oct.; 9–5, Nov.–March.

FEE: $5/adult, $1/children ages 6–14.

TOURS: Group tours by prearrangement.

RESTAURANT: Restaurant providing full menu.

SHOPS: Plants, film, books, and gifts.

WHEELCHAIR ACCESS: Access to most of garden.

SPECIAL ACTIVITIES: Fountain performances in summer. Organ music Oct. and Dec.–April, Sun. afternoons at 2:30. Over three hundred performing events each year—list provided on request. Educational programs on all levels year-round; Longwood also serves as a 2-year internship for University of Delaware graduate students in ornamental horticulture.

---

TIPS: 1. Don't miss:

   a. Every seasonal conservatory show, especially the Chrysanthemum (Nov.) and Christmas Poinsettia shows. The twenty permanent indoor gardens (orchids, roses, tropicals, cacti) are always superb.

   b. Waterlilies, some with pads over seven feet in diameter, in bloom June–Sept.

   c. Topiary garden: one of North America's best.

   d. Summer performances of illuminated fountains are held twice weekly. Summer concerts and plays are offered in the Open Air Theater, modeled after the Villa Gori near Sienna, Italy. The French fireworks and fountain display is held monthly (reservations required); on these evenings the conservatories are kept open until 10:30.

2. Don't miss the two magnificent gardens of Pierre du Pont's cousins in nearby Delaware—Winterthur and Nemours, as well as the restored garden of their great-grandfather, E. I. du Pont, at the Hagley Museum and Library.

# EXCELLENT GARDENS

## ALLENTOWN: MALCOLM W. GROSS MEMORIAL ROSE GARDEN

The Malcolm W. Gross Rose Garden is a 2-acre public garden containing twenty-five hundred rose bushes (sixty varieties) caringly displayed among graceful trees and elegant gazebos. This garden received the All-America Rose Selections Award for Excellence in 1984. Wheelchair accessible. Garden available for weddings. Open daily. Fee: None. Location: Allentown is located 54 miles north of Philadelphia. For further information, write to the Dept. of Parks, 2700 Parkway Blvd., Allentown, PA 18104. Tel.: 215-437-7627.

## AMBLER: AMBLER CAMPUS OF TEMPLE UNIVERSITY

Forty acres of this campus are set aside as an outdoor laboratory for the Department of Horticulture and Landscape Design. Hence the grounds have a varied assortment of well-tended displays, most notably the formal gardens whose long borders are packed with flowering annuals, perennials, and bulbs. The woodland areas contain a carpet of wildflowers in spring. There is also a 3-acre orchard of apple and peach trees, a collection of Japanese cherries, and greenhouses containing seasonal flowers and foliage plants. Grounds open daily, dawn to dusk; greenhouses open Mon.–Fri., 8:30–4:30; closed Sat., Sun., and holidays. Fee: None. Located about 20 miles north of downtown Philadelphia, between U.S. 309 and State Rte. 63. Address: Butler Pike and Meetinghouse Rd., Ambler, PA 19002. Tel.: 215-643-1200.

## CHADDS FORD: BRANDYWINE RIVER MUSEUM

This extensive wildflower garden has been developed over the last decade to complement the 100-year-old grist mill museum. The garden features blue, white, and pink asters, New England asters, blue lobelias, sundrops, black-eyed Susans, cardinal flowers, bluebells, and several varieties of goldenrod. In spring and late summer the walks and meadows are filled with color. The Brandywine River Museum contains collections from area artists, including Andrew and James Wyeth, Maxfield Parrish, Harvey Dunn, and George Cope. There is also an exhibit of the works of Howard Pyle, known as the father of American illustration. A glass tower adjoins the museum and offers lovely views of the meandering Brandywine River. Lectures, workshops, and garden walks scheduled year-round. Wheelchair accessible. Guided tours by prearrangement. Museum shop offers books, wildflower seeds. Restaurant. Garden open daily, dawn to dusk; museum open daily, 9:30–4:30; closed Christmas. Fee: Garden, free; museum, $2.50/adults, $1.25/seniors, students, and children ages 6–12; group rates available. Located on U.S. 1 in Chadds Ford, 28 miles southwest of Philadelphia and 12 miles north of Wilmington. For further information, write to Brandywine River Museum, P.O. Box 141, Chadds Ford, PA 19317. Tel.: 215-459-1900.

## DOYLESTOWN: DELAWARE VALLEY COLLEGE

Opened in 1896 as the National Farm School, the Delaware Valley College's 45-acre main campus offers a formal herb garden, a woodland garden with azaleas and rhododendrons, a dwarf conifer collection (nearly one hundred specimens), a hedge demonstration garden, an arboretum with a pond and spring bulbs and wildflowers, as well as a 200-year-old sassafras and 300-year-old native American sycamore. A greenhouse of 16,000 square feet contains the Kerr Orchid Collection. Peak bloom is in spring. A self-guided tour map is available at the college library. Open daily, dawn to dusk. Fee: None. Location: Doylestown is located at the junction of U.S. 202 and State Rte. 611, 25 miles north of downtown Philadelphia; the college can be found on U.S. 202 at New Britain Rd., about 1 mile west of Doylestown. Address: Doylestown, PA 18901. Tel.: 215-345-1500.

## GLADWYNNE: HENRY FOUNDATION FOR BOTANICAL RESEARCH

This natural 40-acre garden is famous for its collections of native American species and its efforts toward their preservation, propagation, and redistribution. The founder, Mrs. J. Norman Henry, made over a hundred treks across the continent to gather rare specimens from the wild. Described as a "connoisseur's garden," the Henry Foundation for Botanical Research today boasts exceptional collections of native rhododendrons, magnolias, liliums, ilex, and more. Plantings are dispersed along the steep, rocky terrain. Plants are labeled. Peak bloom is in April to May (azaleas and rhododendrons) and September to October (perennials, fall color). Special activities include courses on horticultural topics throughout the year, as well as Rhododendron Day in spring and a Holly Day (check for specific dates). Guided tours available upon request (especially if made in advance). Open Apr.–Oct., Tues. and Thurs. only, 10–4; other times and group tours by appointment. Fee: None. Located in the prestigious Main Line area west of Philadelphia; follow I-76 west to State Rte. 23 west, to Henry La. (turn right) to Stony La. Address: 801 Stony La., Gladwynne, PA 19035. Tel.: 215-525-2037.

---

## HERSHEY: HERSHEY GARDENS

Originally a 3½-acre rose garden developed by Milton Hershey, the founder of Hershey Chocolate, Hershey Gardens today consists of 23 acres, which include an arboretum, an herb garden, and superb flower displays. Spring is this garden's finest hour when tulips (over 50,000), azaleas (125 varieties), dogwoods, cherries, magnolias, crab apples, rhododendrons (50 varieties), peonies (100 varieties), and irises and viburnum are in bloom. Summer is the peak time for the 30,000 roses, the daylilies, annuals, and perennials. In October there is a lovely chrysanthemum display. The arboretum features collections of hollies and Japanese maples. Tours at 11 and 1:30 daily, Memorial Day to Labor Day. Garden Gift Shop offers botanical gifts and educational items for all ages. Hershey Foods Corporation also offers a variety of other interesting attractions: Chocolate World (no fee) presents the story of chocolate, indoor tropical gardens (nearly fifty thousand plantings), and a turn-of-the-century village with gift shops; ZOOAMERICA (fee), a 10-acre walk-through zoo presenting over two hundred animals from five North American regions; and the Hershey Museum of American Life (fee) with displays and collections plus the story of Milton Hershey. Hershey Gardens is open Memorial Day–Labor Day, 9–7; Apr.–May and Sept.–Nov., 9–5; Thanksgiving–Dec. 24, 10–5. Fee: $2.75/adults, $1.50/children ages 12–18 during the Memorial Day–Labor Day season; $2.50/adults, $1.25/children ages 12–18 at other times. Location: Hershey is located on U.S. 422 about 90 miles west of Philadelphia and 15 miles east of Harrisburg; Hershey Information Center is on State

Rte. 743—look for signs. Address: Hershey Information Center, 400 W. Hersheypark Dr., Hershey, PA 17033. Tel.: 717-534-3005.

## LIMA: JOHN J. TYLER ARBORETUM

Situated on 700 acres of rolling hills and streams with 20 miles of hiking paths, the John J. Tyler Arboretum possesses a good collection of pines, a giant sequoia, a very large tulip tree, plus a beautiful array of flowering cherries, magnolias, crab apples, and dogwoods—all of which draw crowds in the spring. There is also a fragrance garden for the visually impaired. Gift and book shop. Open daily, 8–dusk. Fee: None. Location: Lima is located approximately 18 miles west of downtown Philadelphia; the arboretum is located about 1 mile north of the junction of U.S. 1 with State Rte. 352. Address: 515 Painter Rd., P.O. Box 216, Lima, PA 19037. Tel.: 215-566-5431.

## MALVERN: SWISS PINES

A beautifully designed area best known for its lovely Japanese garden. The tea house was crafted in Japan, then assembled here. Swiss Pines also offers a pinetum, a crab apple grove, and rose and herb gardens (over 110 kinds of herbs). Many specimens of heather, azalea, and rhododendron can also be seen. Peak bloom, May. Open mid-Mar.–mid-Dec. Mon.–Fri., 10–4, and Sat., 9–12; closed Sun. and holidays. Fee: None. Location: Malvern is located 20 miles west of downtown Philadelphia, just off U.S. 30; Swiss Pines is about 4 miles north of Malvern on Charleston Rd. (State Rte. 29). Mailing address: P.O. Box 97, Upper Darby, PA 19082. Tel.: 215-933-6916.

## MEADOWBROOK: MEADOWBROOK FARM

Meadowbrook Farm offers a unique combination of experiences. Open daily to the public is the commercial greenhouse containing attractively arranged displays of orchids, ferns, begonias, cacti, and succulents, plus many kinds of foliage plants, topiary (in the form of animals, birds, circles, and pyramids), statuary, and other garden ornaments. Outside the greenhouse are extensive beds of annuals, perennials (250 varieties, some rare), shrubs, and trees. At Meadowbrook's private gardens a different kind of experience is available to groups of fifteen to thirty-five by appointment. The result of four decades of work by horticulturist J. Liddon Pennock and his wife, this private tour offers a lovely sequence of impeccable terraced gardens. Connected by allees and stairways, embellished by pools, fountains, and six elegant gazebos, these gardens contain specimens of oleander, jasmine, hibiscus, gardenias, pansies, primroses, and annuals. Peak bloom in the private garden is in summer. The greenhouse is open Mon.–Sat., 10–5; private garden open to groups by appointment only. Fee: None. Located about 15 miles north of downtown Philadelphia, just off State Rte. 63; from the Pennsylvania Tpk. (I-276) take State Rte. 61 south, to State Rte. 63 east, to Washington La. south. Address: 1633 Washington La., Meadowbrook, PA 19046. Tel.: 215-887-5900.

## MERION: ARBORETUM OF THE BARNES FOUNDATION

For the plant enthusiast, this arboretum possesses over 290 varieties of trees and shrubs from around the world. Landscaped with ferns and wildflowers, Barnes seems more like a pleasant garden than the educational institution that it is. The Barnes Foundation holds a regular schedule of lectures and courses, and the garden's compact 12 acres make it easy to view a surprising number of rare and exotic plants without trudging all over the countryside. In addition, the original estate house holds a nationally famous art collection. Garden open Mon.–Sat., 9:30–4:00, and Sun., 1:30–4:30; closed weekends in July and Aug. Passes required for visits Fri.–Sun. (call for information); all visitors must sign in at office. Fee: None. Located in the Main Line area west of Philadelphia, just across U.S. 1 from St. Joseph's College. Address: 57 Lapsley Rd., Merion, PA 19066. Tel.: 215-664-8880.

## MORRISVILLE: PENNSBURY MANOR

Pennsbury Manor is a faithful re-creation of the seventeenth-century estate of William Penn, the founder and first governor of Pennsylvania (from the Latin, meaning "Penn's Woods"). Although no description of Penn's original grounds is available, the restored gardens were designed by Thomas Sears in the Colonial Revival style typical of Penn's time. Located on the banks of the Delaware River, the garden contains a formal flower garden, a kitchen garden of culinary and medicinal herbs, a vegetable garden, and an orchard. The manor itself provides insight into life during the 1600s, and the barn area contains farm livestock. Special activities include the Market Fair, the Colonial Fair in mid-September, and Holly Night prior to Christmas. Tours last approximately 1½ hours. Open Tues.–Sat., 9–5, and Sun., 12–5; closed Thanksgiving, Christmas, and New Year's Day. Fee: $2.50/adults, $1.75/seniors; $1.00/children ages 6–18; group rates by prearrangement. Located on State Rte. 32 along the Delaware River, 30 miles northeast of Philadelphia, approximately 10 miles north of the Pennsylvania Tpk. (I-276). Address: 400 Pennsbury Memorial La., Morrisville, PA 19067. Tel.: 215-946-0400.

## PHILADELPHIA: BARTRAM'S GARDEN

This 27-acre garden was begun in 1730 by John Bartram, considered by his contemporaries "the greatest natural botanist in the world." Collecting plants from across the colonies, Bartram introduced over two hundred new varieties to Europe, including the sugar maple. Bartram's Garden contained colonial America's most outstanding collection of native plants. Peak bloom in spring and October. Open daily, dawn to dusk. Fee: Garden, none; Bartram house, $1. Located approximately 2 miles west of downtown Philadelphia. Address: 54th St. and Lindbergh Blvd., Philadelphia, PA 19143. Tel.: 215-729-5281.

## PHILADELPHIA: FAIRMOUNT PARK
## HORTICULTURAL CENTER

The largest city park system in America, Fairmount Park offers a variety of horticultural displays across its 8,000 acres. Foremost of these is the Horticultural Center, which presents seasonal displays as well as special pre-Easter, Autumn, and Christmas shows. Lectures, demonstrations, and workshops are also held on a regular basis. Located nearby is the Japanese House and Garden, an authentic reconstruction originally presented in 1954 to the Museum of Modern Art of New York City by the America-Japan Society. Fairmount Park also possesses ten elegant eighteenth-century mansions, completely restored, depicting daily life in an era when Philadelphia was the second largest city in the English-speaking world. The Horticultural Center is open daily, 10–4; closed some holidays. Fee: $.50 donation. Located 2 miles northwest of downtown Philadelphia. Address: Horticulture Drive near Belmont Ave., Fairmount Park, Philadelphia, PA 19131. Tel.: 215-686-1776, ext. 81287.

## PHILADELPHIA: FRIENDS HOSPITAL

Located on the grounds of America's oldest private nonprofit psychiatric hospital (founded in 1813), this garden is best known for 20 wooded acres packed with magnificent azaleas (approximately sixteen thousand bushes, eighty varieties), some specimens over 50 years old and 15 feet high. The grounds also possess a rose garden, beds of flowers, and dogwoods. The gardens represent the Friends Hospital's philosophy of utilizing activity therapy, including horticulture therapy, as part of its treatment of mental illness. Wheelchair access to parts of garden. Plant clinics and plant sales. Gift shop. Wedding pictures permitted by prearrangement. Open only on Garden Days, the last Sun. in April and the first two weekends in May, 12–5. Fee: $2/car (includes free azalea cutting). Located in the northeast section, about 8 miles from downtown Philadelphia. Address: Roosevelt Blvd. at Adams Ave., Philadelphia, PA 19124. Tel.: 215-831-4772 or 215-831-4600.

## PHILADELPHIA: MORRIS ARBORETUM

Located in the lovely Chestnut Hill area, this 175-acre garden and arboretum was started by the Morris family in 1887. Today it possesses some of the rarest and largest trees and shrubs (more than thirty-five hundred kinds) in the Philadelphia area, and one of the best collections of Oriental trees in the eastern United States. Bequeathed to the University of Pennsylvania in 1932, the arboretum serves as both a research center and a public garden. In spring, thousands of visitors come to view the lovely Azalea Meadow and Magnolia Slope. Peak bloom, April–June; autumn color, October. Open daily, Apr.–Oct., 9–5, and Nov.–Mar., 9–4; open till 8 P.M. on Wed., June–Aug.; closed Christmas. Fee: $1. Located about 12 miles north of downtown Philadelphia; take U.S. 422 (Germantown Ave.) north, turn right onto Hillcrest Ave.—entrance is on Hillcrest. Address: 9414 Meadowbrook Ave., Philadelphia, PA 19118. Tel.: 215-247-5777.

## PHILADELPHIA: PENNSYLVANIA HORTICULTURAL SOCIETY GARDEN

Part of the Independence National Historic Park located in old Philadelphia, this authentic eighteenth-century garden offers an attractive formal garden of seasonal flowers, a small orchard (ripening fruit is a rare spectacle indeed in Center City), and an herb garden—entirely constructed of plants descended from those used by our colonial ancestors. Open daily. Fee: None. Located in the heart of old Philadelphia, 1 block from Independence Hall. Address: 325 Walnut St., Philadelphia, PA 19106. Tel.: 215-625-8250.

## PHILADELPHIA: WYCK

Wyck and its garden will be of particular interest to the horticultural expert and garden historian. Wyck dates back to the 1600s and is the oldest house in Philadelphia. The 2½-acre garden was tended by nine generations of the same Quaker family—from the seventeenth century until opened to the public in 1973. The garden's most famous horticultural display is the rose collection, bordered by boxwood. Many of the rose varieties date back to the 1820s and indeed some are believed to have been transported to this country as early as 1750. The garden also contains wildflowers, wisteria, rare shrubs, vegetables, and fruit trees. Open May–Oct., Tues., Thurs., and Sat. only, 1–4 (other hours by appointment). Fee: $1. Located in the Germantown section, about 6 miles north of downtown Philadelphia on U.S. 422 (Germantown Ave.). Address: 6026 Germantown Ave. (at Walnut La.), Philadelphia, PA 19144. Tel.: 215-848-1690.

## PITTSBURGH: PHIPPS CONSERVATORY

Phipps was America's largest conservatory when it was completed in 1893 through the backing of steel magnate Henry Phipps. In 1894 it obtained most of the rare plants used at the Columbian Exposition of the Chicago World's Fair—some of these specimens can still be viewed today. Designed in the Victorian fashion with a central palm court and peripheral greenhouses, the conservatory now extends over 2½ acres and consists of thirteen large show houses and nine growing houses with nearly a half mile of paths winding through permanent displays of tropical jungle, blazing blossoms, a water garden, a Japanese garden, and an outstanding orchid display (many from Thailand). Phipps Conservatory is also famous for its fine Spring, Fall, and Christmas flower shows. The Fall Flower Show, for example, comprises more than seven display greenhouses filled with some four hundred varieties of chrysanthemums. In summer there is an adjacent outdoor water garden filled with tropical lilies, and a colorful flower garden. Gift shop. Open daily, 9–5; hours extended during shows; closed Christmas Day and two days before each flower show. Fee: $1/adults, $.50/children and seniors; for flower shows, $2/adults, $.75/children and seniors. Located near the entrance to Schenley Park. For further information, write to the Dept. of Parks, 400 City County Bldg., Pittsburgh, PA 15219. Tel.: 412-255-2370.

## SLIPPERY ROCK: JENNINGS ENVIRONMENTAL EDUCATION CENTER

A patch of natural prairie rare this far east, the 350-acre Jennings Center possesses flora unusual for Pennsylvania. Amid a vast array of wildflowers, the featured species is the spectacular blazing star, rising up to 6 feet and flowering from the top down. In August thousands of these plants burst into bloom. The Visitor's Center contains displays and exhibits. Classes for all ages are held on a regular basis. Group programs and tours can be arranged for schools, churches, Scouts, or private groups. Open daily, dawn to dusk; Visitor's Center open Mon.–Fri., 8–4. Fee: None. Location: Slippery Rock is located in west-central Pennsylvania about 50 miles north of Pittsburgh, at the junction of State Rtes. 108 and 173, 4 miles east of I-79; the center can be found 4 miles south of Slippery Rock—take State Rte. 173 south, turn onto State Rte. 528. Address: R.D. 1, Slippery Rock, PA 16057. Tel.: 412-794-6011.

## SWARTHMORE: SCOTT ARBORETUM

The site of the national office of the American Association of Botanical Gardens and Arboreta, the Scott Arboretum consists of a series of gardens and an arboretum within the 350-acre campus of Swarthmore College. The arboretum possesses over five thousand kinds of plants, including a rhododendron collection numbering two thousand specimens. Excellent spring bloom also includes daffodils (six hundred kinds), azaleas, lilacs, tree peonies, magnolias, and cherries. Summer color is provided by roses and daylilies. Other displays include a rock garden, a woodland garden, the Harry Wood Memorial garden of contemporary courtyard landscaping, and the Wister Solar Greenhouse. Peak bloom is April to June. Map for self-guided tour available at the Scott Arboretum office on College Ave. Grounds open daily, dawn to dusk; office open Mon.–Fri., 8:30–4:30. Fee: None. Located on State Rte. 320 (Chester Rd.), about 12 miles west of downtown Philadelphia. Address: Swarthmore College, Swarthmore, PA 19081. Tel.: 215-328-8025.

## VALLEY FORGE: VALLEY FORGE NATIONAL HISTORICAL PARK

This 3,000-acre site, where Washington quartered his troops during the bitter winter of 1777-78, today possesses one of America's finest collections of dogwoods and other flowering trees. Over fifty thousand pink and white dogwoods are found here, many of them clustered at Dogwood Grove near the New Jersey monument. Wooded areas also contain rhododendron and moutain laurel. Peak bloom, April to May; fall foliage also impressive. Open daily, dawn to dusk. Fee: None. Located 20 miles northwest of Philadelphia; take I-76 from Philadelphia, exit onto State Rte. 29 north. For further information, write to Valley Forge National Park, P.O. Box 953, Valley Forge, PA 19481. Tel.: 215-783-7700.

## VILLANOVA: APPLEFORD

Once part of a 1682 land grant from William Penn, this 22-acre site is now owned and maintained by Lower Merion Township. Designed by Thomas Sears in the 1920s, the grounds consist of small, immaculate formal gardens enclosed by stone walls and clipped hedges, featuring roses (150 bushes), perennials, annuals, fruit trees, and wisteria. The wooded areas contain rhododendrons, ferns, and wildflowers. There is also a working greenhouse where cut flowers and plants can be obtained. This garden offers color from spring into fall. The house, originally built in 1705 and enlarged later, is filled with antiques and is available for rental for social events or meetings by prearrangement. Garden open daily, dawn to dusk; house open to groups by appointment only. Fee: None. Located in the prestigious Main Line area, 14 miles west of Philadelphia, at 770 Mt. Moro Rd. For further information, write to The Appleford Committee, P.O. Box 182, Villanova, PA 19085. Tel.: 215-525-9430.

# WASHINGTON CROSSING: BOWMAN'S HILL WILDFLOWER PRESERVE

Within Washington Crossing State Park, where Washington and his troops camped prior to the famous raid on Trenton, the 100-acre Bowman's Hill Wildflower Preserve offers two dozen walking trails as well as fine collections of wildflowers, shrubs, trees, and vines native to Pennsylvania. The park is located on the Delaware River where wild azaleas, bluebells, violets, and other wildflowers create a fine display in spring. Autumn foliage is also worth seeing. The Preserve Building holds seasonal exhibits, an annual Christmas exhibit, and a permanent bird, nest, and egg display. Picnicking. Group tours by prearrangement. Wheelchair access to building and one trail. Open daily, 9–sunset; Preserve Building open Mon.–Sat., 9–5, and Sun., 12–5. Fee: None. Located just north of the junction of State Rtes. 32 and 532, about 25 miles north of downtown Philadelphia. For further information, write: Washington Crossing Park Commission, Washington Park, PA 18977. Tel.: 215-862-2924.

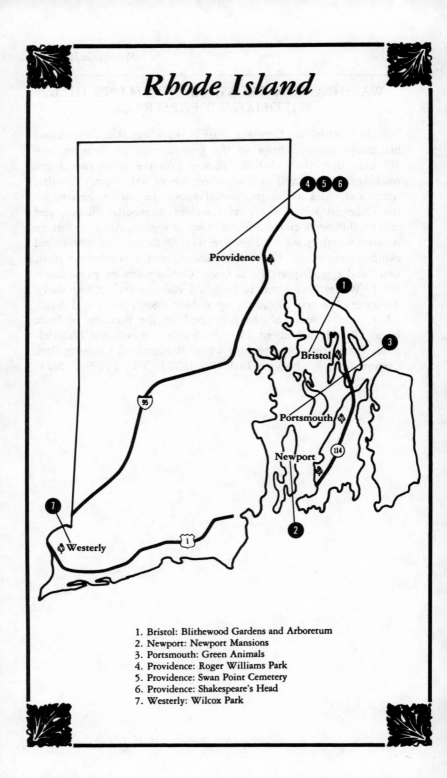

# *Rhode Island*

1. Bristol: Blithewood Gardens and Arboretum
2. Newport: Newport Mansions
3. Portsmouth: Green Animals
4. Providence: Roger Williams Park
5. Providence: Swan Point Cemetery
6. Providence: Shakespeare's Head
7. Westerly: Wilcox Park

# Rhode Island

## EXCELLENT GARDENS

### BRISTOL: BLITHEWOOD GARDENS AND ARBORETUM

This forty-five-room English manor built in 1896 is complemented by 33 gracefully landscaped acres. Overlooking Bristol Harbor, the grounds contain many colorful gardens, and such rare and exotic woody plants as Japanese tree lilacs, yellow-groove bamboo, and the largest giant sequoia east of the Rockies. Plantings include a rose garden, a water garden, a rock garden in Japanese style, a north garden (blue and yellow blossoms only), and masses of bulbs and flowers in bloom April to October. Special events include the Spring Bulb Display (punctuated by fifteen thousand daffodils and other bulbs), plant sale in May, summer evening concerts, and Christmas at Blithewood, when the mansion is decorated. Wheelchair accessible. Gift shop in mansion. Mansion available for weddings and meetings. A full schedule of programs, lectures, exhibits, and workshops are held throughout the year. Gardens open daily, 10–4; mansion open late Apr. to Oct., plus Christmas. Garden fee: $2/adults, $.50/children ages 6–15; mansion and gardens: $4/adults, $1/children ages 6–15; group rates available. Location: Bristol is located in eastern Rhode Island, halfway between Providence and Newport; Blithewood can be found on State Rte. 114, about 1½ miles south of Bristol. Address: Ferry Rd., Bristol, RI 02809. Tel.: 401-253-2707.

### NEWPORT: NEWPORT MANSIONS

America's most impressive group of mansions open to the public, these eight former homes are now owned and operated by the Preservation Society of Newport County. From the 1748 Hunter House to the turn-of-the-century opulence of Cornelius Vanderbilt's seventy-two-room Breakers, or the Elms (modeled after the Chateau d'Asnieres near Paris), these mansions present a unique spectacle of architecture, furnishings, and antiques from America's most lavish era. Most of the mansions once possessed equally lavish gardens, but time has left only three of note. A formal French sunken garden at the Elms includes statuary and fountains, as well as flower beds edged by boxwood. At Rosecliff there is an attractive rose garden, which was restored in 1976, as well as statuary and ornaments by Saint-Gaudens. The once magnificent grounds around the Breakers, which overlook the Atlantic, were designed by Frederick Law Olmsted and still retain the broad lawns and lovely vistas, plus interesting statuary and impressive old trees. Group reservations available. Open: Hours vary for each mansion and each season (check for specifics); in general, most mansions are open Apr.–Oct., daily, 10–5, later in summer; Elms, Chateau-Sur-Mer, and Marble House, open Nov.–Mar. on Sat. and Sun., 10–4. Fee: Cost depends on number of mansions on ticket, from $25/adults and $9/children ages 6–11 for all 8 mansions to $4/adults and $2/children ages 6–11 for just one mansion; group rates (call 401-847-6543). Located along Bellevue and Ochre Point Aves. For further information, write to the Preservation Society of Newport County, 118 Mill St., Newport, RI 02840. Tel.: 401-847-1000.

---

## PORTSMOUTH: GREEN ANIMALS

One of the two finest topiary—the art of shaping shrubbery into geometric or animal forms—gardens in America (the other is Ladew Gardens). Green Animals offers a hundred pruned and trained specimens including a giraffe, an elephant, a cat, a dog, a lion, a donkey, a camel, a peacock, a rooster, and a mountain goat, plus scores of meticulously shaped hedges and pedestals. The animal forms in particular—the giraffe looking down his nose at you, the two-humped camel with his craned neck, the lumbering elephant—are excellent. Bordered by contoured trees, boxed hedges, and flower beds, these green statues appear very lifelike. Indeed, the sculpturing is so realistic that you, and especially your children, will find yourselves responding as if they were truly part of the animal, rather than vegetable, kingdom. Few topiary gardens exist today because topiary requires a lot of work and specialized tools; it is the most labor-intensive form of gardening. Also at Green Animals are formal gardens (annuals and perennials), a vegetable garden, and a collection of fruit trees. The Small Toy Museum is located in the main house. Gift and Garden Shop offers home-grown plants, fruits, and vegetables. Wheelchair accessible. Open daily May–Sept., 10–5. Fee: $4/adults, $2/children ages 6–11;

group rates available. Located on Cory's La. off State Rte. 114, 7 miles north of Newport and 28 miles south of Providence. The garden is connected to Newport by a historic train (recommended). For further information, write to the Preservation Society of Newport County, 118 Mill St., Newport, RI 02840. Tel.: 401-847-1000.

## PROVIDENCE: ROGER WILLIAMS PARK

This 430-acre city park contains four greenhouses, five formal gardens, woodlands, seven lakes, a zoo, and five major Victorian buildings of historic interest, as well as a museum of natural history. There are rose, Japanese, and flower gardens. The greenhouses hold regularly scheduled exhibitions including annual Easter, Chrysanthemum (autumn), and Christmas Flower shows. Roger Williams Park also offers picnicking, playing fields, tennis courts, bridle paths, and in winter, ice skating, sledding, and cross-country skiing. Throughout the year, the park sponsors over a thousand educational and cultural events including concerts, dances, theater, and exhibitions. Weddings may be held here by prearrangement. The park is open daily, 7 A.M.– 9 P.M.; greenhouses open daily 11:00–4:30. Fee: None. Located near the junction of I-95 and State Rte. 10, about 3 miles south of downtown Providence; entrances to park off Broad St., and Montgomery, Elmwood, and Park Aves. For further information, write to the Dept. of Public Parks, Providence, RI 02905. Tel.: 401-785-9450.

## PROVIDENCE: SWAN POINT CEMETERY

Its grounds designed by landscape architects, Swan Point attracts thousands of visitors each year. Against a background of manicured lawns and tall trees, the mature plantings of laurels, rhododendrons and azaleas, tulips, daffodils, and stands of dogwoods, crab apples, and cherries present a very colorful display in spring. Annuals predominate in summer, and in autumn there are chrysanthemums and colorful fall foliage. Interesting monuments date back to the American Revolution. Open daily, 8–5. Fee: None. Located east of downtown Providence on the headwaters of Narragansett Bay. Address: P.O. Box 2446, 585 Blackstone Blvd., Providence, RI 02906. Tel.: 401-272-1314.

## PROVIDENCE: SHAKESPEARE'S HEAD

Two centuries ago the sign of Shakespeare's head atop a high pole indicated the home and printing shop of John Carter. An apprentice to Benjamin Franklin in Philadelphia, Carter later became publisher of the Providence *Gazette* (forerunner of the *Journal*) from 1768 to 1814. The property was condemned in 1937, after years of deterioration, and then rescued by the Shakespeare's Head Association. While clearing the grounds, evidence of the original garden was discovered and from it a faithful restoration emerged. Today the garden possesses three terraces and includes a sunken formal garden with beds of flowers, an herb garden, and a promenade with peonies and flowering crab apples. Albeit small in scope, this garden offers an unexpected oasis in the heart of downtown Providence. Peak bloom is in spring. Open daily, dawn to dusk. Fee: None. Address: 21 Meeting St., Providence, RI 02903. For further information, write to the Providence Preservation Society, 24 Meeting St., Providence, RI 02903. Tel.: 401-831-7440.

## WESTERLY: WILCOX PARK

Listed with the National Register of Historic Places, this public park has recently accumulated a variety of interesting collections. These include an herb garden containing perennial and annual herb beds and two sixteenth-century knot gardens; a rock garden with 130 dwarf conifers from the Gotelli Collection at the National Arboretum (DC); a perennial garden providing blossoms from spring into fall; and a lily pond with a good collection of waterlilies, a fountain, waterfowl, and koi. The park also contains a quality collection of native and rare trees amid its broad lawns and statuary. Group tours by prearrangement. Scheduled activities include summer concerts and festivals. Library. Open daily, dawn to dusk. Fee: None. Location: Westerly is located on U.S. 1 in southwest Rhode Island; Wilcox Park can be found along High and Broad Sts. and Grove Ave. Address: 71½ High St., Westerly, RI 02891. Tel.: 401-348-8362.

# *South Carolina*

## "DON'T MISS" GARDENS

## CHARLESTON: MAGNOLIA PLANTATION AND GARDENS

*One of America's oldest and most beautiful gardens, Magnolia Gardens is world renowned for the brilliant color of its azaleas in spring and for its camellia collection.*

Listed in the National Register of Historic Places, Magnolia Plantation and Gardens dates back to the 1680s when Thomas and Ann Drayton built the original plantation house, the first of its kind in the Carolina colonies. Originally a productive plantation, Magnolia's original gardens were of the formal English style with landscaped lawns and flower beds. In 1836, under the ownership of the Reverend John Grimke Drayton, the garden was redesigned to emphasize the haunting beauty of the tall cypress trees covered with Spanish moss; then it was further embellished with plantings along the waterways and forests. Despite Sherman's torching of the plantation during the Civil War, the fame of the gardens continued to spread. Grimke Drayton finally opened the gardens to the public during the spring months, and hordes of visitors, in their straw hats or long dresses, came up the Ashley River from Charleston by paddlewheel steamer. By 1900, Magnolia Plantation and Gardens was listed as one of America's three major attractions (along with Niagara Falls and the Grand Canyon) by Baedecker's travel guide. Today, these dramatic 50 acres of gardens remain as deservedly famous as ever and are still owned and run by a direct Drayton family descendant in their ninth generation of plantation ownership. Magnolia Plantation and Gardens are presently administered by the Magnolia Plantation Foundation, a non-profit, charitable organization.

LOCATION: On Rte. 61, 10 miles west of Charleston.
ADDRESS: Magnolia Plantation and Gardens, Highway 61, Charleston, SC 29407.
TELEPHONE: 803-571-1266.
HOURS: Daily, 8–6.

# South Carolina

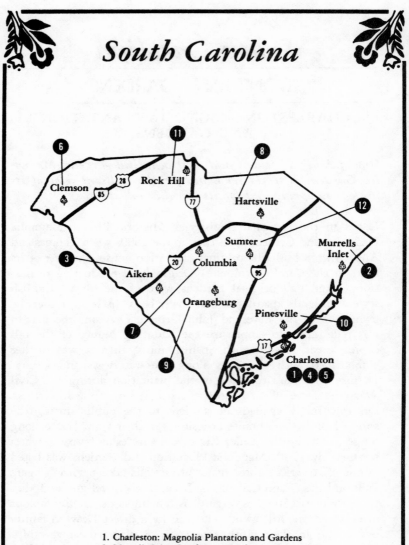

1. Charleston: Magnolia Plantation and Gardens
2. Murrells Inlet: Brookgreen Gardens
3. Aiken: Hopeland Gardens
4. Charleston: Cypress Gardens
5. Charleston: Hampton Park
6. Clemson: Clemson University Horticultural Gardens
7. Columbia: Boylston Gardens
8. Hartsville: Kalmia Gardens of Coker College
9. Orangeburg: Edisto Memorial Gardens
10. Pinesville: Middleton Place
11. Rock Hill: Glencairn Garden
12. Sumter: Swan Lake Iris Gardens

FEE: $6/adult, $4/teens, $3/children ages 4–12.

TOURS: Plantation house tours conducted regularly throughout the day (fee: $2).

RESTAURANT: In basement of Plantation House during spring months. Snack shop open year-round. Picnicking permitted in designated areas.

SHOPS: Gift shop in Plantation House.

WHEELCHAIR ACCESS: Paths accessible to wheelchairs; house not accessible.

SPECIAL ACTIVITIES: Magnolia Plantation and Gardens offers something for everyone, from canoeing and fishing on its lake, to walking or bicycling trails (which encompass the waterfowl refuge, prehistoric burial mound, and plantation slave graveyard), to its petting zoo, its peacocks, and miniature horses less than 3 feet tall.

---

TIPS: 1. Don't miss:

    a. Spring azaleas, among the best in the East with over 250 species, including the Azalea Indica first brought to America by John Grimke Drayton.

    b. Camellias, over 900 varieties, and a camellia maze similar to Thomas Jefferson's at Williamsburg (copied after the one still viewable at Hampton Court, England, created in the sixteenth century for Henry VIII). Magnolia was the first American garden to use camellias outdoors. Peak bloom, Nov.–Mar.

    c. Summer blossoms: A vast array including mimosas, hydrangeas, oleanders, crape myrtles, roses, bedding plants, bougainvilleas, gardenias (named after Charleston botanist and physician Alexander Garden), and more.

    d. The biblical garden, the seventeenth-century herb garden, and a topiary garden filled with friendly hedge animals.

2. The 125-acre Waterfowl Refuge can be viewed from hiking and bicycling trails or by canoe (bicycle and canoe rentals available). A three-tiered observation tower provides excellent views of wildlife and 170 species of birds and waterfowl. The refuge is most active before sunset. The Audubon Swamp Boardwalk offers a twenty-five-minute walk through a cypress swamp with benches and blinds for maximum bird-watching enjoyment.

3. The Plantation House, a historic landmark, contains photos and memorabilia of early plantation life. The upper floor offers the work of local artists.

---

## MURRELS INLET: BROOKGREEN GARDENS

*A unique and beautiful sculpture garden (Frederic Remington, Carl Milles, Daniel Chester French, Augustus Saint-Gaudens, Anna Huntington, and others) within a botanical garden containing over two thousand kinds of plants. For children (and adults) there is a wildlife park and a neighboring public beach.*

Listed in the National Register of Historic Places, Brookgreen Gardens was founded in 1931 by Archer and Anna Huntington. The gardens were created from land originally used as a rice plantation before the Civil War. Styled after the nineteenth-century English natural-landscape design, they incorporated many 200-year-old plantings and native species, thus creating a green and peaceful atmosphere. Two features of the garden are the breathtaking Live Oak Allée, moss-hung oaks in a sea of English ivy, and the original pathways laid out in the shape of a butterfly. Recently, azaleas, magnolias, and other flowering varieties have been planted to provide color, especially in spring. Overall, more than two thousand kinds of plants are found here, including outstanding collections of oaks, hollies, and wildflowers. But Brookgreen's ever expanding collection of statuary is equally impressive, with 449 sculptures by 205 of the greatest names in American art history; this is the finest outdoor collection of American sculpture in the world. And, if this weren't enough, there is also a delightful 40-acre wildlife sanctuary with an otter pond, an alligator swamp, a deer savannah, a fox and raccoon glade, and a walk-through cypress bird sanctuary.

---

LOCATION: Located on the Atlantic coast, on U.S. 17 near Litchfield Beach, 18 miles south of Myrtle Beach and 22 miles north of Georgetown.

ADDRESS: Murrells Inlet, SC 29576.

TELEPHONE: 803-237-4218.

HOURS: Open daily (except Christmas), 9:30–4:45.

FEE: $4/adult, $1/children ages 6–12 (subject to change).

TOURS: Regularly scheduled 45-minute tours of gardens and wildlife park.

RESTAURANT: None on grounds. Picnicking in designated areas.
SHOPS: Museum shop at Visitors Pavilion.
WHEELCHAIR ACCESS: Access to most of garden.
SPECIAL ACTIVITIES: Free slide shows regularly provided at the Education Center Auditorium (special showings by request). Films relating to art, travel, nature, and wildlife shown twice monthly. Year-round schedule of lectures and workshops for all ages. Special guided walks (birding, wildflower). Special teaching programs for teachers and other educators. Grounds available for weddings.

---

TIPS: 1. Peak bloom is in spring. Fall foliage in autumn. Though summers are quite hot here, an early morning visit followed by an afternoon at the beach makes a fine holiday.
2. Brookgreen Gardens is the ideal place for garden/ sculpture lovers. The Wildlife Park also makes it ideal for families.

---

# EXCELLENT GARDENS

---

## AIKEN: HOPELAND GARDENS

Paths run beneath willows and oaks, along pools, around fountains and gazebos, and across the broad lawns of this 14-acre garden. Year-round color can be found in the form of camellias, azaleas, wisteria, dogwoods, magnolias, lilies, crape myrtles, and roses. There is a Touch and Scent Trail for the visually handicapped. The gardens also contain the Thoroughbred Racing Hall of Fame. In summer, Monday evening concerts are performed. Gardens open daily, sunrise to sunset; Hall of Fame open Tues.–Sun., 2–5. Fee: None. Location: Aiken is located at the junction of U.S. 1 and 78 and State Rte. 19, 16 miles east of Augusta and 52 miles southwest of Columbia; the gardens can be found at Whiskey Rd. and Mead Ave. For further information, write to Hopeland Gardens, City of Aiken, P.O. Box 1177, Aiken, SC 29801. Tel.: 803-755-5811.

---

## CHARLESTON: CYPRESS GARDENS

This unusual, enchanting 162-acre forest is filled with moss-covered cypresses growing out of the dark waters of a lake. Once a haven for escaped fugitives or Civil War guerrillas, after 1930 this original rice plantation was turned into a navigable lake and its forest filled with thousands of bulbs and flowering plants. From February to summer the banks of the lake are aglow with blossoms. Displays include an azalea garden, a woodland garden, a camellia garden, a nature preserve, fine plantings of wisteria, and thousands of bulbs (daffodils, bluebells, and snowflakes). The garden can be toured by foot (self-guide brochure available) or guided boat tour (recommended). Gift shop. Outdoor cafe. Open daily, Feb. 15–Apr., 9–5; May–Feb. 14, 8–4. Fee: $4/adults, $3/seniors, $2/children ages 6–16. Located just off U.S. 52, 24 miles north of Charleston; take I-26 north to the U.S. 52/Moncks Corner exit, follow U.S. 52 past Goose Creek, then follow signs to gardens. For further information, write to the Dept. of Leisure Services, Hampton Park, Charleston, SC 29403. Tel.: 803-553-0515.

## CHARLESTON: HAMPTON PARK

Once the site of the East Indian Exposition of 1897, this city park is bordered by avenues of majestic live oaks and contains a rose walk with over a hundred varieties of roses, as well as groupings of azaleas, magnolias, and crape myrtles. There is a reconstructed bandstand and a fountain with jets reaching up to 50 feet. Gulls and geese are willing recipients of handouts. Peak bloom: Mar.–Apr. Picnicking. A cafe offers light meals. Bandstand entertainment during summer. Weddings permitted by prearrangement. Open daily, dawn to dusk. Fee: None. Located off President St. in central Charleston area, about 1 mile northwest of downtown. For further information, write to Hampton Park, Charleston SC 29403. Tel.: 803-724-7321.

## CLEMSON: CLEMSON UNIVERSITY HORTICULTURAL GARDENS

On its 70 acres, the Horticultural Gardens include azaleas, rhododendrons, and camellias, as well as a fern garden, a bog garden, a wildflower garden, a garden of meditation located in a glade with gentle waterfalls and a pagoda, and a 2-acre flower and turf garden with hundreds of varieties of annuals and perennials. Part of the gardens are located on John C. Calhoun's original cotton and tobacco plantation site. There is also a pioneer complex, which contains two log cabins, a grist mill, a collection of antique farm implements, and a colonial herb and vegetable garden. For the handicapped there is the Hortitherapy Garden in which raised beds can be tended from wheelchairs, and the Braille Trail for the visually impaired. Picnicking permitted. Group tours by prearrangement. Gardens available for weddings, meetings, and other group activities. Gardens open daily, sunrise to sunset. (Clemson University also possesses greenhouses, which are located near the Plant and Animal Science Bldg. on East Campus; open daily, 8:30–4:30.) Fee: None. Location: Clemson is located in the far northwest tip of South Carolina on State Rte. 28; the garden is on the east side of the Clemson campus. For further information, write to the Dept. of Horticulture, Clemson University, Clemson, SC 29634. Tel.: 803-656-3403.

## COLUMBIA: BOYLSTON GARDENS

Located on the 9-acre site of the Governor's Mansion, these historic gardens consist of tree-lined paths, secluded garden areas, patterned flower beds and boxwood hedges, plus statuary and fountains. The garden is in the process of restoration (a wedding garden has recently been added), primarily through the efforts of South Carolina's former first lady Ann Riley and local garden clubs. The Governor's Mansion and Boylston House can be toured. Open Mon.–Fri., 9–5—please prearrange visit by calling 803-737-1710. Fee: None. Address: Governor's Mansion, Columbia, SC 29201.

## HARTSVILLE: KALMIA GARDENS OF COKER COLLEGE

In this 28-acre garden of natural woodlands, streams, thickets, and swamp, walking trails lead through azaleas, camellias, and most important, the mountain laurel (*Kalmia latifolia*) for which this garden is named. A festival is held in April featuring arts, crafts, and entertainment. Open daily. Fee: None. Location: Hartsville is located on U.S. 15 about 60 miles northeast of Columbia; the gardens are situated on the bluffs of Black Creek, 2½ miles west of downtown, on Carolina Ave. (Bus Rte. 151). Address: Coker College, Hartsville, SC 29550. Tel.: 803-332-1381, ext. 410.

## ORANGEBURG: EDISTO MEMORIAL GARDENS

Originally an 85-acre swamp along the North Edisto River, this city park is a blaze of color from mid-March to late April. Designed for sheer beauty, the roads and trails are bordered by dense plantings of azaleas and camellias and canopied by trees draped in Spanish moss. Edisto also possesses, in conjunction with the American Rose society and the All-America Rose Selection Committee, an excellent rose garden with seventy-five hundred plants of 100 varieties, in bloom from April to November. The Annual Rose Festival, with exhibits and entertainment, is held the first weekend in May. Picnicking and fishing allowed. Weddings and meetings may be held by prearrangement. Wheelchair access to most areas. Open daily, sunrise to sunset; Garden Dr. open to autos, Mon.–Fri., 8:30–4:30. Fee: None. Location: Orangeburg is located in central South Carolina at the junction of U.S. 21 and 301, 44 miles south of Columbia; the gardens can be found on U.S. 301, about 1 mile south of downtown Orangeburg. For further information, write to the Dept. of Parks, P.O. Box 1321, Orangeburg, SC 29115. Tel.: 803-534-6376.

## PINESVILLE: MIDDLETON PLACE

The first major landscaped garden in America and a National Historic Landmark, Middleton Place today provides an authentic representation of an eighteenth-century plantation and gardens. Designed to emphasize the natural beauty of the area, the gardens consist of broad lawns bordered by clipped hedges, placid lakes, and a succession of landscaped terraces leading from the mansion down to the Ashley River below. Ransacked in the Revolutionary and Civil Wars, the plantation was restored in 1916, at which time thousands of azaleas, magnolias, and dogwoods were added to lend color to the grounds. Today, with its brilliant array in spring, Middleton hosts over a hundred thousand visitors yearly to its gardens and mansion-museum. Wheelchair access to garden, but not mansion. Gift shop. Restaurant. Hours: Garden open daily, 9–5; mansion, Tues.–Sun., 10:00–4:30. Fee: $10.50/adult (includes gardens and house tour), $3.50/children ages 4–12 (an additional $3.50 is charged if child takes house tour). Located on State Rte. 61, 14 miles northwest of Charleston. Address: Rte. 4, Charleston, SC 29407. Tel.: 803-556-6020.

## ROCK HILL: GLENCAIRN GARDEN

Named for a town in Scotland, this private garden was opened to the public in 1940. Deeded to the city of Rock Hill in 1958, the 6-acre garden today offers winding paths along terraced lawns, a reflecting pool and fountain, plus a waterfall, which cascades down stone basins to a lily pond. Plantings include thousands of azaleas (forty varieties), scores of flowering trees (magnolias, dogwoods, redbuds, crape myrtles), and wisteria, daffodils, periwinkles, and other flowering species. Peak bloom is in mid- to late April, during which time Rock Hill hosts its Come See Me week drawing a hundred and fifty thousand visitors. Glencairn also hosts art shows, concerts, and other performances throughout the year. Garden tour guides available upon request. Wheelchair accessible. Weddings held by prearrangement. Open daily, dawn to dusk. Fee: None. Location: Rock Hill is located in north-central South Carolina on I-77/U.S. 21; the garden is in the heart of Rock Hill, at Charlotte Ave. and Crest St. For further information, write to the Dept. of Parks and Recreation, City of Rock Hill, P.O. Box 11706, 155 Johnson St., Rock Hill, SC 29731. Tel.: 803-329-5620.

## SUMTER: SWAN LAKE IRIS GARDENS

This 100-acre park contains informal gardens in a natural setting and a 15-acre lake with white and black swans. The gardens feature the world's largest Japanese iris collection with millions of little blossoms during late May. The gardens also possess extensive azalea and camellia collections, plus lotus, jasmine, gardenia, wisteria, and other attractive flora. Special activities include the Iris Festival in mid-May, the Fall Fiesta of Arts in mid-October, and Christmas Lights in early December. The park has picnic areas, a pavilion, and tennis courts. Wheelchair accessible. Grounds available for weddings. Open daily, 8–sundown. Fees: None. Location: Sumter is located 41 miles east of Columbia in central South Carolina, at the junction of U.S. 15, 521, 76, and 378; the gardens are on W. Liberty St. For further information, write to the Dept. of Parks, Sumter, SC 29150. Tel.: 803-775-5811.

# *Tennessee*

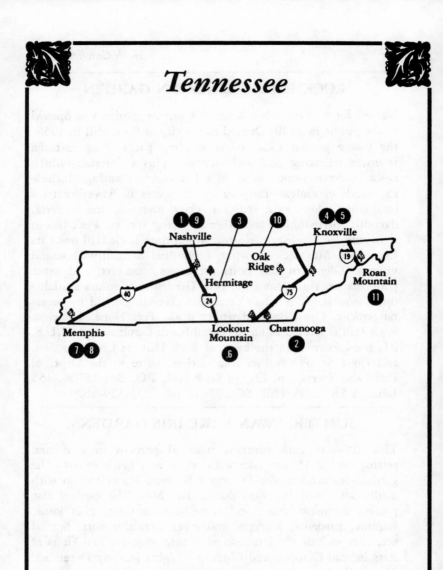

1. Nashville: Cheekwood
2. Chattanooga: Reflection Riding
3. Hermitage: The Hermitage
4. Knoxville: Blount Mansion
5. Knoxville: Racheff Park and Gardens
6. Lookout Mountain: Rock City Gardens
7. Memphis: Dixon Gallery and Gardens
8. Memphis: Memphis Botanic Garden
9. Nashville: Opryland Hotel Conservatory
10. Oak Ridge: University of Tennessee Arboretum
11. Roan Mountain: Roan Mountain State Park

# *Tennessee*

## "DON'T MISS" GARDENS

### NASHVILLE: CHEEKWOOD

*A joining of the garden arts and fine arts can be found at Cheekwood, where handsome grounds and excellent floral collections surround its Fine Arts Center housing nineteenth- and twentieth-century paintings and sculpture.*

Also known as the Tennessee Botanical Gardens and Fine Arts Center, Cheekwood was originally the estate of Mr. and Mrs. Leslie Cheek. The stately Georgian-style mansion was built around 1930 out of limestone quarried on the grounds, and was filled with artifacts from English estates. In 1957 the 55-acre estate was donated for the establishment of a center for the horticultural and fine arts—dual functions which continue to be splendidly fulfilled at Cheekwood.

The paths leading through the gardens and broad lawns offer fine vistas; there are terraced gardens with packed flower beds, lily ponds and waterfalls, hillsides covered with blossom-laden trees, wildflower walks and natural forest, statuary and fountains. Collections include roses, herbs, daffodils, perennials, wildflowers, and native plants, irises, peonies, azaleas, boxwood, magnolias, and dogwoods. There is a garden of scent and taste for the visually impaired, and a Japanese garden is at present under construction. Botanic Hall, with its tropical atrium and sculptured fountains, presents exhibits and flower shows on an ongoing basis. Next door are Cheekwood's four greenhouses with collections of orchids and camellias, as well as a notable replica of a Central American cloud forest. The Cheek mansion now serves as the Fine Arts Center and contains a permanent collection specializing in nineteenth- and twentieth-century American artists (Wyeth, Warhol, Grooms, Cloar, and others), plus collections of Worcester porcelain, Old Sheffield silver plate, and Oriental snuff bottles.

LOCATION: 8½ miles southwest of downtown Nashville, adjacent to Percy Warner Park; from the I-40 loop take U.S. 70 to the west, continue on U.S. 70 south, turn left on Belle Meade Blvd., right on Page Rd., right on Forrest Park Dr.

ADDRESS: Forrest Park Dr., Nashville, TN 37205.

TELEPHONE: 615-352-5310.

HOURS: Tues.–Sat., 9–5, and Sun., 1–5. Closed major holidays.

FEE: $2.50/adults, $1/children ages 7–17; group rates available.

TOURS: Group tours by prearrangement.

RESTAURANT: Pineapple Room Restaurant serves lunch, 11–2. Picnicking permitted.

SHOPS: Museum Shop contains gifts and collectibles, as well as books on gardening and art.

WHEELCHAIR ACCESS: Access to most of garden and most parts of buildings.

SPECIAL ACTIVITIES: A year-round schedule of classes and programs on gardening and the fine arts. Concerts, art, and garden exhibits also presented regularly.

TIPS: 1. Color is at its peak in spring when the redbuds, dogwoods, wildflowers, and spring bulbs burst into bloom. Good color also visible throughout summer and peaks again in the fall foliage season.
2. Cheekwood hosts several superb flower shows held annually by local garden societies: Camellia Show (early March), Daffodil Show (late March, early April), Rose Show (late May), Wildflower Week (late April), and Trees of Christmas (December).

# EXCELLENT GARDENS

## CHATTANOOGA: REFLECTION RIDING

A 300-acre nature preserve possessing an excellent variety of wildflowers and shrubs in an English landscape setting. Viewable by foot or car, the park features dramatic wildflowers from spring into autumn, coupled with azaleas, mountain laurels, rhododendrons, asters, ferns, and flowering trees. There is also a nature center offering displays, workshops, and educational programs for all ages. Open daily, Mon.–Sat., 9–5, and Sun., 1–5; closed holidays. Fee: $1.50/adults, $1/children ages 4–17 and seniors. Location: Chattanooga is located in southeast Tennessee; the garden is 4 miles southwest of downtown Chattanooga; take I-24 to Brown's Ferry Rd., go south toward Tiftonia, turn left onto Cummings Hwy. (U.S. 41), turn right onto Garden Rd. Address: Chattanooga Nature Center, Rte. 4, Garden Road, Chattanooga, TN 37409. Tel.: 615-821-1160.

## HERMITAGE: THE HERMITAGE

This historic home of Andrew Jackson, complete with its 1-acre period garden, is now caringly maintained by The Ladies Hermitage Association. The garden was designed for President Jackson's wife, Rachel, and possesses over fifty varieties of flowering plants and herbs, including hickory and magnolia trees planted during Jackson's lifetime. Group tours by prearrangement. Wheelchair accessible. Open daily, 9–5; closed Thanksgiving and Christmas. Fee: $3.75/adults, $1.25/children ages 6–13; group rates available. Located about 12 miles east of downtown Nashville, just off Lebanon Pike (U.S. 70). Address: 4580 Rachel's La., Hermitage, TN 37076. Tel.: 615-889-2941.

## KNOXVILLE: BLOUNT MANSION

Blount Mansion was built in 1792 and was the site of the drafting of the Tennessee State Constitution. In 1960 the garden was redesigned with the help of Colonial Williamsburg's landscape architects in the Colonial Revival style, the style in fashion in the late eighteenth century. Today the garden consists of formal beds of herbs, wildflowers, annuals, and perennials, with a lengthy boxwood walk serving as the central axis. The garden is very colorful in spring, during which time it offers special activities as part of Knoxville's annual Dogwood Arts Festival. The Blount Mansion, a Registered National Historic Landmark, is furnished in the eighteenth-century manner and provides an interesting look into frontier life as lived by the prosperous. Open Apr.–Oct., Tues.–Sat., 9:30–5:00, and Sun., 2–5; Nov.–Mar., Tues.–Sat. only, 9:30–4:30. Fee for house and garden: $2.25/adults, $.75/children ages 6–12; group rates available. Located in central Knoxville, just off I-40. Address: 200 W. Hill Ave., P.O. Box 1703, Knoxville, TN 37901. Tel.: 615-525-2375.

## KNOXVILLE: RACHEFF PARK AND GARDENS

As owner of the Knoxville Iron Company, Ivan Racheff donated this 3-acre piece of property to the Tennessee Federation of Garden Clubs, Inc., in 1970, providing a welcome patch of greenery in Knoxville's industrial area. The garden is primarily naturalistic in design and is best known for its thousands of daffodils and tulips in April, when it serves as a featured garden during Knoxville's annual Dogwood Arts Festival. Other displays include a wildflower garden, butterfly garden, cutting garden, and a memorial wall and fountain. An annual plant and craft sale is held in early October, and in December the Old Fashioned Greens Tea. Group tours welcome. Gift shop. Classes and programs on gardening topics. Open Mon.–Fri., 9–4; also open weekends during the April festival. Fee: None. Located at 1943 Tennessee Ave. For further information, write to Tennessee Federation of Garden Clubs, Inc., 6905 Cresthill Dr., Knoxville, TN 37919.

## LOOKOUT MOUNTAIN: ROCK CITY GARDENS

Initially developed as a private garden with a dramatic backdrop of sheer cliffs and stunning vistas, Frieda and Garnet Carter opened their gardens to the public in 1932. Over the years a variety of tourist displays have been added, including gift shops, restaurant, deli, Fudge Kitchen, Deer Park, New Street Fair, and for children, the Fairyland Caverns and Mother Goose Village. The garden itself contains four hundred different wildflowers and shrubs native to this mountainous area. In spring, azaleas, rhododendrons, and flowering trees create sparkling color amid the fantastic rock outcroppings. Autumn color is also impressive. The vistas from Lover's Leap and other viewing points are outstanding. On a clear day, seven states can be seen from one overlook (North Carolina, South Carolina, Florida, Alabama, Tennessee, Kentucky, Virginia). A special visitor's guide is available for the disabled. June 21–Labor Day, open 8–sundown; the rest of the year, 8:30–sundown; closed Christmas. Fee: $6/adults, $3/children ages 6–12; group rates by prearrangement. Located 5 miles west of Chattanooga; take I-24, follow Lookout Mtn. exit to State Rte. 58 to Lookout Mtn. Address: Rock City, Dept. B, Lookout Mtn., TN 37350. Tel.: 404-820-2531.

## MEMPHIS: DIXON GALLERY AND GARDENS

This superb 17-acre city garden was designed in the naturalistic style to complement the Georgian home of Margaret and Hugo Dixon. The garden consists of native woodland, open terraces, and vistas, underplantings of azaleas and dogwoods, plus intimate flower beds and gardens to provide color year-round. There is also a greenhouse containing over two hundred varieties of camellias. The Dixon museum possesses collections of Impressionist and Post-Impressionist paintings, and English art and antiques. Wheelchair accessible. Group tours by prearrangement. Open Tues.–Sat., 11–5, and Sun., 1–5. Fee: $1/adults, $.50/students and seniors; admission free on Tues. and during special lectures or tours. Located on Park Ave. between Getwell and Perkins, across from Audubon Park, about 6 miles east of downtown Memphis. Address: 4339 Park Ave., Memphis, TN 38117. Tel.: 901-761-5250.

## MEMPHIS: MEMPHIS BOTANIC GARDEN

Located in Audubon Park, this 87-acre garden contains a host of notable displays. Perhaps best known for its 4-acre Japanese garden surrounding Lake Biwa, Memphis Botanic also offers the 7-acre Ketchum Memorial Iris Garden, a 4-acre wildflower garden, and a 10-acre arboretum. Other attractions include magnolia, dogwood, and azalea trails, a fern glen, and gardens of cacti, perennials, conifers, dahlias, and daylilies. Peak bloom is in spring; good color also in fall. The conservatory at the Goldsmith Civic Garden Center has a tropical plant collection, a camellia house, and also produces seasonal displays. The Garden Center contains a library, gift shop, and meeting rooms available to garden clubs and plant societies. Educational programs are scheduled throughout the year. Wheelchair accessible. Weddings and receptions by prearrangement. Outdoor gardens open daily, 8:30–sundown; Garden Center open Mon.–Fri., 9:00–4:30, and Sat.–Sun., 1:00–4:30. Fee: None. Located in Audubon Park between Park and Southern Aves., just east of Memphis State University, about 6 miles east of downtown Memphis. Address: 750 Cherry Rd., Memphis, TN 38117. Tel.: 901-685-1566.

## NASHVILLE: OPRYLAND HOTEL CONSERVATORY

Winding paths and elevated walkways meander through the 2-acre, glass-roofed interior of the new Opryland Hotel. The conservatory contains over ten thousand plants representing 216 species, as well as terraces, statuary, ravines, rocky coves, a waterfall, and a 72-foot sculpture fountain. Wheelchair accessible. Restaurant and lounge. Weddings by prearrangement. Fashion shows, art exhibits and musical programs are frequently held here. Open daily, all hours. Fee: None. Address: 2802 Opryland Dr., Nashville, TN 37214. Tel.: 615-899-6600.

## OAK RIDGE: UNIVERSITY OF TENNESSEE ARBORETUM

The University of Tennessee Arboretum is a 250-acre educational and research center containing over seven hundred species and varieties of flora, including major collections of azaleas, magnolias, dogwoods, hollies, willows, and pines. There are 7½ miles of roads and 2½ miles of trails. Good color in spring and fall. Group tours by prearrangement. Open daily to sunset. Fee: None. Location: Oak Ridge is located 24 miles west of Knoxville on State Rte. 62; the arboretum can be found just off Rte. 62, 2 miles from the American Museum of Science and Energy. Address: University of Tennessee Agricultural Experimental Station Arboretum, 901 Kerr Hollow Rd., Oak Ridge, TN 37830. Tel.: 615-483-8721.

## ROAN MOUNTAIN: ROAN MOUNTAIN STATE PARK

Located near the top of the 6,300-foot mountain is perhaps North America's finest display of Catawba rhododendrons. Early travelers reported rhododendron thickets so dense they were impassable. Peak bloom is in mid-June. Open daily, dawn to dusk. Fee: None. Location: The town of Roan Mountain is located on U.S. 19E in eastern Tennessee, 6 miles west of the North Carolina state line and 20 miles southeast of Elizabethton; the state park can be found on State Rte. 143, about 6 miles south of the town. For further information, write to State of Tennessee, Dept. of State Parks, 701 Broadway, Nashville, TN. Tel.: 615-742-6667.

# Vermont

## EXCELLENT GARDENS

### BURLINGTON: UNIVERSITY OF VERMONT AGRICULTURAL STATION

Containing a wide array of shrubs, trees, and flowering plants, this 100-acre research center has as its main goal the testing of all manner of flora for cold-climate hardiness. There is an All-America Selections annual garden, as well as crab apples, lilacs, daylilies, fruit trees, and vegetables. Open warm months, Mon.–Fri., 8–4. Fee: None. Located on State Rte. 7 (Pearl St.). Address: Burlington, VT. Tel.: 802-658-9166.

### LONDONDERRY: THE COOK'S GARDEN

Two acres of trial gardens, the Cook's Garden is owned and managed by a private enterprise selling mail-order plants, seeds, and supplies. Located on a hillside farm in the Green Mountains, it is utilized for developing and testing a wide variety of salad crops, vegetables, fruits, herbs, and flowering plants. The public is invited to visit, and seeds, plants, produce, jams and jellies, maple syrup, and garden supplies can be purchased. Open May–Oct., Tues.–Sun., 10–6. Fee: None. Location: Londonderry is located in southern Vermont at the junction of State Rtes. 11 and 100; the Cook's Garden can be found off Landgrove Rd., 2 miles west of Londonderry; follow the signs from State Rte. 11. For further information, write to The Cook's Garden, P.O. Box 65, Londonderry, VT 05148. Tel.: 802-824-3400.

### NORTH BENNINGTON: THE PARK-MCCULLOUGH HOUSE

This Victorian estate has parklike lawns, flower-filled urns, and vine-covered trellises, plus a herb garden, colonial garden of blossoming annuals and perennials, vegetable garden, lily pool, and a greenhouse. The mansion house, listed in the National Register of Historic Places, was erected in 1865 and contains parquet floors, marble mantels, paintings, sculptures, and original furnishings. Other buildings include a children's playhouse and a stable with original carriages and sleighs. Garden classes,

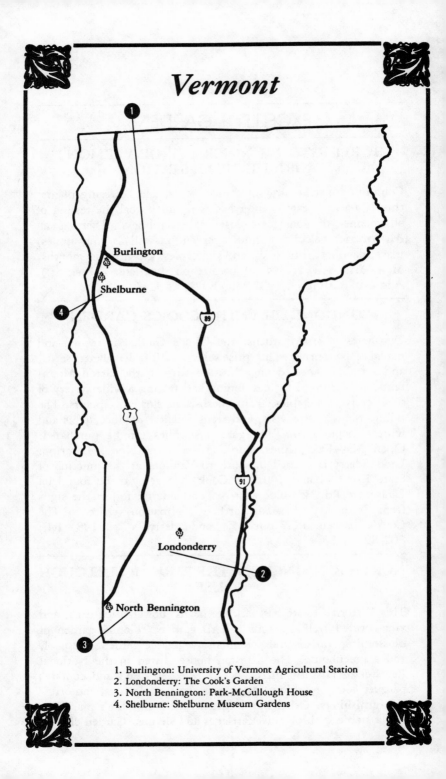

# Vermont

Burlington

Shelburne

89

7

91

Londonderry

2

North Bennington

3

1. Burlington: University of Vermont Agricultural Station
2. Londonderry: The Cook's Garden
3. North Bennington: Park-McCullough House
4. Shelburne: Shelburne Museum Gardens

lectures, seminars, concerts, and art exhibitions are offered on a regular basis. Special activities include an Open Gardens Day (June), October Festival Week for Children, Christmas Open House. Garden accessible to wheelchairs. Gift shop. Garden and house available for weddings and garden parties. Open late May to Oct., Sun.–Fri., 10–4, and Sat., 10–2. Check for current fees. Location: North Bennington is located on State Rte. 67 in the far southwest corner of Vermont, 4 miles above Bennington; the garden is on West St. at the top of the hill. Address: North Bennington, VT 05257. Tel.: 802-442-2747.

## SHELBURNE: SHELBURNE MUSEUM GARDENS

Vermont's most popular tourist attraction, with over 4 million visitors in 40 years, Shelburne Museum consists of thirty-five buildings offering fine collections of Americana (quilts, duck decoys, cigar store statuary, weathervanes, carousel animals, and other folk arts) on 45 carefully groomed acres. The gardens include a medicinal herb garden adjacent to the nineteenth-century apothecary shop, and a garden of culinary and dye plants next to the textile building. Best of all, however, is the lilac collection consisting of four hundred plants representing ninety varieties. In late May, a Lilac Sunday is held when the lilacs are at peak bloom. In addition, there are flowering trees, roses, and a small formal garden. This family attraction is given a top rating by the Michelin Guide. Open daily, mid-May–mid-Oct., 9–5; winter months, open Sun. only, 11–4. Fee: $9/adults, $3.50/children ages 6–15; group rates available. Located on U.S. 7, 7 miles south of Burlington. Address: Shelburne, VT 05482. Tel.: 802-985-3346.

# *Virginia*

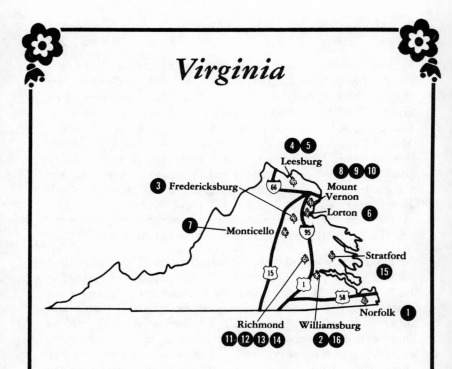

1. Norfolk: Norfolk Botanical Gardens
2. Williamsburg: Colonial Williamsburg
3. Fredericksburg: Kenmore
4. Leesburg: Morven Park
5. Leesburg: Oatlands
6. Lorton: Gunston Hall
7. Monticello: Monticello
8. Mount Vernon: Mount Vernon
9. Mount Vernon: River Farm
10. Mount Vernon: Woodlawn Plantation
11. Richmond: Agecroft Hall
12. Richmond: Bryan Park Azalea Gardens
13. Richmond: Maymount Foundation
14. Richmond: Virginia House
15. Stratford: Stratford Hall
16. Williamsburg: Carter's Grove Plantation

# *Virginia*

## "DON'T MISS" GARDENS

### NORFOLK: NORFOLK BOTANICAL GARDENS

*One of America's finest azalea displays, plus excellent collections of camellias, rhododendrons, and roses amid beautifully landscaped grounds.*

Begun as a WPA project in 1938, two hundred persons were employed to clear the 175 acres and plant four thousand azalea bushes. The azalea collection now numbers nearly a quarter million and serves as the basis for an annual Azalea Festival during the third week of April. This festival salutes the NATO Organizations, and its queens have included Lucy Baines Johnson, Linda Byrd Johnson, Tricia Nixon, and Susan Ford.

But Norfolk Botanical possesses much more than its azaleas; of equal interest are the award-winning rose garden that covers 3½ acres and contains 4,000 plants; the camellia collection of more than 750 varieties; and the four rhododendron gardens. More than 25,000 tulips blossom in the spring, and more than 50,000 annuals flower throughout summer. The Scented Garden offers the aromas of lavender, peppermint, bayberry, and others. Annual festivals and shows are held throughout the year. These include the Orchid Show (every other March), Camellia Show (mid-March), Shower of Flowers Show (every other April), Aquarium Show (September), Bird Show (October), and a Christmas Flower Show. There is also an annual Scottish Festival held the Fourth Saturday in June.

LOCATION: On Airport Rd. off Azalea Garden Rd., near the Norfolk International Airport, 6 miles northeast of downtown Norfolk.

ADDRESS: Botanical Gardens, Norfolk, VA 23518.

TELEPHONE: 804-853-6972.

HOURS: Daily, 8:30–sunset.

FEE: $1. Free for senior citizens of Norfolk.

TOURS: Narrated 30-minute tours by train or canal boat ($1.50).

RESTAURANT: Fast-food restaurant. Picnic area with tables and grills.

SHOPS: Gift shop.

WHEELCHAIR ACCESS: Accessible. Wheelchairs available.

SPECIAL ACTIVITIES: The garden serves as a training ground for horticultural students. There is a nineteen-hundred-volume library. Courses, workshops, and lectures are offered to the public throughout the year. Weddings held by prearrangement.

---

TIPS: 1. Don't miss the azaleas which peak Apr.–May.
2. The boat or train tours are particularly helpful in getting oriented to the garden before setting out on its 12 miles of paths.
3. An excellent view can be obtained from the observation tower.
4. Norfolk Botanical has a program through which one may donate a tree or bench (with a plaque) in memory of a loved one.

---

## WILLIAMSBURG: COLONIAL WILLIAMSBURG

*America's most authentic and most extensive colonial gardens— over one hundred large and small gardens that serve as an essential part of the world-famous Williamsburg restoration.*

The restoration of Colonial Williamsburg was begun in 1926. Its first buildings opened to the public in 1932. Its creators (The Reverend William Goodwin provided the motivation, John D. Rockefeller, Jr., the money) spared no effort in unearthing the original plan of the town through archeological digs, library searches, and examinations of historical documents and private letters. This research provided information on everything from the sizes of the lots and designs of the gardens to such particulars as the forms and materials of the fences. History was also on the restorers' side because when Williamsburg ceased being the capital of Virginia in 1781, it also ceased to grow. Eighty-eight original buildings still stood when the restoration began, and many streets and public green remained very much as they were when Thomas Jefferson attended nearby William and Mary College.

It was the same William and Mary—the Dutch sovereigns who were invited to rule England in 1689—whose tastes are reflected in today's gardens at Williamsburg. Both William and Mary had an eye for horticulture. They refashioned many of the royal gardens in the Dutch style of sections bordered by clipped hedges, topiary (shaped bushes), and flower designs. Witness, for example, the 10 acres of gardens at the Governor's Palace (the name "Palace" was given by the citizens who disdained the kingly extravagance of the royal governor). If this garden had been designed in the eighteenth instead of the seventeenth century, we would see the later English "naturalized" garden of broad lawns and open vistas. Instead we have a number of small gardens separated by hedges, a multitude of round or geometrically shaped bushes, a maze, a bowling green, a ballroom garden for entertaining visiting dignitaries, formal beds of tulips and other colonial flowers, and a maze designed by Thomas Jefferson (after the one at Hampton Court, created in the sixteenth century for Henry VIII and still viewable today).

In all, 90 of Colonial Williamsburg's 175 acres are given over to gardens large and small. All of the plantings are of species known in the 1700s when Williamsburg was one of America's foremost "green country towns." Unlike America's other country-town cities of the same era (Philadelphia perhaps being the most famous), the Williamsburg that a million visitors a year see today varies little from the town Jefferson, Henry, and Washington inhabited.

---

LOCATION: On U.S. 64 and 60, midway between Richmond and Norfolk.

ADDRESS: P.O. Box C, Williamsburg, VA 23187.

TELEPHONE: 804-229-1000.

HOURS: Visitor center open 8:30–8:00; most buildings open 9–5, later in summer.

FEE: Basic admission is $14.50/adult, $7.25/children ages 6–12; price varies according to specific tour. An unlimited, 1-year pass is about 50% higher.

TOURS: No garden tours. The Governor's Palace is viewed by guided tour.

RESTAURANT: Several restaurants, taverns, bakeries.

SHOPS: Dozens of shops provide a wide vareity of gifts, crafts, and mementos. Bookstore at the visitor center.

WHEELCHAIR ACCESS: Access to most of historic area. Ask for free brochure guide for the handicapped.

SPECIAL ACTIVITIES: Concerts, plays, parades, dances, exhibitions, and evening programs every week. A Williamsburg Garden Symposium is held each spring.

---

TIPS: 1. In addition to the Governor's Palace Gardens, don't miss Williamsburg's other excellent early American gardens: the George Wythe House, the Norton-Cole House, the Orlando Jones House, the Prentis House, the Alexander Craig House, the Powell-Waller House, and the recently completed Lila Acheson Wallace Garden adjacent to the DeWitt Wallace Decorative Arts Gallery.

2. Peak garden periods are spring (tulips, daffodils, and other spring flowers) and autumn (excellent fall foliage). Summer can be quite hot and humid—and crowded.

3. A historical film (recommended), *Williamsburg—The Story of a Patriot,* is shown at the Visitors' Center.

4. Colonial Williamsburg is America's foremost colonial restoration. For young and old, it is an excellent experience in American history. Although it is more expensive than most gardens, one can easily spend a full day or more in seeing its many attractions.

---

# EXCELLENT GARDENS

---

## FREDERICKSBURG: KENMORE

Built in 1752, Kenmore was the home of Betty Washington, the only sister of George Washington. The extensive gardens and grounds were gradually sold off or became overgrown until 1929, when the Garden Club of Virginia began its excellent restoration. It was to finance the work that Historic Garden Week of Virginia was begun and private gardens opened to the public. This has since become an annual event, which has benefited many Virginia gardens. The Kenmore Garden covers an entire city block. It is a naturalized garden with lawns, tree-lined paths (allees), ancient boxwood hedges, a flower garden, an herb garden, and two domed pavilions. Only plant materials known to have existed in the eighteenth century are used. The manor contains period furnishings, porcelains, silver, and portraits. Tea and gingerbread are served in the kitchen to all guests as part of the house tour. Open Apr.–Oct., daily, 9–5; Nov.–Mar., daily, 9–4; closed Dec. 24, 25, 31, Jan. 1. Fee: $2.50/adult, $1/children ages 6–16; group rates available. Location: Fredericksburg is located on I-95, 48 miles south of Washington, DC; from I-95 take State Rte. 3 (William St.) east

to Washington Ave. Address: 1201 Washington Ave., Fredericksburg, VA 22401. Tel.: 703-373-3381.

---

## LEESBURG: MORVEN PARK

Morven Park is an eighteenth-century, 1,200-acre estate known
for its elegant Greek Revival mansion and its boxwood garden.
The garden area consists of lawns and stately trees, extensive
boxwood hedges and parterres, seasonal flowers, and a reflecting
pool. The mansion, which started as a farmhouse in 1781,
contains interesting antiques, artwork, and sixteenth-century
tapestries. Also in the mansion is the Museum of Hounds and
Hunting, which offers artifacts, paintings, and a 20-minute film
tracing the history of fox hunting. On the grounds is a carriage
museum with a collection of over a hundred carriages, carts, and
an antique fire engine dating from the turn of the century.
Group tours by prearrangement. Wheelchair access to garden
and first floor of mansion. Picnicking. Weddings held in garden
by prearrangement. Open Memorial Day–Labor Day, Tues.–
Sat., 10–5, and Sun., 1–5; open weekends only in May and
Sept.; groups can visit during other months by prearrangement.
Fee: $3.50/adult, $3/seniors, $1.75/children; group rates avail-
able. Location: Leesburg is located on State Rte. 7, 35 miles
northwest of Washington, DC. Address: Rte. 3, Box 5, Leesburg,
VA 22075. Tel.: 703-777-2414.

---

## LEESBURG: OATLANDS

Built in 1804, this magnificent 260-acre estate has terraced
English-style gardens, with 150-year-old boxwood spiced by a
succession of blossoms (tulips, daffodils, perennials) from spring
through fall. The impressive mansion, a National Historic
Landmark, is filled with period pieces and antiques. There is a
gift shop and a mini-menagerie including llamas, goats, and
donkeys. Group tours by prearrangement. Weddings, receptions,
group activities by prearrangement. Open daily, Apr.–Dec.
15—check for hours. Fee: $4/adult, $3/seniors or children ages
7–18; group rates available. Location: Leesburg is located on
State Rte. 7, 35 miles northwest of Washington, DC; Oatlands
can be found 6 miles south of Leesburg on U.S. 15. Address:
Rte. 2, Box 352, Leesburg, VA 22075. Tel.: 703-777-3174.

## LORTON: GUNSTON HALL

Gunston Hall was the home of George Mason, who in 1776 drafted the Virginia Declaration of Rights, which later served as model for the Bill of Rights. Mason designed Gunston Hall—including its elaborate gardens with extensive parterres and boxwood hedges. In 1949 the estate was bequeathed to the Commonwealth of Virginia, to be managed by the National Society of the Colonial Dames of America. The gardens have been restored under the care of the Garden Club of Virginia. In this restoration only plants of the colonial era have been used. With their flower parterres and boxwood allee, these gardens bear some resemblance to those at Williamsburg. Both are in the eighteenth-century Dutch-English style. Most historic of all is the boxwood hedge—220 years old, 12 feet high, and almost a football field in length. This impressive walkway, paved with crushed oyster shells, forms the main axis of the garden from the mansion out toward the Potomac ½ mile beyond, where sailing ships once docked to load Mason's crops for Europe. Graceful gazebos at the lower end of the garden provide fine views of the parterre garden, deer park area, and river. There is also a nature trail through woodlands to the river where many species of birds and wildflowers (and sometimes a deer at dusk) can be seen. The Gunston Hall mansion has been faithfully restored with furnishings dating from before 1792, many belonging to Mason himself. Wheelchair access to lower floor of house; because garden paths are paved with cracked shells, wheelchair mobility is difficult. Gift shop. Open daily, 9:30–5:00; closed Christmas. Fee $3.00/adult, $2.50/seniors; $1/children 6–15; group rates available. Located 20 miles south of Washington, DC; take U.S. 1 south, turn east onto State Rte. 242 and follow to Gunston Hall. Address: Lorton, VA 22079. Tel.: 703-550-9220.

## MONTICELLO: MONTICELLO

Ever the architect, Thomas Jefferson designed these gardens as he prepared to step down from the presidency. "I am fond of placing handsome plants or fragrant, those of mere curiosity I do not aim at." Jefferson's garden consisted of pleasant walks over terraces and lawns, along flower beds and borders. The garden fell into decay after its founder's death, but in 1939 the Garden Club of Virginia undertook its restoration. Combined with a tour of the famous house, the gardens offer an enjoyable and historically fascinating experience. Open daily, Mar.–Oct., 8–5, and Nov.–Feb., 9:00–4:30; closed Christmas. Fee: $5/adult, $1/ children ages 6–11. Location: Charlottesville is located in central Virginia on U.S. 64 and 29, about 70 miles northwest of Richmond; Monticello can be found 2 miles southeast of downtown Charlottesville just off State Rte. 53. Address: Monticello, VA. For further information, write to Monticello, P.O. Box 316, Charlottesville, VA 22902. Tel.: 804-295-2657.

## MOUNT VERNON: MOUNT VERNON

The original garden was designed and planted under the watchful eyes of George Washington. After his death, the gardens gradually fell into disrepair until rescued in 1853 by the Mount Vernon Ladies' Association of the Union. Today the superb restoration of the Mount Vernon Gardens serves as a premier example of eighteenth-century landscaping. The house opens onto a courtyard, with a bowling green beyond. The Serpentine Walk meanders amid graceful trees (ten of which survive from colonial times) and colorful underplantings. The rose garden, restored in 1934, contains species available during Washington's life. All plant materials used in the impressive kitchen garden and flower garden are descendants or close relatives of those mentioned in Washington's diaries or in publications of the late eighteenth century. The Green House, an orangery, used for the winter care of citrus and certain greens, has been faithfully reconstructed. Of course, after seeing the garden, you will want to visit the great man's mansion, plantation, and tomb. A sales shop is located near the flower garden offering plants, seeds, film, and mementoes. Open daily, Mar.–Oct., 9–5, and Nov.– Feb., 9–4. Fee: $4/adult, $3.50/senior, $2/children ages 6–11; there is an open house (no fee) on the third Monday in Feb. Located on State Rte. 235 just off U.S. 1, at the south terminus of the Mt. Vernon Memorial Hwy., 8 miles south of Alexandria and 16 miles south of downtown Washington. Address: Mount Vernon, VA 22121. Tel.: 703-780-2000.

## MOUNT VERNON: RIVER FARM

Originally settled in the seventeenth century and later owned and worked by George Washington, River Farm became the headquarters of the American Horticultural Society in 1973.

Today, River Farm offers a collection of display gardens including an Idea Garden, with beds maintained in cooperation with the American Dahlia Society, the American Hemerocallis Society, the American Ivy Society, the American Iris Society, the American Marigold Society, the Cactus and Succulent Society, the Dominion Chrysanthemum Society, and the North American Lily Society. Additional displays include a dwarf fruit tree orchard, a water garden, a shade garden, a wildflower meadow, a woodland walk, a ballroom yard, a demonstration fruit orchard, and a rose garden with over three hundred All-America Rose Selections bushes. The historic house, part of which dates back to the original 1757 structure, has been refurbished with antiques and reproductions from the colonial era. Group tours and slide shows by prearrangement; self-guided tour brochure available upon request. Special activities include Spring Open House, Spring Lecture Series, Autumn Festival, Christmas Open House, and other programs and lectures. Main house may be rented for horticulturally related functions. Established in 1922 for the furthering of horticulture in the United States, the American Horticultural Society promotes plant conservation, educational programs, and garden tours throughout the country. The American Horticultural Society also specializes in answering questions from amateur and professional gardeners. River Farm is open Mon.–Fri., 8:30–5:00; closed Sat., Sun., and holidays. Fee: None (Adopt-a-Plant program for those wishing to make donations). Located at 7931 East Boulevard Dr., just off the George Washington Memorial Pkwy, east of Alexandria on the way to Mount Vernon. For further information, write to American Horticultural Society, P.O. Box 0105, Mount Vernon, VA 22121. Tel.: 703-768-5700.

## MOUNT VERNON: WOODLAWN PLANTATION

Originally part of Mount Vernon, Woodlawn Plantation and its 20-acre garden have been carefully restored. The parterre gardens contain old-fashioned roses, and there are nature trails through native woodlands. Peak bloom is in late May. Group tours by prearrangement. Wheelchair accessible. Open daily, 9:30–4:30; closed Thanksgiving, Dec. 25, and Jan. 1. Fee: $4/adult, $3/children under 18. Located on U.S. 1, just past Mount Vernon, 9 miles south of Alexandria and 17 miles south of downtown Washington. Address: 9000 Richmond Hwy., Mount Vernon, VA 22121. Tel.: 703-557-7881.

## RICHMOND: AGECROFT HALL

Built in the late 1400s, this authentic Tudor mansion was transported to the United States in 1926 and reconstructed on the banks of the James River. To augment the manor, a period garden was developed, including an excellent herb garden using only those species known to exist in Elizabethan England. The 23-acre grounds also include a sunken garden, a knot garden, a formal flower garden, and several pleasant walks. The manor is filled with furnishings and art of the Tudor era. Group tours by prearrangement. Open Tues.–Fri., 10–4, and Sat.–Sun., 2–5. Fee: $2/adult, $1.50/seniors, $1/students; group rate available. Located in the Windsor Farms area, east of downtown Richmond, just off U.S. 195; take Cary St. west, turn left on Canterbury Rd., which curves into Sulgrave Rd. Address: 4305 Sulgrave Rd., Richmond, VA 23221. Tel.: 804-353-4241.

## RICHMOND: BRYAN PARK AZALEA GARDENS

Located in this large city park is a 17-acre area packed with over forty-five thousand azalea bushes (more than fifty species). Begun in 1952 with small cuttings from other public and private gardens, the Bryan Park azaleas are a show in themselves from mid-April to mid-May, attracting two hundred thousand visitors during that time. A favorite feature is a huge, 35-foot cross of white and red azaleas. Other blooms include camellias in early spring, crab apples and dogwoods in mid-spring, crape myrtles and southern magnolias in summer, and American hollies bright with red berries in fall. The grounds can be viewed by foot or car. Wheelchair accessible. Picnicking. Gardens available for weddings. Open daily, dawn to dusk. Fee: $2/car, weekends and holidays in spring and summer only; other times, free. Located in Bryan Park at the end of Bellevue Ave. off Hermitage Rd., 5 miles north of downtown Richmond. For further information, write to the Dept. of Parks, City of Richmond, 900 E. Broad St., Richmond, VA 23219. Tel.: 804-780-8785.

## RICHMOND: MAYMOUNT FOUNDATION

Listed with the National Register of Historic Places, this estate garden was developed in the early 1900s by Major and Mrs. James Dooley. Today, the handsome 105-acre garden offers quality color in all seasons in the form of tulips, wisteria, candytufts, roses, annuals, perennials, dahlias, crocuses, and osmanthus. Specialty gardens include an Italian garden with statuary and water cascades, a daylily garden (123 varieties), an herb garden, an English courtyard garden, a rhododendron row with plants over 30 feet tall, and over two hundred species of native and exotic trees, many rare. Of particular merit is the 6-acre award-winning Japanese stroll garden with tea house, pond with koi, bog area, waterfalls, and a meditation area. The grounds also contain a Victorian mansion filled with the Dooley's collections of furnishings and fine arts. There is also a carriage collection from the late nineteenth and early twentieth century, and carriage rides through the grounds are available. The Children's Farm has bison, bears, racoons, beavers, elk and deer, as well as barnyard animals. Picnicking permitted. Snack bar. Gift shop. Wheelchair accessible. Group tours by prearrangement. Garden open Mar.–Oct., daily, 10–7; Nov.–Feb., daily, 10–5. Check for mansion hours. Fee: None for garden; $2.50 donation requested for mansion. Address: 1700 Hampton St., Richmond, VA 23220. Tel.: 804-358-7166.

## RICHMOND: VIRGINIA HOUSE

Owned and operated by the Virginia Historical Society, Virginia House possesses 1½ acres of rose, azalea, perennial, and water gardens. There is a fine view of the James River, and in spring over 2,500 bulbs and 1,500 annuals bring color to the garden. The house is an English Tudor manor dating back to 1565 (many of its stones are actually from the Priory of the Holy Sepulchre, 1125) which was brought here and reassembled in the 1920s. Open to individuals and groups by appointment only (call at least 2 days in advance): Mon.–Sat., 10–4, and Sun., 1–4. Fee: $1.50/adult, $.75/children under 12. Location: See directions to Agecroft Hall, located nearby. Address: 4301 Sulgrave Rd. (near Wakefield Rd.), Richmond, VA 23221. Tel.: 804-353-4251.

## STRATFORD: STRATFORD HALL

Built in the 1720s, Stratford Hall was the birthplace of Robert E. Lee, as well as two signers of the Declaration of Independence (Richard Henry Lee and Francis Lightfoot Lee). Today it offers an authentic example of a colonial plantation, including two garden areas, fine vistas, and a woodland trail. The East Garden, restored in the 1930s by the Garden Club of Virginia, represents a typical eighteenth-century terraced English garden, with flower parterres outlined by English boxwood, and several flowering trees (cherries, magnolias, crape myrtles). The West Garden possesses beds of herbs, vegetables, and flowers using only plant materials known to have grown in the colonial period. Other features include a reproduced period orchard, a large grape arbor, and wildflowers along woodland trails. To the north of Stratford Hall is a view of the 6-mile-wide Potomac. Stratford Hall itself is filled with historical furnishings such as portraits, antiques, and a 250-year-old plantation kitchen. Guided tours through the Hall. Gift shop. Open daily, 9–5; closed Christmas. Fee: $3/adult, $1/children. Located on State Rte. 214, just off State Rte. 3, 6 miles west of the town of Montross, 60 miles northeast of Richmond and 90 miles southeast of Washington. Address: Stratford, VA 22558. Tel.: 804-493-8038.

---

# WILLIAMSBURG: CARTER'S GROVE PLANTATION

One of the foremost homes of the colonial period, this handsome brick mansion (built in 1750) was once part of a plantation of more than 300,000 acres. Today the grounds are still extensive (more than 700 acres) and contain an annual flower garden, vegetable and herb gardens of the period, and lovely vistas to the James River. The mansion (viewed by guided tour) is a living museum of colonial life, owned and operated by the Colonial Williamsburg Foundation. The Reception Center provides an introductory film, exhibits, and a gift shop. Open daily, 9–5. Fee: $6/adults ($4 with a Colonial Williamsburg general admission ticket). Located on U.S. 60, 6 miles southeast of Williamsburg. For further information, write to the Colonial Williamsburg Foundation, P.O. Box C, Williamsburg, VA 23185. Tel.: 804-229-1000.

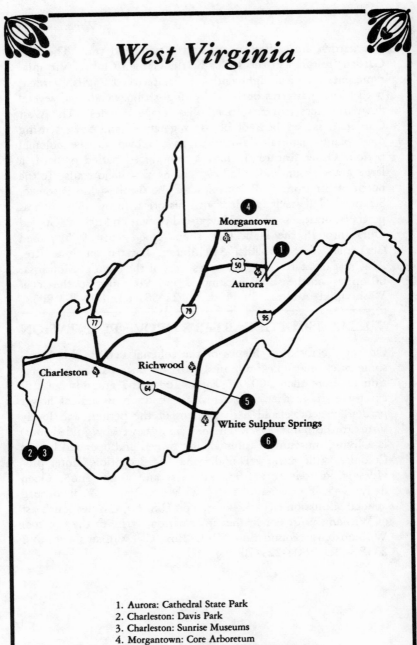

# West Virginia

1. Aurora: Cathedral State Park
2. Charleston: Davis Park
3. Charleston: Sunrise Museums
4. Morgantown: Core Arboretum
5. Richwood: Cranberry Glades Botanical Area
6. White Sulphur Springs: The Greenbrier

# West Virginia

## EXCELLENT GARDENS

### AURORA: CATHEDRAL STATE PARK

A rare and imposing stand of majestic hemlocks, with individual trees up to 90 feet high and 21 feet around. Vast underplantings of wildflowers (fifty species), ferns and mosses, and acres of rhododendron flowering June–July. Picnic area and playground. Open daily, 6 A.M.–10 P.M. Fee: None. Location: Aurora is located on U.S. 50, about 40 miles southeast of Morgantown, near the Maryland border. Address: Rte. 50, Aurora, WV 26705. Tel.: 304-735-3771.

### CHARLESTON: DAVIS PARK

This pleasant public park offers a gazebo and statuary, a rose garden containing several hundred bushes, and a broad green edged with shrubs and flowering plants. The park hosts many public activities including concerts, and is available to the public for educational or cultural activities. Open daily, daylight hours. Wheelchair accessible. Fee: None. Located along Lee and Capitol Sts. For further information, write: Municipal Beautification Dept., City of Charleston, P.O. Box 2749, Charleston, WV 25330. Tel.: 304-341-8000.

### CHARLESTON: SUNRISE MUSEUMS

A museum complex embodying two art museums, a historic home and a children's museum. On the grounds are rose and herb gardens, plus bedding flowers in season. Group tours of museums by prearrangement. Open Tues.–Sat., 10–5, and Sun., 2–5; closed Mon. and holidays. Fee: $2/adult, $1/students and seniors; no fee on Sun. Address: 746 Myrtle Rd., Charleston, WV 25314. Tel.: 304-344-8035.

### MORGANTOWN: CORE ARBORETUM

Located on the Evansdale campus of West Virginia University, this 75-acre arboretum contains over five hundred types of plants, including the largest Chinkapin Oak in the state. Wildflowers in abundance, hundreds of kinds of birds, many forms of wildlife, and fine views of the Monongahela River can be seen from the 3½ miles of trails. Open daily, dawn to dusk. Fee: None. For further information, write to the Dept. of Biology, P.O. Box 6057, West Virginia University, Morgantown, WV 26506. Tel.: 304-293-5201.

## RICHWOOD: CRANBERRY GLADES BOTANICAL AREA

This unique ecological area consisting of bog forest and grass-land is made accessible by a ½-mile boardwalk. Wild orchids, jasmine, rhododendrons, mosses, and several carnivorous plants can be seen, plus many rare varieties swept down from Canada some 10,000 years ago by advancing glaciers. Wheelchair accessible. Visitor Center offers exhibits, slide show. Guided tours June–Aug., Sun., 2 P.M.; group tours by prearrangement. Visitor Center open daily, 9:30–5:00; Memorial Day–Labor Day; open May and Sept., Sun. only. Fee: None. Location: Visitor Center located just off State Rtes., 39 and 150 in east-central West Virginia, between Mill Point and Richwood. Address: Cranberry Mountain Visitor Center, U.S. Forest Service, Richwood, WV 26261. Tel.: 304-653-4826 (summer) or 304-846-2695 (other months).

## WHITE SULPHUR SPRINGS: THE GREENBRIER

This five-star resort, located on 6,500 acres in the Allegheny Mountains, offers 12 acres of formal gardens and walkways. Plantings are arranged for maximum color from March through October. Flowering varieties include crocuses, hyacinths, daffodils, forsythias, tulips, lilacs, azaleas, rhododendrons, snow-balls, hydrangeas, and chrysanthemums. Flowering trees include cherries, magnolias, crab apples, dogwoods, and redbuds. Excellent boxwood adds definition to the garden. Weddings can be held in the garden by prearrangement. In addition, several very rare wild species such as box huckleberry, mountain pimpernel, and swordleaf phlox, are said to be found in the wooded areas 2 miles west of the hotel. Rhododendrons grow naturally here and light up the forest in April and May. In addition to the landscaped gardens, Greenbrier offers virtually everything a vacationer could desire: hotel rooms or guest houses or cottages, spa, indoor and outdoor tennis courts and pools, horseback riding, hiking and jogging trails, carriage or sleigh rides, a championship golf course, bowling, fishing, trap shooting, a shopping arcade, a medical diagnostic center, and special weekend programs and packages. There is also a large conference center. Gardens open daily, all hours. Garden fee: None. Located off I-64 in southeast West Virginia, just a few miles from the Virginia state line. Address: White Sulphur Springs, WV 24986. Tel.: 800-624-6070 or 304-536-1110.

# *Wisconsin*

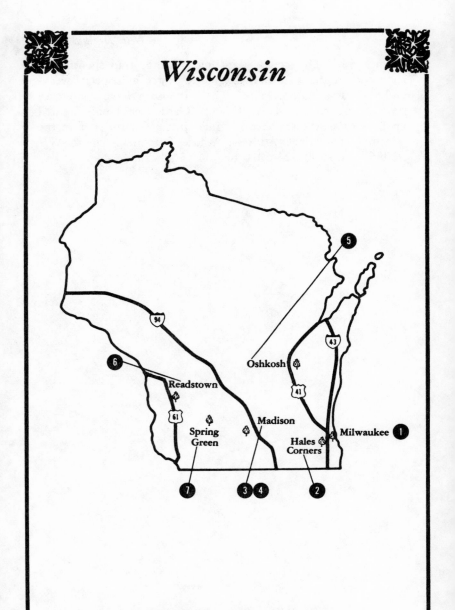

1. Milwaukee: Mitchell Park Horticultural Conservatory
2. Hales Corners: Boerner Botanical Gardens
3. Madison: Olbrich Gardens
4. Madison: University of Wisconsin at Madison Arboretum
5. Oshkosh: Paine Art Center and Arboretum
6. Readstown: Jones Arboretum and Botanical Gardens
7. Spring Green: House on the Rock

# *Wisconsin*

## "DON'T MISS" GARDENS

## MILWAUKEE: MITCHELL PARK HORTICULTURAL CONSERVATORY

*A superb conservatory consisting of three large domes offering beautiful displays year round.*

Each year over half a million visitors are attracted by the magnificent displays at the Mitchell Park Conservatory. Possessing a combination of permanent and rotating displays, the conservatory is best known for its Show Dome exhibitions. Five breathtaking shows (Winter, Easter, Summer, Fall, and Christmas) span the calendar. Each show uses different designs and props, so visitors see something entirely new season to season, year to year. The dome, nearly the size of half a football field and the height of a seven-story building, is packed with blossoms of every type and hue.

The other two domes contain permanent collections. The Tropical Dome holds over twelve hundred species of tropical plants, including over four hundred species of orchids and a fine collection of Hawaiian ferns. At least fifty types of plants are blooming in this dome every day of the year. The Arid Dome offers displays from five different desert regions across the globe. Over 300 species of cacti and hundreds of species of succulents, including 145 from Madagascar alone, can be seen here.

LOCATION: In Mitchell Park, just off 27th St. in central Milwaukee.
ADDRESS: 524 S. Layton Blvd., Milwaukee, WI 53215.
TELEPHONE: 414-649-9800.
HOURS: Open Sept.–May, Mon.–Fri., 9–5, and Sat.–Sun., 9–8; June–Aug., Sat.–Thurs., 9–8, and Fri., 9–5.
FEE: $2/adult; $1/children under age 18. Milwaukee County residents: free Mon.–Fri. before 10:30. Group rates available.
TOURS: By prearrangement. Staff available for questions, 10–3.
RESTAURANT: None on premises. Picnicking facilities in nearby park.
SHOPS: Extensive array of books, plants, artwork.
WHEELCHAIR ACCESS: Yes.

SPECIAL ACTIVITIES: Lectures and classes, art shows and concerts, special exhibits by local horticultural clubs. Conservatory available for weddings, receptions, social events, meetings.

TIPS: 1. Don't miss:
   a. Any of the Show Dome's five displays. The Christmas and Winter Shows are particularly stirring because of the contrast to the barrenness outdoors.
   b. In summer the gardens surrounding the conservatory are lovely, especially the sunken garden with its flower beds and lily pond.

# EXCELLENT GARDENS

## HALES CORNERS: BOERNER BOTANICAL GARDENS

This lovely outdoor park contains dazzling flower gardens and America's largest collection of flowering crab apple trees. Located in Whitnall Park, the gardens were built during the Great Depression by the CCC and WPA, and aided by the donation of plant materials from Arnold Arboretum. Today the gardens consist of a 400-acre arboretum and 40 acres of landscaped plantings including an All-America Rose Selections Garden (5,000 plants), All-America Selections Flower Trail Garden, an incredible lilac garden (over 1,100 plants, 400 species) bordered by 50,000 tulips (175 varieties), plus excellent collections of lilies, dahlias, chrysanthemums, begonias, and irises (456 kinds). The crab apple collection consists of 1,105 trees (237 species), and the herb garden (1,500 types) is one of the largest and finest of its kind. There is also a rock garden, a bog garden, a shrub mall, a perennial garden, and in the arboretum, hedge and turf displays, nature trails, wildflowers, and collections of evergreens and dwarf shrubs. The garden is patterned so that there is continual bloom from April to November. Peak bloom is April–May (tulips, lilacs, crab apples); the rose garden peak is June–August. Garden shop offers plants, gifts, books. Wheelchair access to most of garden. Full schedule of classes and lectures, Plant Doctor Clinics, art exhibits and crafts workshops, plant sales, concerts. Weddings and receptions by prearrangement. Open mid-Apr.–mid-Nov., 8–sunset. Fee: None.

Located in Whitnall Park, 8 miles southwest of downtown Milwaukee; take W. Forest Home Ave. (State Rte. 24), turn south onto 92nd St.; entrance is between Grange and College Aves. Address: 5879 S. 92nd St., Hales Corners, WI 53130. Tel.: 414-425-1130.

## MADISON: OLBRICH GARDENS

Still in the process of development, Olbrich Gardens packs a bountiful display within its 12 acres. Divided into a variety of gardens and flower beds, displays include an All-America Display Garden, All-America Rose Show Garden, a Dahlia Show Garden, plus daylily, hibiscus, chrysanthemum, herb, rock, and wildflower gardens. The flower beds also offer vast arrays of colorful annuals. Special exhibits include a Rose Show (June), a Dahlia Show (Labor Day weekend), a Chrysanthemum Show (November), and a Holiday Show (December). The Garden Center holds special plant sales, and includes a display gallery, library, and meeting and reception rooms. Wheelchair accessible. Picnic area. Open June–Sept., daily, 9–sunset; Oct.–May, Mon.–Fri., 9–5. Fee: None. Location: Madison is located in south-central Wisconsin, 77 miles west of Milwaukee; the garden can be found in Olbrich Park at the north end of Lake Monana, 2½ miles from downtown Madison. Address: 3330 Atwood Ave., Madison, WI 53704. Tel.: 608-226-4731.

## MADISON: UNIVERSITY OF WISCONSIN AT MADISON ARBORETUM

Each year nearly a quarter of a million people visit this 1,260-acre arboretum of diverse collections and displays. Unlike most arboreta, this one has grouped its natural collections into the form of plant *and* animal communities native to Wisconsin. Such communities include prairies (105 acres, three hundred species, plus the world's oldest restored tall-grass prairie), deciduous forests (120 acres with brilliant fall foliage), conifer forests, and wetlands (250 acres along Lake Wingra). In addition are 50 acres of horticultural gardens, which include excellent collections of viburnums (over eighty species), lilacs, and crab apples (one of the Midwest's finest). Free tours on Sundays, April to October; group tours by prearrangement. Exhibits, slide programs, guide books, and library, plus a full schedule of classes and lectures available at the McKay Center. Garden open daily 7 A.M.–10 P.M.; McKay Center open Mon.–Fri., 9–4, and Sat.–Sun., 12:30–4:00. Fee: None. Location: Madison is located in south-central Wisconsin, 77 miles west of Milwaukee; the arboretum can be found just off the Beltline Hwy. (U.S. 14 and 151), directly south of Lake Wingra. Address: 1207 Seminole Hwy., Madison, WI 53711. Tel.: 608-263-7888.

## OSHKOSH: PAINE ART CENTER AND ARBORETUM

The arboretum is actually a collection of display gardens including an alpine garden, a garden in white, and a wildflower garden filled with bulbs and primroses in spring. There is also a rose garden (150 bushes) and an herb garden, as well as a formal garden packed with Dutch bulbs in spring and flowering annuals and perennials in summer. Good color April into September; good autumn foliage into late October. The Paine Mansion contains antique furnishings and exceptional wood-carved walls and banister. Group tours by prearrangement; school groups free. Classes, activities, and exhibitions held regularly. Open Tues.–Sat., 10:00–4:30, and Sun., 1:00–4:30; closed Mon. and holidays. Fee: $2. Location: Oshkosh is located on Lake Winnebago in east-central Wisconsin, 85 miles north of Milwaukee; the arboretum can be found on Algoma Blvd. (State Rte. 110), just west of the junction with Congress Ave. (State Rte. 21). Address: 1410 Algoma Blvd., Oshkosh, WI 54901. Tel.: 414-235-4530.

## READSTOWN: JONES ARBORETUM AND BOTANICAL GARDENS

Established in 1974 to test the hardiness of trees, shrubs, and perennials in this climate, the Jones Arboretum and Botanical Garden offers collections of ferns, hostas, lilies, and wildflowers amid its 128 acres. There is also a perennial garden, a rose garden, an herb garden, and a Japanese garden. Guided tours by prearrangement. Wheelchair accessible. Many kinds of plants grown in the garden are available for purchase. Open May 15 to Sept. 15, daily, 8 A.M. to 8 P.M. Fee: None. Located on U.S. 14, about 3 miles west of Readstown and 90 miles west of Madison, 40 miles southeast of La Crosse. Address: Readstown, WI 54652. Tel.: 608-629-5553.

# SPRING GREEN: HOUSE ON THE ROCK

House On the Rock is Wisconsin's foremost tourist attraction, visited by over six hundred thousand people annually. Originally just a thirteen-room modernistic house built upon a 60-foot chimney rock 450 feet above Wyoming Valley, today there are also sculptured gardens consisting of boldly designed terraces, waterfalls, huge planters, and massed plantings. Flowers are selected for color, and varieties include tulips, daylilies, impatiens, marigolds, begonias, geraniums, hydrangeas, ferns, giant dahlias, daffodils, irises, foxgloves, primroses, blazing stars, plus perhaps the grandest collection of amaryllis anywhere. The grounds contain shops and restaurants, all uniquely designed to blend into the incredible scenery. Contained within are collections of Americana including organs, stained glass, Tiffany lamps, apothecary bottles, dolls, and the world's largest carousel. Open Apr.–mid-Nov., 8–dusk. Fee: $10/adults, $6/children ages 7–12, $1/children ages 4–6; group rates available. Location: Spring Green is located 40 miles west of Madison in south-central Wisconsin; the garden can be found on State Rte. 23, 8 miles south of Spring Green. Address: Spring Green, WI 53588. Tel.: 608-935-3639.

# PART TWO

# Garden Listings:

# Eastern

# Canada

# Maritime, Ontario, Quebec Provinces

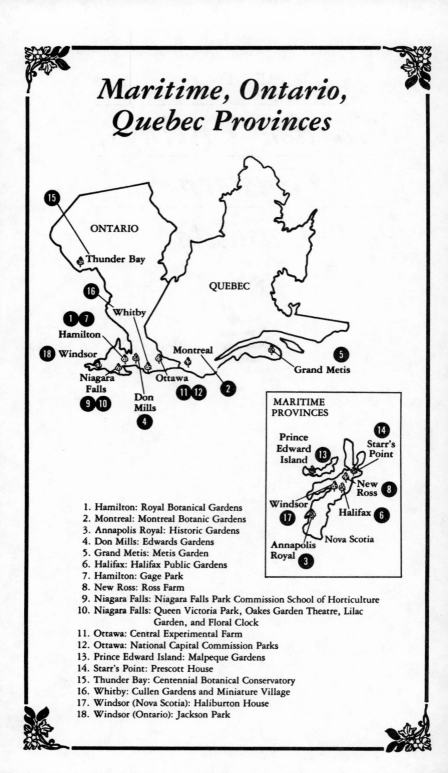

1. Hamilton: Royal Botanical Gardens
2. Montreal: Montreal Botanic Gardens
3. Annapolis Royal: Historic Gardens
4. Don Mills: Edwards Gardens
5. Grand Metis: Metis Garden
6. Halifax: Halifax Public Gardens
7. Hamilton: Gage Park
8. New Ross: Ross Farm
9. Niagara Falls: Niagara Falls Park Commission School of Horticulture
10. Niagara Falls: Queen Victoria Park, Oakes Garden Theatre, Lilac Garden, and Floral Clock
11. Ottawa: Central Experimental Farm
12. Ottawa: National Capital Commission Parks
13. Prince Edward Island: Malpeque Gardens
14. Starr's Point: Prescott House
15. Thunder Bay: Centennial Botanical Conservatory
16. Whitby: Cullen Gardens and Miniature Village
17. Windsor (Nova Scotia): Haliburton House
18. Windsor (Ontario): Jackson Park

# Maritime, Ontario, and Quebec Provinces

## "DON'T MISS" GARDENS

### HAMILTON, ONTARIO: ROYAL BOTANICAL GARDENS

*A top-flight research institution with many superb collections (irises, lilacs, orchids, tulips) presented via an array of individualized gardens spread across 2,000 acres of Ontario woodland.*

"Where art and science meet" is the Royal Botanical Gardens motto, and it fits. Established during the Great Depression on forgotten gravel pits, this garden today combines its dual role as tourist attraction and botanical garden with admirable skill. Since it is not one centralized garden but a collage of displays splashed across the Ontario countryside (to see them all, a car is a necessity), the gardens are best described in their component parts.

Hendrie Park contains thousands of modern and old-fashioned roses, a scented garden, a medicinal garden, a clematis collection, and a lavish trial garden. In the Laking Garden is perhaps North America's largest iris display (over a quarter of a million blossoms in season), hundred of types of peonies, followed in summer by colorful perennials of virtually every color, shape, and texture. The 40-acre arboretum, situated along the Cootes Paradise wildlife refuge, offers a wide variety of native trees, flowering trees (dogwoods, magnolias, redbuds, and crab apples) and a superb lilac collection (over seven hundred kinds). The rock garden is famous for its dramatic rock formations, ponds, ninety thousand tulips in spring, and tens of thousands of begonias, impatiens, and summer annuals—even the parking lot here is landscaped. The Royal Botanical Gardens Centre holds excellent indoor collections and seasonal displays.

LOCATION: Royal Botanical Gardens Centre is at 680 Plains Rd. West (Rte. 2), between the cities of Hamilton and Burlington, 35 miles south of Toronto.
ADDRESS: P.O. Box 399, Hamilton, Ontario, Canada L8N 3H8.

TELEPHONE: 416-527-1158.

HOURS: Gardens open daily, sunrise to sunset; Centre shop hours vary—check for times.

FEE: Free ($2 parking fee at rock garden; small fee for indoor Mediterranean garden).

TOURS: For groups by prearrangement.

RESTAURANT: Refreshments available at Rock Garden and at Hendrie Park.

SHOPS: Floral Art Shop in Royal Botanical Gardens Centre.

WHEELCHAIR ACCESS: Access to majority of gardens.

SPECIAL ACTIVITIES: A 15-acre Children's Garden tended by local youth. A full range of classes, lectures, concerts, and exhibitions. The library is open to the public, and an auditorium is available for weddings and receptions. There are horticultural programs for the disabled and a speakers' bureau for interested groups.

---

TIPS: 1. The schedule of bloom extends from April to October. Highlights include the arboretum's flowering trees in April, lilacs in May; Rock Garden tulips in April and May; irises and peonies in Laking Garden in June; summer annuals in Hendrie Park and Rock Garden in August; autumn color in October, plus much more. Schedule of highlights available upon request.

2. This is a very large garden, impossible to be seen at one time without becoming numbed by its diverse beauty. We recommend touring only a few gardens at each visit and saving the rest for another day—especially since the gardens are designed to blossom at various times of the season.

3. Winter offers some unique attractions, from cross-country skiing and maple syrup displays to the indoor floral shows.

4. The Plant Clinic's diagnostic service invites you to bring or mail samples and questions.

---

# MONTREAL, QUEBEC: MONTREAL BOTANICAL GARDEN

*One of the world's great gardens, Montreal Botanical Garden possesses ten greenhouses and thirty outdoor gardens containing some twenty-six thousand species of plants. Its bonsai and penjing (Chinese bonsai) collections are unsurpassed in North*

*America, and its orchids, begonias, and gesneriads are also exceptional.*

Nearly 2 million people visit the Montreal Botanical Garden each year, and for a very good reason. The depth, diversity, and sheer beauty of its displays outrank any other Canadian garden and rival the best of the United States. The outdoor gardens include a rose garden (eight thousand bushes), a heath garden (with rhododendrons in bloom in June), a perennial garden (asters, phlox, dahlias, delphiniums), a flowery brook (irises, daylilies, peonies), a vegetable test garden, an economic plants garden, an annual test garden (nearly five hundred species of annuals), a medicinal plant garden, a poisonous plant garden, an alpinum (a rock garden of Alpine plants), an arboretum (junipers, crab apples, beeches, and others representing three thousand varieties of woody plants), a shade garden, native habitats, and a children's garden tended by local youngsters. The ten conservatories, including the new exhibition hall, offer seasonal flower shows (spring, fall, Christmas), plus excellent collections of orchids (1,700 species), bromeliads (400 species and varieties), begonias (365 species and varieties), gesneriads (264 species), Japanese bonsai (75 plants), and Chinese penjing (345 plants). Other permanent greenhouse displays include cacti and succulents, ferns, and tropical economic plants. The main entrance to the conservatories, the Molson Hospitality Pavilion, is dedicated to public education and services. For anyone traveling in the area, this garden is a must.

---

LOCATION: On the corner of Sherbrooke St. (Rte. 138) and Pie IX Blvd., across from Montreal Olympic Stadium and near metro station Pie IX.

ADDRESS: 4101 Sherbrooke St. East, Montreal, Quebec H1X 2B2.

TELEPHONE: 514-872-1454.

HOURS: Outdoor gardens open daily, sunrise to sunset. Conservatories open daily, 9–6.

FEE: No fee for outdoor gardens and grounds. Conservatories, $3/adult, $1.50/children under 17 and seniors; group rates available.

TOURS: Train tour of grounds ($1/adult, $.50/children). Sologuide (recorder) tour of conservatory, $2; conservatory group tours by prearrangement.

RESTAURANT: On grounds.

SHOPS: Souvenir boutique in conservatories.

WHEELCHAIR ACCESS: All grounds are accessible.

---

TIPS: 1. Peak bloom for outdoor gardens extends from mid-May to mid-Sept. (crab apples, annuals, perennials, roses), though excellent color can be found anytime from spring into fall.

2. The bonsai, orchid, bromeliad, and begonia collections are, by themselves, worth a visit. In addition, the Spring (tulips, daffodils), Chrysanthemum (autumn), and Christmas (poinsettias and Jerusalem cherry trees) shows are very impressive.

---

# EXCELLENT GARDENS

---

## ANNAPOLIS ROYAL: HISTORIC GARDENS

Opened in 1981, this 10-acre garden reflects the rich history of the Annapolis Royal area, which was settled before Jamestown or Quebec. Theme gardens include a rose garden (2000 plants, 300 varieties) with a rose maze; a perennial garden with blossoms spring to fall; a nineteenth-century Victorian garden with circular paths and interlocking flower beds; an eighteenth-century English garden with parterres; and a seventeenth-century Acadian cottage and kitchen garden. There are paths through woodlands and a lookout over a 50-acre wildfowl sanctuary. The town also offers an historic park and Fort Anne. Group garden tours by prearrangement. Restaurant and snack area. Wheelchair accessible. Weddings by prearrangement. Open daily, dawn to dusk, June–Oct. Fee: $3/adults, $1.50 seniors and children. Location: Annapolis Royal is located in southwestern Nova Scotia, at the junction of Rtes. 1 and 8; a ferry from St. John lands at Digby, 18 miles south of Annapolis Royal; the gardens are found just off Saint George St. (Rte. 8), near Prince Albert Rd. (Rte. 1). For further information, write to Annapolis Royal Development Commission, P.O. Box 278, Annapolis Royal, N.S. B0S 1A0. Tel: 902-532-5104.

---

## DON MILLS, ONTARIO: EDWARDS GARDENS

This lovely 27-acre garden offers paths along sweeping lawns and wide vistas, over rustic bridges across pools, streams, and a river, and under sprawling shade trees. Displays include an extensive rock garden and fine collections of flowering flora, including roses, lilies, irises, peonies, rhododendrons, and azaleas. Also on the grounds is the Civic Garden Centre, which offers flower shows sponsored by local garden clubs, courses, and workshops, library, bookshop and gift shop, plus rooms for weddings or meetings. A snack bar is located in the garden. Wheelchair access to garden and buildings. Garden open 24 hours daily; Garden Centre open Mon.–Fri., 9:30–4:00, and Sat.–Sun., 1–4. Fee: None. Located about 3 miles north of downtown Toronto. Address: 777 Lawrence Ave. East, Don Mills, Ontario M3C 1P2. Tel.: 416-445-1552.

## GRAND METIS, QUEBEC: METIS GARDEN

This fascinating 45-acre garden was the creation and passion of Elsie Reford. From 1928 to 1958, Ms. Reford experimented with plants from around the world, gathering over fifteen hundred species (lilies, rock plants and small shrubs, rhododendrons, crab apples, and more than five hundred species of perennials), some of them unknown this far north. The Villa Reford was built in 1887 and today contains a museum, local crafts shop, snack bar, and lounge. Open early June–mid-Sept., daily, 8:30 A.M.–10 P.M. Garden fee: $3.50/automobile; Villa Reford, $1/adult, $.50/children ages 8–18. Located on Rte. 132 on the south bank of the St. Lawrence River, about 200 miles northeast of the city of Quebec. For further information, write to Metis Gardens, P.O. Box 242, Mont-Joli, Quebec G5H 3L1. Tel.: 418-775-2221.

## HALIFAX, NOVA SCOTIA: HALIFAX PUBLIC GARDENS

Begun in the 1830s, the Halifax Public Gardens are among North America's finest examples of Victorian gardens. Located in central Halifax, these lovely gardens consist of a myriad of small gardens and bedding areas interspersed among specimen trees, ponds, fountains, statuary, and an ornate bandstand. Plantings include daffodils, tulips, fuschias, begonias, dahlias, roses, delphiniums, poppies, and mass plantings of annuals and geraniums. There is an extensive collection of trees, many rare. Concerts in summer. Snack bar. Wedding pictures can be taken in the park. Self-guide brochure. Wheelchair accessible. Open

May–Nov. 15, 8–sunset daily. Fee: None. Located at Spring Garden Rd. and South Park St. For further information, write to the City of Halifax Parks Division, Halifax, Nova Scotia B3J 3A5. Tel.: 902-421-6551.

## HAMILTON, ONTARIO: GAGE PARK

Gage Park is Hamilton's horticultural park. The 77-acre park contains five greenhouses with permanent displays (including a tropical collection) and a chrysanthemum show consisting of more than sixty thousand blooms (130 varieties). The outdoor park contains a rose garden (5,000 bushes) and collections of lilacs and perennials. The park also has a Children's Museum, as well as playing fields, a running track, a bowling green, a children's playground and wading pool, and picnic areas. A variety of concerts and festivals are presented in summer. Group tours by prearrangement. Wheelchair accessible. Wedding portraits permitted. Greenhouses open 9–3 daily, 9–8 during chrysanthemum show the first two weeks of November Outdoor park open daily, dawn to dusk. Fee: None. Location: Hamilton is located on Lake Ontario about 40 miles south of Toronto; Gage Park is located in central Hamilton off Main St.; the greenhouses can be found off Lawrence Rd. For further information, write to Dept. of Parks, Hamilton, Ontario L8N 3T4. Tel.: 416-526-4627.

## NEW ROSS, NOVA SCOTIA: ROSS FARM

This museum farm offers an educational experience for the entire family. Features include wagon rides, farm animals that can be petted, barrel-making demonstrations, collections of farm implements, restored buildings, and workshops. The garden consists of a sizable vegetable garden and herb garden, plus small flower garden. Open May 15–Oct. 15, daily 9:30–5:30. Fee: None. Located on Rte. 12 in central Nova Scotia, about 50 miles west of Halifax. Address: New Ross, Nova Scotia B0J 2MO. Tel.: 902-389-2210.

## NIAGARA FALLS, ONTARIO: NIAGARA PARKS COMMISSION SCHOOL OF HORTICULTURE

The 100-acre campus of the Niagara Parks Commission School of Horticulture contains gardens and landscaped areas as an outdoor laboratory for its students. Displays consist of colorful and interesting plant materials, including annuals, perennials, shrubs, and trees. Excellent color can be found from April into October. Flowering types include bulbs, lilacs, rhododendrons, irises, peonies, roses, chrysanthemums, plus Japanese cherry trees. Special displays include a rock garden, a vegetable garden, a natural garden, an herb garden, an arboretum, an ornamental fountain and pool, ponds and foot bridges, bird pens, and greenhouses. Wheelchair accessible. Group tours. Gift shop located in the Visitor Reception Center. Facilities for weddings and meetings. Open daily, daylight hours. Fee: None. Located on the Niagara Pkwy., 5 miles north of the Canadian Horseshoe Falls and Queen Elizabeth Park. For further information, write to P.O. Box 150, Niagara Falls, Ontario L2E 6T2. Tel.: 416-356-8554.

## NIAGARA FALLS, ONTARIO: QUEEN VICTORIA PARK, OAKES GARDEN THEATRE, LILAC GARDEN, AND FLORAL CLOCK

Owned and maintained by the Niagara Parks Commission, Queen Victoria Park not only offers excellent views of the falls, but also acres of splendidly colorful gardens from spring to fall. In late April, half a million golden daffodils burst into bloom, the largest mass planting of this species in North America. These are soon followed by tulips, annuals (a hundred forty thousand of them), perennials and dahlias by the thousands, plus exquisite carpet bedding displays. The rose garden has four thousand bushes of all types. The park also maintains a popular conservatory (almost a third of a million visitors annually) with a permanent tropical display and seasonal flower shows (spring daffodils and tulips, Easter lilies, fall chrysanthemums, Christmas poinsettias), plus a greenhouse that produces over a hundred thousand bedding plants each year for the outdoor gardens. Near the daffodil plantings is the Oakes Garden Theatre, designed like a Greek and Roman amphitheatre, containing colorful formal gardens, rock gardens, and sloping terraces. The Queen Victoria Park area contains several restaurants, shops, and tourist services. Wheelchair access to most areas. In early May the Annual Grand Blossom Festival is held. Seven miles up Niagara Parkway is the Lilac Garden and the famous Floral Clock. Over twelve hundred bushes (250 varieties) fill the 8-acre Lilac Garden; peak bloom is in late May. The Floral Clock is the world's largest and is made of twenty-five thousand plants. All outdoor gardens are open daily, dawn to dusk; Queen

Elizabeth Park Conservatory open daily, 9:30–4:15 (later in summer—check for hours), closed Christmas. Fee: None. Location: Queen Elizabeth Park is located on the Canadian side of the Niagara River, directly above the falls. For further information, write to the Niagara Parks Commission, P.O. Box 150, Niagara Falls, Ontario L2E 6T2. Tel.: 416-356-2241.

## OTTAWA, ONTARIO: CENTRAL EXPERIMENTAL FARM

Originally created to improve farming practices in Canada, the farm possesses flower gardens, an arboretum, and greenhouses, in addition to its experimental fields, stables, and laboratories. The Ornamental Gardens contain displays of annual and perennial blossoms of virtually every variety compatible with Ottawa's climate, plus a rock garden, lilac walk, and roses. The greenhouse features tropical plants, and the arboretum offers more than two thousand varieties of trees and shrubs—including crab apples and magnolias, azaleas, and rhododendrons. The greenhouse hosts an annual Chrysanthemum Show in autumn. The farm's other displays include livestock barns, an observatory, and a Tally-Ho Wagon Ride. Group tours by prearrangement at least 1 month in advance. Gardens available for weddings. Grounds open daily, 8:30–dusk; conservatory open daily, 9–4. Fee: None. Located off Carling Ave. and Prince of Wales Dr. (Rte. 16), about 2 miles south of downtown Ottawa. For further information, write to the Ottawa Research Station, Bldg. 50, Ottawa, Ontario K1A OC6. Tel.: 613-995-5222.

## OTTAWA, ONTARIO: NATIONAL CAPITAL COMMISSION PARKS

More than 3 million bulbs and flowering plants make Ottawa one of North America's most colorful cities in spring. Beginning in World War II, when Ottawa was the haven of the Dutch royal family, tulips and other bulbs were planted by the thousands at various sites. Today nearly 2 million tulips burst into bloom, along with hundreds of thousands of daffodils, from late April through May. The most impressive displays can be found at Dows Lake and Commissioners' Park (tulips) and at Rockcliffe Rockeries (daffodils). Earlier in spring (late March to April), thousands of crocuses and scillas can be enjoyed at Parliament Hill and Commissioners' Park. In June, irises, lilacs, and crab apple trees are in bloom, and in summer it's the two hundred thousand annuals and perennials. A festival of spring is held in mid-May with workshops, a marathon, and other activities. Wheelchair access to most areas. Boat cruise on Rideau Canal goes past the heart of the capital with its thousands of blossoms. Parks open sunrise to sunset. Fee: None. Further information and maps can be obtained by visiting or writing to Canada's Capital Information Center, 14 Metcalfe St. (at Wellington), Ottawa, Ontario. Tel.: 800-267-0450, or for local calls, 232-1234.

## PRINCE EDWARD ISLAND: MALPEQUE GARDENS

Excellent collections of dahlias (400 cultivars), begonias, and roses punctuate the 5-acre Malpeque gardens. Additional collections include a wide array of perennials, a dwarf orchard, and a sunken garden. There is also a windmill, a children's mini-farm, and a beehive. Group tours by prearrangement. Snack bar and dairy bar. Gift shop. Open June 15–Sept. 1, daily, 8:30–dusk; Sept. 2–Oct. 15, daily, 9–5. Fee: $2; group rates available. Location: Malepeque is located on Rte. 20 in northcentral Prince Edward Island, 6 miles north of Kensington. For further information, write to Malpeque Gardens, Kensington R.R. 1; P.E.I. C0B 1M0. Tel.: 902-836-5418.

## STARR'S POINT, NOVA SCOTIA: PRESCOTT HOUSE

Designated a National Historic Site, the 1814 Prescott House was the home of Charles Ramage Prescott, a horticulturist best known for the introduction of superior varieties of apples to the area. The 50-acre estate with its period garden later fell into disrepair, only to be restored in the early 1940s by Prescott's great-granddaughter, Mary Allison Prescott. Today the garden contains a sunken rock garden and beds of bulbs, annuals, and perennials. There are also several notable specimen trees, including a 200-year-old elm, 11 feet in diameter, and an old Gravenstein apple tree of the kind that Prescott introduced to Nova Scotia. The Prescott House, now owned and maintained by the Nova Scotia Museum Complex, has also been restored with original furniture and other period pieces. Open May 15–Oct. 15, daily, 9:30–5:30. Fee: None. Located in northcentral Nova Scotia, about 60 miles northwest of Halifax; take Rte. 101 to Rte. 358 to Starr's Point. Address: Starr's Point, Nova Scotia. Tel.: 902-542-3984.

## THUNDER BAY, ONTARIO: CENTENNIAL BOTANICAL CONSERVATORY

Constructed in 1967, this ½-acre conservatory contains a Tropical House and Cactus House. There is also a Show House in which flower shows are offered Easter, summer, November (chrysanthemums), and Christmas (poinsettias). Group tours by prearrangement. Weddings by prearrangement. Wheelchair accessible. Open daily, 1–4; closed some holidays. Fee: None. Location: Thunder Bay is located on Lake Superior, on Rtes. 11 & 17 in Western Ontario, about 25 miles north of the U.S. border. Address: 1601 Dease St., Thunder Bay, Ontario P7C 5H3. Tel.: 807-622-7036.

## WHITBY, ONTARIO: CULLEN GARDENS AND MINIATURE VILLAGE

An historic village of one hundred buildings is reproduced in miniature amid 22 acres of profusely colorful gardens. Thousands of blossoms can be seen spring through fall, including daffodils (100,000) in April, tulips (65,000) in May, annuals (84,000) and roses (10,000) in summer, and chrysanthemums in September. The garden also contains topiary and a floral peacock. Group tours by prearrangement. Wheelchair accessible. Programs and festivals scheduled year round. Shops, restaurant, snack bar. Bed and breakfast inn. Open late April to mid-Oct., daily, 9 A.M. to 9 P.M.; mid-Oct. to early Jan., daily, 10 to 9. Fee: $5/adult, $4/seniors and students, $2.50/children ages 3–12. Location: Whitby is located about 25 miles east of Toronto; from Rtes. 2 or 401 take Rte. 12 north, turn left on Taunton Rd. Address: 300 Taunton Rd. West, Whitby, Ontario L1N 5R5. Tel.: 416-668-6606 or 416-294-7965.

## WINDSOR, NOVA SCOTIA: HALIBURTON HOUSE

Another historical home maintained by the Nova Scotia Museum Complex, this 1836 structure was built by Thomas Haliburton, legislator and humorist. Haliburton and his wife had a keen interest in horticulture and laid out colorful grounds for their home. After a century of neglect, the house and grounds have been restored with a small flower garden, rose garden, and beds of annuals and perennials. Also of interest are exhibits of Haliburton's writings and, especially, his timeless sayings: "raining cats and dogs," "quick as a wink," "barking up the wrong tree," "drank like a fish," and "the early bird gets the worm." Open May 15–Oct. 15, daily, 9:30–5:30. Fee: None. Located in Windsor in central Nova Scotia, on Clifton Ave. just off Rte. 101, approximately 40 miles northwest of Halifax. Address: Windsor, Nova Scotia. Tel.: 902-798-2915.

# WINDSOR, ONTARIO: JACKSON PARK

This 65-acre all-purpose park possesses two noteworthy gardens among its playing fields and picnic areas. The Queen Elizabeth II Gardens (previously known as the Sunken Gardens) are extensive formal gardens oriented around a central pool and fountain. From spring to early fall, the flower beds are packed with colorful blossoms (thirty thousand spring bulbs, forty thousand summer annuals). Directly adjacent is the Lancaster Memorial Rose Garden, named for the reliable Canadian Royal Air Force Lancaster Bomber of World War II. This garden contains over 12,500 rose bushes representing five hundred varieties, one of Canada's largest collections. Open 24 hours daily. Fee: None. Location: Windsor is located at the southwest tip of Ontario, across from Detroit; Jackson Park is located on Tecumseh Rd. in central Windsor. Also noteworthy is Coventry Gardens, a pleasant waterfront park descending toward the Detroit River via a series of flower-filled terraces. The center-piece of this garden is the Charles Brooks Memorial Peace Fountain, a unique fountain that floats in the river and shoots varying patterns of water 70 feet high and 180 feet in diameter. At night the jets are embellished by multicolored lights. Open 24 hours (the fountain is in operation 11 A.M. to 11 P.M., mid-May to mid-Oct.). Fee: None. Location: Coventry Gardens can be found on Riverside Drive East at Pillette Rd. in central Windsor. For further information regarding Jackson Park or Coventry Gardens, write to the Dept. of Parks, 2450 McDougall St., Windsor, Ontario N8X 3N6. Tel.: 519-255-6270.

PART THREE

*Garden Listings:*

*Special*

*Gardens*

# Family Fun: Attractions for Children

In addition to splendid floral displays, these 91 gardens offer entertainment or special displays geared toward families with young children or teenagers.

## ALABAMA

**Ave Maria Grotto, Cullman:** An unusual garden displaying 125 miniature buildings and shrines from world history (Pantheon, Hanging Gardens of Babylon, Old Jerusalem, and more).

**Noccalula Falls, Gadsden:** Pioneer village, military museum, shops, western shows, zoo, picnicking—as well as a 10-acre botanical garden.

**Oakleigh, Mobile:** Small playground.

**Jasmine Hill Gardens, Montgomery:** Fine replicas of Greek sculpture, recommended for children or young adults with an interest in art.

## CONNECTICUT

**Bruce Park, Greenwich:** All-purpose park with recreational facilities, picnicking, concerts in summer.

**Pardee Rose Garden, Hamden:** Located in East Rock Park, a recreational park for all ages.

**Elizabeth Park, Hartford:** Large playground in all-purpose park. Classes and workshops for all ages. In summer, concerts, country dance, and other entertainment.

## DELAWARE

**Hagley Museum and Library, Wilmington:** Fascinating restoration of nineteenth-century industrial village, with powder mill, machine shop, steam engine, exhibits, and entertainment.

# FLORIDA

**Florida Cypress Gardens, Cypress Gardens:** A first-class family attraction with shows, rides, entertainment, spectacular ski shows, and much more.

**Morikami Park, Delray Beach:** Children's Activity Days in June, July, and August, with folk tales, origami, activities.

**Thomas A. Edison Winter Home, Fort Myers:** Includes a museum of the great inventor's work and his antique car collection.

**Everglades National Park, Homestead:** A unique natural setting, viewable by car or boat, full of water plants, animals, and birds.

**Corkscrew Swamp Sanctuary, Immokalee:** Fascinating excursion into a natural Florida swamp.

**Bok Tower Gardens, Lake Wales:** Serene gardens where you can feed the ducks and listen to the carillon (bells).

**Caribbean Gardens, Naples:** Tropical animals and birds amid a lush setting, with a zoo next door.

**Sunken Gardens, Saint Petersburg:** A very popular tropical garden with rare birds and unusual animals.

**Ringling Museums, Sarasota:** Fascinating collection of the famous company's circus artifacts.

**Sarasota Jungle Gardens, Sarasota:** Exotic birds and wildlife amid lush surroundings; petting zoo, Reptile Show, and Jungle Bird Circus.

**Parrot Jungle, South Miami:** Extensive parrot collection in a tropical setting.

**Busch Gardens, Tampa:** This garden is well-known for its amusement park and animal displays.

# GEORGIA

**Callaway Gardens, Pine Mountain:** A first-class resort offering fine lodgings and activities from golf to horseback riding to sailing and more.

**State Botanical Garden of Georgia, Athens:** Classes for all ages, Christmas storytelling hour, slide shows.

Okefenokee Swamp Park, Waycross: Walking trails through this National Wildlife Refuge. Boat tour into the swamp.

## ILLINOIS

Chicago Park District, Chicago: The Lincoln Park Conservatory is located in Lincoln Park, which offers beaches, playing fields, a golf course, and the Lincoln Park Zoo.

Lake of the Woods Botanic Garden, Mahomet: Pioneer museum with 5,000 artifacts and antiques from firearms to furnishings.

Cantigny, Wheaton: First Division Museum (military museum).

## INDIANA

Foellinger-Freimann Botanical Conservatory, Fort Wayne: Jungle Garden Halloween on October 31.

Garfield Park Conservatory, Indianapolis: Haunted Conservatory on October 31.

## KENTUCKY

Lexington Cemetery, Lexington: Historical monuments; tour guide brochure specifically geared to children.

## MARYLAND

Cylburn Arboretum, Baltimore: Children's Nature Museum and Bird Museum.

Ladew Topiary Garden, Monkton: Superb topiary (shrubbery shaped into the form of animals or geometric designs), delightful for young and old.

## MASSACHUSETTS

Longfellow National Historic Site, Cambridge: Tours of the famous poet's home.

Garden in the Woods, Framingham: Classes for all ages.

Adams National Historic Site, Quincy: Historic home of Presidents John Adams and John Quincy Adams.

Heritage Plantation, Sandwich: Interesting collections of antique cars, military miniatures, antique firearms, hand tools, lithographs, and a hand-carved 1912 carousel.

**Old Sturbridge Village, Sturbridge:** Historical houses restored as a living museum of Americana, offering displays and entertainment.

# MICHIGAN

**Anna Scripps Whitcomb Conservatory, Belle Isle, Detroit:** Located in Belle Isle Park where there is an aquarium, picnicking, and a host of outdoor activities in all seasons.

**Veldheer Tulip Gardens, Inc., Holland:** Tulip Time Festival in May offers festivities and entertainment, windmills and Dutch drawbridges. Also on the grounds is the Wooden Shoe Factory (tour).

# MISSISSIPPI

**Palestinian Gardens, Lucedale:** Non-denominational garden contains scale models of cities of the Holy Land including Jerusalem, Jericho, Bethlehem, and Tiberias.

# NEW HAMPSHIRE

**Strawbery Banke, Portsmouth:** Historic restoration of buildings and gardens of old Portsmouth.

# NEW JERSEY

**Lemming's Run and Colonial Farm: Cape May Court House:** The seventeenth-century farm offers a log cabin and farm animals.

**Willowwood Arboretum, Gladstone:** Children's Garden, plus classes and programs for all ages.

**Frelinghuysen Arboretum, Morristown:** Classes and programs for all ages.

**Cora Hartshorn Arboretum and Bird Sanctuary, Short Hills:** Programs designed for children and teenagers.

# NEW YORK

**New York Botanical Garden, Bronx, New York City:** Programs for all ages. The famous Bronx Zoo is next door.

**Brooklyn Botanic Garden, Brooklyn, New York City:** World-famous Children's Garden where children are taught how to grow vegetables, plus other children's programs.

The Brooklyn Museum and Prospect Park are located nearby.

**Farmers' Museum, Cooperstown:** A restoration of historical buildings containing displays of Americana.

**Queens Botanical Garden, Flushing:** Classes and programs for all ages.

**Roosevelt Rose Garden and Gravesite, Hyde Park:** Historic home of President Franklin D. Roosevelt.

**Mohonk Gardens, New Paltz:** Mohonk Mountain House is a resort hotel offering golf, swimming, tennis, horse trails, ski trails, and many other activities for young and old.

**Biblical Garden at the Cathedral of St. John the Divine, New York City:** Garden of plants mentioned in the Bible; plants accompanied by quotes from scriptures.

**Stone-Tolan House, Rochester:** Faithful restoration of a 1790's farmstead.

## NORTH CAROLINA

**Elizabethan Gardens, Manteo:** Located on Roanoke Island, the site of the Lost Colony, near historic Fort Raleigh and the Colony Waterside Theatre.

**Tanglewood Park, Clemmons:** A 1,150-acre family resort offering activities for all ages.

## OHIO

**Stan Hywet Hall and Gardens, Akron:** Dances, shows, exhibits, travelogues; Christmas open house and readings.

**Garden Center of Greater Cleveland, Cleveland:** Programs and classes for all ages.

**Krohn Conservatory, Cincinnati:** Conservatory safari for ages 5-12.

**Franklin Park Conservatory and Garden Center, Columbus:** Witches Walk Halloween; classes for children and teenagers.

**Holden Arboretum, Mentor:** Maple syrup-making demonstration in winter.

**Toledo Zoo, Toledo:** Garden and conservatory on zoo grounds; price of admission includes all.

# PENNSYLVANIA

**Longwood Gardens, Kennett Square:** Fantastic fountain shows and outdoor concerts in summer.

**Hershey Gardens, Hershey:** In addition to the gardens, exhibits include Chocolate World, ZOO AMERICA, Hershey Museum of American Life, and a turn-of-the-century village.

**Pennsbury Manor, Morrisville:** Faithful restoration of William Penn's 1600's plantation including farm implements and livestock barn.

**Jennings Environmental Education Center, Slippery Rock:** Displays and exhibits, plus classes for all ages.

**Valley Forge National Historical Park, Valley Forge:** Historic encampment of the Revolutionary Army during the bitter winter of 1777–78.

**Bowman's Hill Wildflower Preserve, Washington Crossing:** Located at the site of Washington's daring 1777 crossing of the Delaware to raid the British at Trenton.

# RHODE ISLAND

**Blithewood Gardens and Arboretum, Bristol:** Christmas wreath making, doll exhibit, plus other classes and programs for children and adults.

**Green Animals, Portsmouth:** Superb topiary of a score of animals (elephant, giraffe, camel), delightful for every member of the family, plus the Small Toys Museum.

**Roger Williams Park, Providence:** City park with picnicking, lakes, and a zoo. The Christmas Show in the greenhouse has a 20-foot Talking Snowman.

# SOUTH CAROLINA

**Magnolia Plantation and Gardens, Charleston:** Bicycle trails, canoeing and fishing on the lake, miniature horses, a petting zoo, and a wildlife refuge.

**Brookgreen Gardens, Murrells Inlet:** Excellent collection of American sculpture (recommended for older children or young children with an interest in art), plus a wildlife park and an adjacent public beach.

**Cypress Gardens, Charleston:** Enchanting excursions by boat through a moss-draped forest.

**Clemson University Horticultural Gardens, Clemson:** Pioneer complex with log cabins, grist mill, and a collection of antique farm implements.

## TENNESSEE

**Reflection Riding, Chattanooga:** Exhibits and classes for all ages.

**The Hermitage, Hermitage:** Historic home of President Andrew Jackson.

**Rock City Gardens, Lookout Mountain:** Tourist attraction offering Mother Goose Village, Fairyland Caverns, Deer Park, Fudge Kitchen, as well as lovely spring and autumn color, interesting rock formations, and excellent vistas.

## VERMONT

**Shelburne Museum Gardens, Shelburne:** Popular family attraction offering interesting displays and collections (quilts, decoys, cigar store statuary, weathervanes, carousel animals and other folk arts), plus entertainment and activities.

## VIRGINIA

**Colonial Williamsburg, Williamsburg:** World-famous restoration of colonial America. An enjoyable and educational experience for all ages.

**Oatlands, Leesburg:** Mini-zoo with llamas, goats, and donkeys.

**Monticello, Monticello:** Historic home of President Thomas Jefferson.

**Mount Vernon, Mount Vernon:** Historic home of George Washington.

**Maymount Foundation:** Children's farm with bison, bears, elk, racoons, and barnyard animals, plus a carriage collection and carriage rides.

## WEST VIRGINIA

**Sunrise Museums, Charleston:** Art museums plus a Children's Museum.

Cranberry Glades Botanical Area, Richwood: Classes for all ages.

The Greenbrier, White Sulphur Springs: A resort hotel offering activities for all ages including carriage rides, horseback riding, sports of all kinds, plus much more for the entire family.

## WISCONSIN

House on the Rock, Spring Green: Popular tourist attraction with displays (glasswares, dolls, world's largest carousel) for all ages.

## EASTERN CANADA

Montreal Botanic Gardens, Montreal: Children's Garden where children grow plants and vegetables.

Gage Park, Hamilton: Children's Museum, playing fields, and picnicking.

Ross Farm, New Ross: Restored nineteenth-century farm offering exhibits, collections and demonstrations, plus wagon rides and a petting barn.

Queen Victoria Park, Niagara Falls: Excellent views of Niagara Falls from this all-purpose park.

Central Experimental Farm, Ottawa: Observatory, livestock barns, Tally-Ho Wagon Ride.

National Capital Commission Parks, Ottawa: The boat cruise on Rideau Canal is a pleasant way to see the Capitol as well as the spring tulips.

Haliburton House, Windsor, Nova Scotia: Unique museum devoted to the serious and satirical works of Thomas Haliburton, famous for such sayings as "raining cats and dogs," "quick as a wink," "barking up the wrong tree," and "the early bird catches the worm."

Cullen Gardens and Miniature Village, Whitby: An unusual display of a village of 100 buildings reproduced in miniature.

Jackson Park, Windsor, Ontario: Picnicking and playing fields. Also located in Windsor is the Coventry Gardens with its fountain display on the Detroit River.

# Free Gardens:
# No Entrance Fee

This listing consists of 176 gardens that require no entrance fee.

## ALABAMA

Birmingham Botanical Garden, Birmingham

De Soto State Park, Fort Payne

Noccalula Falls Park Botanical Garden, Gadsden (no fee in late autumn and winter)

Mobile Botanical Gardens, Mobile

Oakleigh, Mobile

## CONNECTICUT

Bristol Nurseries, Inc., Bristol

Caprilands Herb Farm, Coventry

Logee's Greenhouses, Danielson

Bruce Park, Greenwich

Pardee Ross Garden, Hamden

Elizabeth Park, Hartford

White Flower Farm, Litchfield

Olive and George Lee Memorial Garden, New Canaan

Connecticut Arboretum at Connecticut College, New London

Bartlett Arboretum, Stamford

Harkness Memorial State Park, Waterford

## DELAWARE

Rockwood Museum and Gardens, Wilmington (no fee for gardens, small fee for tour of mansion)

## DISTRICT OF COLUMBIA

Dumbarton Oaks (free for seniors on all Weds; free for all visitors Nov–Mar)

United States National Arboretum

Bishop's Garden

Franciscan Monastery

Kenilworth Aquatic Gardens

United States Botanic Garden

## FLORIDA

Alberts and Merkel Bros., Inc., Boynton Beach

Morikami Park, Delray Beach

Cummer Gallery of Art, Jacksonville

Ravine Gardens State Park, Palatka

Four Arts Garden, Palm Beach

Eden State Gardens, Point Washington (no fee for garden, fee for tour of mansion)

Mounts Horticultural Learning Center, West Palm Beach

Slocum Water Gardens, Winter Haven

## GEORGIA

State Botanical Garden of Georgia, Athens

Atlanta Botanical Garden, Atlanta

Cator Woolford Memorial Garden, Atlanta

Massee Lane, Fort Valley

Lockerly Arboretum, Milledgeville

Thomasville Nurseries, Inc., Thomasville

## ILLINOIS

Chicago Park District, Chicago (includes outdoor parks and conservatories)

Merrick Park Rose Garden, Evanston

Shakespeare Garden, Evanston

Chicago Horticultural Society Botanic Garden, Glencoe (no admission fee, but $1 parking fee per automobile)

Lilacia Park, Lombard: Free except during "Lilac Time" in early May

Washington Park Botanical Garden, Springfield

Cantigny, Wheaton

## INDIANA

Garfield Park Sunken Gardens, Indianapolis (outside the Conservatory)

Hillsdale Gardens, Indianapolis

Christy Woods, Muncie

Purdue Horticulture Gardens, West Lafayette

## KENTUCKY

Bernheim Forest, Arboretum and Nature Center, Clermont

Lexington Cemetery, Lexington

Kentucky Botanical Gardens, Louisville

## MAINE

Wild Gardens of Acadia, Bar Harbor

Merry Gardens, Camden

Merryspring, Camden

Asticou Azalea Garden, Northeast Harbor

Asticou Terraces, Northeast Harbor

Deering Oaks Rose Garden, Portland

## MARYLAND

Brookside Gardens, Wheaton

Baltimore Conservatory Complex, Baltimore

Cylburn Arboretum, Baltimore

Sherwood Gardens, Baltimore

Lilypons Water Gardens, Lilypons

Hampton, Towson

## MASSACHUSETTS

Arnold Arboretum, Jamaica Plain

Isabella Stewart Gardner Museum, Boston ($2 donation is requested but not required)

Longfellow National Historic Site (garden free, $.50 fee for house)

Mount Auburn Cemetery, Cambridge

Glen Magna, Danvers (garden free, fee for mansion)

Great Hill Farm, East Marion

Jeremiah Lee Mansion, Marblehead

Botanic Garden of Smith College, Northampton

Adams National Historic Site, Quincy (no fee for garden; guided tour of house costs $.50)

Ropes Mansion and Garden, Salem (no garden fee; small fee for mansion)

Berkshire Garden Center, Stockbridge (no fee Nov–Apr)

Wellesley College, Wellesley

Stanley Park, Westfield

Case Estates, Weston

## MICHIGAN

Anna Scripps Whitcomb Conservatory, Belle Isle, Detroit

Michigan State University Horticulture Gardens, East Lansing

Veldheer Tulips, Holland (free except in May)

Dow Gardens, Midland

## MISSISSIPPI

Wister Gardens, Belzoni

## NEW HAMPSHIRE

Prescott Park Formal Garden, Portsmouth

## NEW JERSEY

Rudolf W. van der Goot Rose Garden of Colonial Park, East Millstone

Leonard J. Buck Garden, Far Hills

Willowwood Arboretum, Gladstone

Fischer Greenhouses, Linwood

Acorn Hall, Morristown

Frelinghuysen Arboretum, Morristown

Rutgers Display Gardens, New Brunswick

Skylands, Ringwood (free Nov–Apr, free for seniors year round)

Cora Hartshorn Arboretum and Bird Sanctuary, Short Hills

Reeves-Reed Arboretum, Summit

Presby Memorial Iris Gardens, Upper Montclair

## NEW YORK

Brooklyn Botanic Garden, Brooklyn, New York City (Conservatories and Japanese Garden free on weekdays, other gardens free everyday)

Planting Fields Arboretum, Oyster Bay (free on weekdays, Sept–Apr)

Buffalo and Erie County Botanical Garden, Buffalo

George Landes Arboretum, Esperance

Queens Botanical Garden, Flushing

Legg Dahlia Gardens, Geneva

Clermont State Historic Park, Germantown

Cornell Plantations, Ithaca

Cary Arboretum, Millbrook

Biblical Garden at the Cathedral of St. John the Divine, New York City

Wave Hill, New York City (free on weekdays)

Mt. Hope Cemetery, Rochester

Dr. E. M. Mills Memorial Rose Garden, Syracuse

## NORTH CAROLINA

Coker Arboretum, Chapel Hill

North Carolina Botanical Garden, Chapel Hill

University of North Carolina at Charlotte Botanical Gardens, Charlotte

Campus Arboretum of Haywood Technical College, Clyde

Sarah P. Duke Gardens, Durham

Bicentennial Garden, Greensboro

North Carolina State University Arboretum, Raleigh

Greenfield Gardens, Wilmington

Reynolda Gardens, Winston-Salem

## OHIO

Kingwood Center, Mansfield

Cox Arboretum, Dayton

Ault Park, Cincinnati

Krohn Conservatory, Cincinnati

Mt. Airy Arboretum, Cincinnati

Spring Grove Cemetery, Cincinnati

Cleveland Cultural Gardens and Rockefeller Park Greenhouses, Cleveland

Garden Center of Greater Cleveland, Cleveland

Lake View Cemetery, Cleveland

Franklin Park Conservatory and Garden Center, Columbus

Park of Roses, Columbus

Lakeview Park Rose Garden, Lorain

Dawes Arboretum, Newark

George P. Crosby Gardens, Toledo

Inniswood Botanical Garden and Nature Preserve, Westerville

Secrest Arboretum, Wooster

Fellows Riverside Gardens, Youngstown

## PENNSYLVANIA

Malcolm W. Gross Memorial Rose Garden, Allentown

Ambler Campus of Temple University, Ambler

Delaware Valley College, Doylestown

Henry Foundation for Botanical Research, Gladwynne

John J. Tyler Arboretum, Lima

Swiss Pines, Malvern

Arboretum of the Barnes Foundation, Merion (by appointment)

Bartram's Garden, Philadelphia

Pennsylvania Horticultural Society Garden, Philadelphia

Jennings Environmental Education Center, Slippery Rock

Scott Arboretum, Swarthmore

Valley Forge National Historical Park, Valley Forge

Appleford, Villanova

Bowman's Hill Wildflower Preserve, Washington Crossing

## RHODE ISLAND

Roger Williams Park, Providence

Swan Point Cemetery, Providence

Shakespeare's Head, Providence

Wilcox Park, Westerly

## SOUTH CAROLINA

Hopeland Gardens, Aiken

Hampton Park, Charleston

Clemson University Horticultural Gardens, Clemson

Boylston Gardens, Columbia (by appointment)

Kalmia Gardens of Coker College, Hartsville

Edisto Memorial Gardens, Orangeburg

Glencairn Garden, Rock Hill

Swan Lake Iris Gardens, Sumter

## TENNESSEE

Racheff Park and Gardens, Knoxville

Dixon Gallery and Gardens, Memphis (free on Tue only)

Memphis Botanic Garden, Memphis

Opryland Hotel Conservatory, Nashville

University of Tennessee Arboretum, Oak Ridge

Roan Mountain State Park, Roan Mountain

## VERMONT

University of Vermont Agricultural Station, Burlington

The Cook's Garden, Londonderry

## VIRGINIA

Mount Vernon, Mount Vernon (free on 3rd Mon in Feb only)

Bryan Park Azalea Gardens, Richmond (free except $2/car on weekends and holidays in spring and summer)

Maymount Foundation, Richmond (no garden fee; $2.50 donation requested for mansion tour)

## WEST VIRGINIA

Davis Park, Charleston

Sunrise Museums, Charleston

Core Arboretum, Morgantown

Cathedral State Park, Aurora

Cranberry Glades Botanical Area, Richwood

The Greenbrier, White Sulphur Springs

## WISCONSIN

Mitchell Park Horticultural Conservatory, Milwaukee

Boerner Botanical Gardens, Hales Corners

Olbrich Gardens, Madison

University of Wisconsin at Madison Arboretum, Madison

Jones Arboretum and Botanical Gardens, Readstown

## CANADA

Royal Botanical Gardens, Hamilton

Montreal Botanic Gardens, Montreal (outdoor gardens free, fee for Conservatory)

Edwards Gardens, Don Mills

Halifax Public Gardens, Halifax

Gage Park, Hamilton

Ross Farm, New Ross

Niagara Falls Park Commission School of Horticulture, Niagara Falls

Queen Victoria Park, Oakes Garden Theatre, Lilac Garden and Floral Clock, Niagara Falls

National Capital Commission Parks, Ottawa

Central Experimental Farm, Ottawa

Prescott House, Starr's Point

Centennial Botanical Conservatory, Thunder Bay

Haliburton House, Windsor (Nova Scotia)

Jackson Park, Windsor (Ontario)

# Wedding Gardens: Facilities for Weddings, Receptions, or Wedding Portraits

These eighty-three gardens offer facilities for weddings, wedding receptions or wedding portraits, as well as for other social affairs or meetings. All require appointments, and some charge fees. If one of the gardens in the main text interests you, but is not listed here, it still might be worthwhile to inquire at the specific garden since policies and facilities do change from time to time.

## ALABAMA

**Birmingham Botanical Garden, Birmingham**

**Bellingrath Gardens and Home, Theodore**

**Arlington House and Garden, Birmingham:** Weddings and receptions in house or garden.

**Jasmine Hill Gardens and Restaurant, Montgomery:** Special Wedding Garden with wedding arch of jasmine.

## CONNECTICUT

**Bruce Park, Greenwich**

**Pardee Rose Garden, Hamden**

**Elizabeth Park, Hartford**

## FLORIDA

**Washington Oaks State Gardens, Marineland**

**Leu Gardens, Orlando**

**Ravine Gardens State Park, Palatka:** 4 acres where weddings can be held, plus facilities in the Civic Center Auditorium for receptions or other affairs.

**Marie Selby Botanical Garden, Sarasota**

## GEORGIA

**Callaway Gardens, Pine Mountain:** This famous resort contains facilities for weddings, receptions, business meetings, and other affairs.

**State Botanical Garden of Georgia, Athens:** Conservatory and grounds available for weddings, receptions, affairs, or meetings.

**Cator Woolford Memorial Garden, Atlanta**

**Thomasville Nurseries, Inc., Thomasville**

## ILLINOIS

**Chicago Park District, Chicago:** Weddings can be held in outdoor gardens as well as Garfield Park and Lincoln Park Conservatories.

**Merrick Park Rose Garden, Evanston**

**Shakespeare Garden, Evanston**

**Washington Park Botanical Garden, Springfield**

## INDIANA

**Foellinger-Freimann Botanical Conservatory, Fort Wayne**

**Purdue Horticulture Gardens, West Lafayette**

## KENTUCKY

**Kentucky Botanical Gardens, Louisville:** Wedding garden will be part of new, permanent gardens, beginning 1987-88.

## MAINE

**Asticou Azalea Garden, Northeast Harbor**

**Deering Oaks Rose Garden, Portland**

## MARYLAND

**Brookside Gardens, Wheaton:** Weddings held in the lovely Formal Gardens.

**Baltimore Conservatory Complex, Baltimore:** Weddings held in conservatory.

**McCrillis Gardens and Gallery, Bethesda**

**London Publik House and Gardens, Edgewater:** Weddings held in outdoor gardens of this historic building.

**Hampton, Towson**

---

## MASSACHUSETTS

**Arnold Arboretum, Jamaica Plain:** Visitors Center available for weddings, receptions, meetings and affairs.

**Mount Auburn Cemetery, Cambridge:** Chapel and gardens available for weddings.

**Jeremiah Lee Mansion, Marblehead:** Historic home and garden available for weddings and parties.

**Ropes Mansion and Garden, Salem**

**Naumkeag, Stockbridge:** Elegant mansion available for wedding ceremonies (no receptions or parties).

**Old Sturbridge Village, Sturbridge:** Historic village with facilities for weddings, receptions, affairs, or meetings.

**Wellesley College, Wellesley**

**Case Estates, Weston:** Lovely outdoor gardens for weddings and receptions.

---

## MICHIGAN

**Matthai Botanical Garden, Ann Arbor**

**Michigan State University Horticulture Gardens, East Lansing**

**Grand Hotel, Mackinac Island:** Elegant historic hotel has facilities for weddings, receptions, parties, and meetings.

---

## MISSISSIPPI

**Wister Gardens, Belzoni:** Outdoor gardens available for weddings.

**Mynelle Gardens, Jackson:** Garden available for weddings, receptions, and meetings.

## NEW HAMPSHIRE

**Prescott Park Formal Garden, Portsmouth:** Outdoor gardens available for weddings.

**Strawbery Banke, Portsmouth:** Historic restoration with gardens for weddings.

## NEW JERSEY

**Frelinghuysen Arboretum, Morristown:** Facilities for weddings, receptions, affairs, and meetings.

**Skylands, Ringwood:** Gardens available for weddings and receptions.

**Reeves-Reed Arboretum, Summit**

## NEW YORK

**George Landis Arboretum, Esperance**

**Queens Botanical Garden, Flushing:** Beautiful Wedding Garden with a gazebo, willow trees, waterfall, and a profusion of blossoms.

**Bailey Arboretum, Lattingtown:** Grounds available for wedding portraits.

**Mohonk Gardens, New Paltz:** Mohonk Mountain House is a full-service hotel and resort with facilities for weddings, receptions, meetings, and other affairs.

**Dr. E. M. Mills Memorial Rose Garden, Syracuse**

## NORTH CAROLINA

**Tanglewood Park, Clemmons**

**Bicentennial Garden, Greensboro**

**Elizabethan Gardens, Monteo**

**Greenfield Gardens, Wilmington**

**Orton Plantation, Wilmington:** Beautiful wedding garden for weddings, receptions, and affairs.

## OHIO

**Stan Hywet Hall and Gardens, Akron:** Auditorium available in historic mansion for weddings, receptions, meetings.

Spring Grove Cemetery, Cincinnati: Attractive chapel available for weddings.

Franklin Park Conservatory and Garden Center, Columbus

Park of Roses, Columbus

Dawes Arboretum, Newark

## PENNSYLVANIA

Malcolm W. Gross Memorial Rose Garden, Allentown: Weddings held in rose garden.

Appleford, Villanova

## RHODE ISLAND

Blithewood Gardens and Arboretum, Bristol: English manor house available for weddings, meetings.

Roger Williams Park, Providence

## SOUTH CAROLINA

Brookgreen Gardens, Murrels Inlet: Lovely grounds available for weddings.

Hampton Park, Charleston

Clemson University Horticultural Gardens, Clemson

Boylston Gardens, Columbia: Located on the site of the Governor's Mansion, where a new Wedding Garden has been created.

Edisto Memorial Gardens, Orangeburg: Facilities for weddings and meetings.

Glencairn Garden, Rock Hill

Swan Lake Iris Gardens, Sumter: Grounds available for weddings.

## TENNESSEE

Opryland Hotel Conservatory, Nashville

## VERMONT

Park-McCullough House, North Bennington: Gardens and house available for weddings, receptions, parties, meetings.

## VIRGINIA

**Norfolk Botanical Gardens, Norfolk:** Weddings in lovely outdoor garden.

**Oatlands, Leesburg:** Magnificent mansion with garden available for weddings, receptions, affairs, and meetings.

**Bryan Park Azalea Gardens, Richmond:** Beautiful spring garden available for weddings.

## WEST VIRGINIA

**Cathedral State Park, Aurora**

**The Greenbrier, White Sulphur Springs:** Full-service hotel and resort with facilities for weddings, receptions, meetings, and other affairs.

## WISCONSIN

**Mitchell Park Horticultural Conservatory, Milwaukee:** Conservatory available for weddings, receptions, affairs.

**Boerner Botanical Gardens, Hales Corners:** Lovely gardens available for weddings, receptions, affairs.

**Olbrich Gardens, Madison:** Garden Center offers facilities for weddings, receptions, affairs, meetings.

## EASTERN CANADA

**Royal Botanical Gardens, Hamilton:** Facilities for weddings.

**Historic Gardens, Annapolis Royal**

**Edwards Gardens, Don Mills:** Facilities for weddings, receptions, meetings.

**Gage Park, Hamilton:** Wedding portraits permitted.

**Queen Victoria Park, Oakes Garden Theatre, Lilac Garden, Niagara Falls**

**Niagara Falls Park Commission School of Horticulture, Niagara Falls:** Gardens available for wedding pictures.

**Central Experimental Farm, Ottawa:** Gardens available for weddings.

**Centennial Botanical Conservatory, Thunder Bay**

# Winter Gardens: Those That Shine in Winter

Winter is a harsh time for all but the most southerly of America's gardens. Nevertheless, this problem may be circumvented by offering beautiful conservatory collections or seasonal shows. Some of these shows, as seen at Longwood (Pennsylvania) and Duke (New Jersey), for example, rank among the finest floral displays in the world.

In the South the effect of winter is more variable. In such states as Georgia, North and South Carolina, Alabama, Louisiana, Mississippi, and Tennessee, many gardens are able to maintain presentable displays through December and January. The majority, however, experience a period of dormancy during this time, although not of the magnitude seen in more northern latitudes. On the other hand, spring generally comes early to these states, and some of America's finest outdoor displays can be found here from mid-February through March.

Florida is a different story. Most of its gardens are at their best in winter and, in most cases, at their worst in summer when stifling heat wilts both plants and visitors. For this reason we have listed the Florida gardens en mass, since nearly all of these gardens are winter gardens.

## ALABAMA

**Birmingham Botanical Garden, Birmingham:** One of the Southeast's largest conservatories (orchids, ferns, tropicals), a Desert House, and a Camellia House containing hundreds of specimens (125 varieties).

**Bellingrath Gardens and Home, Theodore:** Lovely poinsettia show in December followed by blooming of the vast camellia collection (January and February), then azaleas and other spring flora beginning in late February.

**Ave Maria Grotto, Cullman:** The garden's most impressive display is its unique miniature buildings—interesting any time of year.

## CONNECTICUT

**Caprilands Herb Farm, Coventry:** Greenhouses packed with herbs (more than 300 varieties).

**Logee's Greenhouses, Danielson:** Collections of begonias, geraniums, tropical plants, African violets, and more.

**East Rock Park, Hamden (see Pardee Rose Garden):** Conservatory with permanent displays and seasonal shows.

**Elizabeth Park, Hartford:** Seasonal shows held in greenhouse.

**Bartlett Arboretum, Stamford:** Seasonal shows held in greenhouse.

## DISTRICT OF COLUMBIA

**United States Botanic Garden:** A ¾-acre conservatory with collections of orchids, palms, begonias, cacti, and bromeliads, plus seasonal shows.

## FLORIDA

All gardens.

## GEORGIA

**Callaway Gardens, Pine Mountain:** The new John A. Sibley Horticultural Complex offers excellent indoor displays and seasonal shows.

**State Botanical Garden of Georgia, Athens:** Conservatory Complex with tropical and other plant displays.

**Massee Lane, Fort Valley:** Fine collection of winter-blooming camellias (peak bloom February to March).

## ILLINOIS

**Chicago Park District, Chicago:** First-class conservatory shows at Garfield Park (4 acres under glass) and Lincoln Park (3 acres under glass) conservatories.

**Ladd Arboretum, Evanston:** Trails open for cross-country skiing in winter.

**Chicago Horticultural Society Botanic Garden, Glencoe:** Ten greenhouses with permanent collections, plus a variety of plant society shows (orchids, bonsais, and others).

**Washington Park Botanical Garden, Springfield:** Quality conservatory displays and seasonal shows.

# INDIANA

**Foellinger-Freimann Botanical Conservatory, Fort Wayne:** Quality indoor exhibits and seasonal shows.

**Garfield Park Conservatory and Sunken Gardens, Indianapolis:** Quality indoor exhibits and seasonal shows.

**Christy Woods, Muncie:** Conservatory exhibits including a superb orchid collection.

# MARYLAND

**Brookside Gardens, Wheaton:** Excellent conservatory exhibits and shows.

**Baltimore Conservatory Complex, Baltimore:** Historic conservatory offering indoor displays and seasonal shows.

**London Publik House and Gardens, Edgewater:** An outdoor winter garden highlighting winter plants, fruits and flowers, plus camellias in bloom in late February.

# MASSACHUSETTS

**Isabella Stewart Gardner Museum, Boston:** Charming courtyard garden within the museum, offering seasonal displays.

**Botanic Garden of Smith College, Northampton:** Lyman Plant House holds collections of palms, ferns, orchids, begonias, and more.

**Berkshire Garden Center, Stockbridge:** Greenhouses and a Sap House where maple syrup is made.

**Lyman Estate and Greenhouses, Waltham:** Four greenhouses as part of this historic mansion.

**Wellesley College, Wellesley:** The Margaret C. Ferguson Greenhouses offer a variety of collections (orchids, ferns, tropicals), and spring and fall shows.

# MICHIGAN

**Anna Scripps Whitcomb Conservatory, Belle Isle, Detroit:** Excellent conservatory exhibits and seasonal shows. The conservatory is located in Belle Isle Park, which offers ice skating, sledding, sleigh rides, plus an indoor aquarium and museum.

**Fernwood, Niles:** Small conservatory containing orchids, cacti, bromeliads, and more.

**Dow Gardens, Midland:** Small conservatory with tropical and desert plant collections, plus an Easter and Christmas display.

**Hidden Lake Gardens, Tipton:** Small conservatory with permanent collections.

## MISSISSIPPI

**Wister Gardens, Belzoni:** Garden House Greenhouse display, plus outdoor camellias blooming in late winter.

**Mynelle Gardens, Jackson:** Camellia collection blooming in late winter.

## NEW HAMPSHIRE

**Fuller Gardens, North Hampton:** Conservatory collection of tropical and desert plants.

**Prescott Park Formal Garden, Portsmouth:** Outdoor Christmas display includes over two miles of Christmas lights.

## NEW JERSEY

**Duke Gardens, Somerville:** Conservatory with superb permanent displays of gardens of different cultures from around the world.

**Fischer Greenhouses, Linwood:** Vast collection of African violets.

## NEW YORK

**New York Botanical Garden, Bronx, New York City:** Excellent permanent displays and seasonal shows in the Haupt Conservatory.

**Brooklyn Botanic Garden, Brooklyn, New York City:** Excellent conservatory displays (orchids, bonsai) and seasonal shows.

**Planting Fields Arboretum, Oyster Bay:** One and a half acres of superb indoor collections of camellias and orchids, plus seasonal shows.

**Buffalo and Erie County Botanical Garden, Buffalo:** Indoor exhibits and seasonal shows of high quality.

**Sonnenberg Gardens, Canandaigua:** Conservatory displays.

**Boscobel Restoration, Garrison:** Conservatory with good collections of orchids and orange trees.

**Cary Arboretum, Millbrook:** Greenhouse with tropical collection.

**Gardens of the Cloisters, New York City:** Three small indoor medieval gardens of horticultural interest.

**Wave Hill, New York City:** Greenhouse displays.

**Lyndhurst, Tarrytown:** Gothic mansion greenhouse is in process of restoration.

## NORTH CAROLINA

**University of North Carolina at Charlotte Botanical Gardens, Charlotte:** Permanent displays in the McMillan Greenhouse including orchids, African violets, desert and tropical plants. Open by appointment (call 704-597-4055).

**Reynolda Gardens, Winston-Salem:** Conservatory offers permanent displays and Christmas open house.

## OHIO

**Stan Hywet Hall and Gardens, Akron:** Seasonal flower shows in conservatory plus Christmas activities in hall.

**Kingwood Center, Mansfield:** Seven greenhouses offer diverse indoor displays and seasonal shows.

**Cox Arboretum, Dayton:** Greenhouse display.

**Krohn Conservatory, Cincinnati:** Permanent displays and 6 excellent seasonal shows.

**Cleveland Cultural Gardens and Rockefeller Park Greenhouses, Cleveland:** Rockefeller Park Greenhouses offer indoor displays and seasonal shows.

**Garden Center of Greater Cleveland, Cleveland:** Year-round displays and indoor collections.

**Franklin Park Conservatory and Garden Center, Columbus:** Permanent displays and seasonal shows.

**Toledo Zoo, Toledo:** Tropical display, orchids, ferns, palms, plus Easter and Christmas shows.

## PENNSYLVANIA

**Longwood Gardens, Kennett Square:** Four acres of the world's finest permanent displays and conservatory shows.

**Ambler Campus of Temple University, Ambler:** Small greenhouse.

**Delaware Valley College, Doylestown:** Small greenhouse.

**Hershey Gardens, Hershey:** Indoor tropical gardens with over 50,000 plantings.

**Meadowbrook Farms, Meadowbrook:** Retail nursery with orchids, begonias, ferns, succulents, and cacti.

**Fairmount Park Horticultural Center, Philadelphia:** Fine indoor displays and seasonal shows.

**Phipps Conservatory, Pittsburgh:** Excellent permanent displays and seasonal shows.

**Scott Arboretum, Swarthmore:** Small greenhouse.

## RHODE ISLAND

**Roger Williams Park, Providence:** Greenhouses with permanent displays and seasonal shows; the Christmas Flower Show has a 20-foot Talking Snowman. Outdoors, the park offers sledding, skating, and cross-country skiing.

## SOUTH CAROLINA

**Magnolia Plantation and Gardens, Charleston:** Camellia collection blooming in late winter.

**Brookgreen Gardens, Murrells Inlet:** Excellent sculpture collection viewable year round.

## TENNESSEE

**Cheekwood, Nashville:** Greenhouses and display house offer permanent collections (orchids, camellias, rain forest) and excellent seasonal shows.

**Dixon Gallery and Gardens, Memphis:** Greenhouse with excellent camellia collection.

**Memphis Botanic Garden, Memphis:** Tropical and camellia collections, seasonal shows.

**Opryland Hotel Conservatory, Nashville:** The 2-acre interior of the Opryland Hotel is filled with plants, statuary, and a waterfall.

## WISCONSIN

**Mitchell Park Horticultural Conservatory, Milwaukee:** Superb conservatory displays (orchids, ferns, tropicals) and seasonal shows.

**Olbrich Gardens, Madison:** Lovely seasonal shows.

## CANADA

**Royal Botanical Gardens, Hamilton:** Indoor floral exhibitions and shows, plus skiing, maple syrup making, and other activities.

**Montreal Botanic Gardens, Montreal:** Ten conservatory buildings hold impressive displays of bonsai, orchids, African violets, and more, plus excellent seasonal shows.

**Gage Park, Hamilton:** Greenhouses with permanent displays and an autumn chrysanthemum show.

**Queen Victoria Park, Niagara Falls:** Conservatory with fine displays and seasonal shows.

**Central Experimental Farm, Ottawa:** Greenhouse with tropical flora.

**Centennial Botanical Conservatory, Thunder Bay:** Permanent displays and seasonal shows.

# Glossary

**Allee:** A single, broad, paved or gravel walk, bordered by generous turf strips and enclosed by high planting. An allee is a glorified garden walk or promenade. It was a common feature of Italian Renaissance gardens.

**Annual:** A plant that naturally completes its life within one year from germination to seeding and death.

**Arboretum:** An ample area set aside for the growing, maintenance, proper labeling, study, and effective display of all the different kinds of woody ornamental trees, shrubs, vines, and other wood plants that can be grown in a given area.

**Cultivar:** Progeny of a clone. The result of selective hybridization, creating a type of plant known only via cultivation and which may or may not be reproduced from seed.

**Gazebo:** A garden structure of Dutch origin for comfort and conversation. A characteristic feature of old Dutch gardens where it was built of brick or stone, gazebos today are made from a variety of materials and styled in unusual or elegant forms to complement a garden design.

**Herbaceous:** Not woody; any plant, annual, biennial, or perennial, hardy or nonhardy, deciduous or evergreen, without woody tissues in its stems.

**Horticulture:** Comprises any activity having to do with the growing of ornamentals, vegetables, fruits, or plants prized for their general interest. The study of horticulture is closely associated with many biological and physical sciences which are tapped for information concerning the growing and arrangement of plants for man's use and appreciation.

**Hybrid:** A variety or individual resulting from the crossing of two species. The result of cross-fertilization; a cross.

**Parterre:** A geometric arrangement of ornamental, shaped beds, separated by a pattern of walks or turf areas. Variations in parterre design are unlimited, the simplest form being four beds arranged symmetrically around a central ornamental feature.

**Perennial:** A plant that persists more than two years.

**Pergola:** A structure designed to offer a shaded passageway from one building to another, or from one garden feature to another.

**Species:** A natural botanical unit; composed of individuals that exhibit characters distinguishing them from all other units within a genus, still not differing from one another beyond the limits of a recognizable and integrated pattern of variation.

# *About the Authors*

---

## EVERITT L. MILLER

---

Having spent over 40 years in the field of horticulture, Everitt Miller is the professional's professional. Mr. Miller graduated from the State University of New York in 1939 with a degree in landscape design. After serving as the landscape manager for a commercial nursery, in 1946 he became manager of the magnificent Planting Fields estate on Long Island (New York), now the nationally renowned Planting Fields Arboretum.

In 1956 Mr. Miller was summoned to the internationally famous Longwood Gardens (Pennsylvania), where he first headed the Department of Horticulture and later became Assistant Director. From 1979 to 1984 he served as Longwood's Director and was responsible for over two hundred employees who tended the thousand acres visited each year by 650,000 people from all over the globe.

During his career Mr. Miller has also held a directorship in the American Camellia Society, the American Horticultural Society, the American Association of Botanical Gardens and Arboreta Inc., and the American Rhododendron Society. In 1981 he was awarded the Gold Medal of the Pennsylvania Horticultural Society, and in 1983 the Liberty Hyde Bailey Award of the American Horticultural Society. Recently retired from the Directorship of Longwood Gardens, Mr. Miller remains quite active as a horticultural consultant, lecturer, author of horticultural articles, and current president of the American Horticultural Society. In addition, being an accredited horticultural judge, he regularly serves in the judging of flower shows and competitions both in the United States and abroad.

# DR. JAY S. COHEN

A physician by profession, Dr. Cohen is an amateur garden enthusiast. Having practiced as both a general physician, researcher (Medical Director of the UCLA Research Project in 1973, America's first university acupuncture research facility), and psychiatrist, he is a firm believer and active participant in the stress-reducing qualities of gardening. In addition, Dr. Cohen is an experienced author who has written several works of fiction and nonfiction, as well as many articles on a variety of topics, including wildflowers and public gardens. He is a member of the Garden Writers Association of America and the American Horticultural Society. He also grows prize-quality roses, ferns, and fuschias at his home.

# Have We Overlooked Someone?

In preparing *The American Garden Guidebook, Volume One*, we have used every means possible to identify and contact eligible gardens. We consulted every available research source and sent out over six hundred inquiries. Still, since the number of high-quality gardens is large and the area covered broad, we realize we may have overlooked some deserving gardens. If you are aware of such a garden, please let us know so that we may remedy the oversight in our next edition. Our goal is to present every garden of merit, so we are most appreciative of information from our readers. Just drop us a note with the garden's name and address (and telephone number, if possible), and we will take it from there. We appreciate your help, and we hope that you have found *The American Garden Guidebook* both informative and useful.

*Everitt L. Miller and Jay S. Cohen*